A Tiger *in the* Kitchen

a memoir of food

and family

Cheryl Lu-Lien Tan

voice

Hyperion   New York

Library of Congress Cataloging-in-Publication Data

Tan, Cheryl Lu-Lien.
    A tiger in the kitchen : a memoir of food and family / Cheryl Lu-Lien Tan.
        p. cm.
    Summary: "A book about the author's quest to recreate the dishes of her native
Singapore during one Lunar Calendar year, as a way to connect food and family
with her sense of home"— Provided by publisher.
    ISBN 978-1-4013-4128-2 (pbk.)
    1. Cooking, Singaporean—Anecdotes.   2. Tan, Cheryl Lu-lien.   I. Title.

    TX724.5.S55T36 2011
    641.595957—dc22

                                                                    2010035210

Book design by Betty Lew

FIRST EDITION

10   9   8   7   6   5   4   3   2

THIS LABEL APPLIES TO TEXT STOCK

A Tiger *in the*
Kitchen

For Daddo, Mommo, and Daffo,
who loved me enough to let me go.

And for Mike,
who caught me on the other side.

A TIGER *in the*

KITCHEN

FAMILY TREE

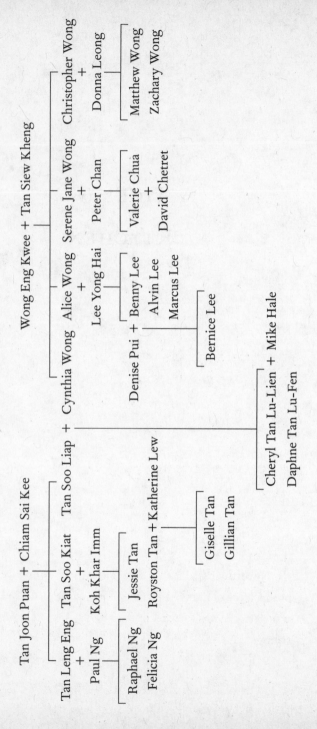

PROLOGUE

I distinctly remember the moment that I knew: I should have been less of a rebel.

I was in my twenties. I was feeling on top of the world as a fashion writer for the *Baltimore Sun,* a paper I had aspired to work at for years.

And I had decided to teach myself to cook.

Even though I had grown up in Singapore, a somewhat traditional place despite its modern, impressive skyline and reputation as a Southeast Asian economic powerhouse, I had deftly managed as a child to avoid setting foot in the kitchen to learn the wifely skills that my girlfriends were encouraged to pick up.

Instead, I had poured my teenage energies into raku pottery, ballet, Chinese brush painting. Basic fried rice? I hadn't the faintest clue how to put that together.

Nevertheless, I had a Singaporean grandmother who was both a force of nature and a legendary cook. And so I believed it was in my blood to excel in the kitchen—or at least kill myself trying.

What unfolded was a series of rather unfortunate episodes.

Fried rice was so burned that brown, charred chunks of rice seared themselves almost permanently to the wok. (How was *I* supposed to know that nonstop stirring action was essential to the process?) A stab at fried noodles yielded an inedible, gelatinous mass. (Periodically peering into a pot of boiling water, apparently, was not the way to tell if noodles were getting gummy and overcooked.) An Oreo cheesecake pie I attempted for Thanksgiving turned out so lumpy that one guest gently inquired if I owned a whisk. (Hello, if I needed one, perhaps the recipe printed on the back of the piecrust label should have said so?)

The pièce de résistance, however, was a dish of hello dollies I very enthusiastically attempted after spying the recipe on a bag of chocolate chips at the grocery store. All morning one Saturday I slaved, opening cans, mixing and assembling. As the bars baked in the oven, the heady smell of chocolate, condensed milk, and coconut started filling my Washington, D.C., kitchen. I began to envision the afternoon that lay before me: I would walk into my friend's home perhaps wearing gingham oven mitts and a matching red and white apron, bearing my baking dish of delicious hello dollies. My friends would inhale the bars, grabbing at seconds—thirds, even! But when they showered me with compliments for my baking, I would merely blush, coyly turn my head, and wave them away with the elegance of Princess Diana.

This, I thought to myself, would be what they call "nailing it."

Naturally, this was not how it went. In a frantic rush, I had gotten to my friend's apartment with no mitts and no apron. And when I sliced into the pan to cut up the bars, my knife emerged dripping with a slick, brown and taupe goo flecked with bits of white coconut. As I watched my friends politely lick at the liquid mounds of chocolate and condensed milk I had scooped onto paper napkins—I had avoided serving plates, having had a fervent, if misguided belief in the solid nature of my bars—I realized, I am not the cook my grandmother was.

Growing up in Singapore, I had taken my Tanglin ah-ma for granted.

My paternal grandmother, whom I called Tanglin Ah-Ma because she once lived in the Tanglin neighborhood of Singapore, was a true legend in the kitchen. A slender, birdlike woman with a nest of short, wavy hair that she kept pulled back from her face with black bobby pins, my Tanglin ah-ma was a mystery to me when I was growing up. We rarely visited her, and when we did, my inability to speak any Teochew, the Chinese dialect that she spoke, meant we mostly sat around with me feeling her eyes scan over me, inspecting this alien, Westernized granddaughter she had somehow ended up with. During these visits, I would learn small things about her—that she kept a wooden, rectangular block that functioned as a pillow, for example. It was a habit that Singaporean Chinese of a certain generation, who had had no access to plush feather pillows, were clinging to. However many times I saw or touched her wooden pillow, though, I never understood it.

While we didn't have the words to communicate, Tanglin Ah-Ma spoke eloquently to me, to her family, by feeding us all. She would routinely rise in the early hours of the morning to fire up the charcoal stove in order to put breakfast on the table. Soy-sauce-braised duck, hearty salted vegetable soups, and even tricky *bak-ʐhang*, the pyramid-shaped glutinous rice dumplings wrapped in bamboo leaves that require such work few women bother to make them at home anymore—Ah-Ma churned them out with such skill that an ever-growing circle of relatives, friends, and then friends of friends would regularly request them.

The crowning moment for my Tanglin ah-ma, however, was Chinese New Year, a time of great feasting in Singapore when people devote entire days to hopping from house to house, catching up with friends and relatives while stuffing themselves with platters of noodles, candy, and above all, cookies.

Amid the sanctioned bacchanalia, one indulgence was supreme for me: pineapple tarts. Each year, I looked forward to the bite-size cookies that are the hallmark of the festivities. And I considered myself a connoisseur of the treats, which comprise a buttery shortbread base topped with a dense, sweet pineapple jam. As we traveled from house to house, I would attack the tarts first, choosing not to sully my palate or waste calories on other, lesser snacks. And at each home, I would, inevitably, be disappointed. The tarts would always be too crumbly, too salty, or not crumbly enough. None compared to my Tanglin ah-ma's tarts—this was, simply, fact.

Despite my love for the tarts, however, I never bothered to learn how to make them. As a child, I had been steadfastly determined not to pick up any womanly skills, least of all cooking. I was more intent on reading, writing, learning about the world—and plotting how I was to eventually go forth and conquer it.

Cooking, I thought, could always come later. Blithely, I

assumed that I would someday ask my Tanglin ah-ma to teach me how to make her pineapple tarts. And then, when I was eleven, she died.

Watching the disaster that was my hello dollies unfold that afternoon in Washington, I felt a sudden pang of regret.

Over the next ten years, as I ventured more deeply into the kitchen, growing ever more ambitious—and, I'd like to think, skilled—this kernel of yearning would only grow. Each stew I made, each cookie I baked only made me wonder what my Tanglin ah-ma would have thought. Nothing I baked or cooked, of course, compared in my mind to anything she made.

I had missed the opportunity to get to know her recipes, to get to know her. By now, I'd achieved the success I'd craved as a child—I was based in New York City, covering fashion for *The Wall Street Journal*, one of the largest newspapers in America. And yet, no matter how high I climbed, the hole stubbornly remained.

I started to think about home—which, to me, isn't just New York, or Singapore, or anywhere in between. Home, rather, is rooted in the kitchen and the foods of my Singaporean girlhood—the intoxicating fog of turmeric and lemongrass seeping into the air as bright orange slabs of *otak*, a curried fish mousse, steam on the stove, or the scent of sliced mackerel and minced ginger doused in white pepper drifting out of the kitchen, heralding a hearty breakfast of fish porridge.

After almost sixteen years in the United States, I realized I had, indeed, become *ang moh* (a Chinese term that means "red hair," implying Westernized). I did not know, after all, how to make these dishes, the food of my people. They aren't recipes that you'll find in Chinese cookbooks; many are uniquely Singaporean and, in some cases, regarded as not "special" enough to put on restaurant menus. Because of recent generations of women just like me who were intent on avoiding cooking, some of these recipes are slowly fading from the culinary awareness.

In the dead of winter, in a city that's just too far away from the sound of banana tree leaves rustling in the tropical breezes, I started to dream. In my daydream, my Tanglin ah-ma is there. She's come to me with a piece of paper bearing her cherished recipes. When I open my eyes, it becomes clear that it's time.

And so I decided to take a leap. I journeyed home to Singapore, finally ready after all these years to learn to cook, to learn about my family, to learn to be a woman—but intent on doing it on my own terms.

On the other side of the world were my maternal grandmother, my aunts, my mother. Patiently, they stood by with arms open—ready to welcome me into the kitchen.

CHAPTER ONE

I was born in the Year of the Tiger with a lucky star over my head and a knife in my hand.

Based on the time I was born and the fact that I was a dynamic and aggressive Tiger, I was already destined to be sharp, intelligent, and incredibly ambitious. But with the additional star to guide me, I was headed for a sparkling future, one that I would sail through with ease, gathering money and a great deal of success along the way.

Instead, the moment I pushed into this world, growling and crying, I took the knife in my hand and stabbed at the star, snuffing it out. In that moment, a fighter was created—a person who knew she would have to work doubly hard to compensate for her dead lucky star, often stubbornly wandering off, heeding no one, and charting a path of her own.

This is the story that my family's fortune-teller tells. And for years, much of it appeared to be true.

Despite the fact that I'm female, I'd always been raised to be somewhat masculine.

Before I was born, my parents chose my name: Brendan.

Because I was the firstborn of the eldest son in a traditional Chinese family in Singapore, there was plenty of hope that I would be male. A son who would carry the family name, a child in whom my father would nurture his ambitions.

Well, I'm female. So my dad, Soo Liap Tan—a practical man who ended up with two daughters—made do with what he got.

Singapore, an island city-state of almost 5 million that straddles the equator, for all its modernity remains a rather old-fashioned Asian society in some ways. Boys are valued. But while girls aren't bad things, you generally don't expect too much of them.

My father believes this to a certain extent, but he's also ambitious. So when his firstborn arrived and it was a girl, he adjusted accordingly.

When I was six, he gave me a dictionary of legal terms. "You don't have to look at it now," he said. "But if you want to look anything up, it's there." I never touched it, but the message was clear. I was headed for law school. My father pressed me to read voraciously, to be good at math, and never once told me I had to clean or learn how to cook in order to be a good wife. He never let me beat him at Scrabble and raised me with all the love a Chinese parent wasn't supposed to show. He challenged me to be outspoken, to question authority, and to always, always let creativity be my guide.

But above all, he told me stories. As much as he encouraged me to shirk my female role in society, he wanted me to know and understand my culture, my heritage, my family. He wanted me to be Chinese, to never forget from where I came.

From the time I was a child, it had been impossible to escape the tales of my ancestors. These oral history outbursts often came when I least expected them. "Dad, I landed this big interview today——" I would start, before being interrupted with his pleased response to praiseworthy things. "Yes! You are Teochew. Aiyah, don't you know, our people are known for being pirates, smugglers, and great businessmen. [The Hong Kong billionaire] Li Ka-shing is Teochew, you know!" (I always thought Dad was exaggerating until we visited Shantou, China, many years later and I realized that the area my father's family is from is like the Sicily of China. Some of the major triads in Asia first blossomed in Guangdong.)

Much later, when I was in my early twenties and called to tell my parents about a new boyfriend, there was a sudden silence after I mentioned his name. "Nakamura . . . ," my dad said quietly. "My two sisters were killed by the Japanese, you know!" (I would have to tell him several times that the boyfriend was a third-generation American and could not possibly have been responsible for the Japanese occupation of Singapore during World War II.)

But the longer stories of my father's boyhood, of his family's hopes and dreams for all he'd become, would emerge as we huddled over late-night suppers of take-out noodles from Singapore's hawker stands after my mother and sister, Daphne, had gone to bed. The slippery fried shrimp noodles we adored came sprinkled with chewy circles of squid. The noodles, wrapped in industrial-strength wax paper, were generally so greasy that the oil penetrated the paper, filling it with dark spots. I always looked forward to the moment when we would carefully peel back the wax paper and steam would rise, fogging up our glasses.

It didn't matter that we couldn't see—we just grabbed our chopsticks and stabbed away at the mound. When the noodles disappeared and the toothpicks were put aside, Dad would begin. "When I was a boy, my grandfather used to hoist me onto his shoulders and lead me through his banks and factories and say, 'All this will be yours one day.'" As the firstborn son of the eldest son, my father had been expected to succeed my great-grandfather. "And then the war came," Dad would continue. "We lost all the money when he died."

These unfulfilled dreams and childhood disappointments were threads that had raced through my father's life for decades. We could never drive past pockets of Singapore without him sighing and murmuring, "My grandfather's company used to have warehouses along this whole stretch, you know! Aiyah . . . you could have been born into a rich family." Specters of this unled life fueled my father's ambitions, leading him to plunge into a lucrative career working for a string of beverage and luxury goods distribution companies after casting aside an early dream to spend his life teaching high school mathematics at Saint Joseph's Institution, the alma mater that had been his refuge from a tumultuous home life. The more his father— a man whose major accomplishment in life was to drink and gamble away the family money—beat him, the more my father had turned to schoolwork and idyllic Saturdays building campfires and volunteering as a Boy Scout. "I saved all my pocket money and bought my father a birthday card once, you know," my father said late one night as we sat in the kitchen, mirroring each other with our legs propped up, still rubbing our bellies over the feast we had just had. "You know what he did? He tore up the card and slapped me for wasting money! You are so lucky your father is not like that."

And indeed, he wasn't. The kind of father he was was involved in showing me a world beyond the one most children would know. With insomnia as a shared affliction, we would stay up way past my bedtime, sitting in our bright living room, quietly reading. We discussed international politics, the economy, whether Liverpool or Arsenal was going to win the English Premier League that year. One afternoon, I emerged from my first-grade classroom in a weathered colonial building along busy Victoria Street near downtown Singapore to find my father's car waiting for me just outside the gates. "Come, we're going for lunch," he said, whisking me into the car. I assumed we were going to a hawker center for a quick meal before he had to jet back to work. Instead, minutes later, I found myself sliding into a chair at the Western restaurant of the posh Dynasty Hotel, nervously smoothing down the starched, white tablecloth before me as I wondered why we were there. It wasn't my birthday—or his. And I couldn't think of any special reason that would have earned such a treat. We were simply having lunch, it turned out—an excuse to show me what it was like to eat at a nice restaurant without my mother ordering for me or family members grabbing pieces of chicken with chopsticks and filling my plate. Terrified that I might do something wrong, I ordered the item on the menu that I had eaten and understood before—a large bratwurst. I remember it being delicious, but not as delicious as the feeling of being an adult, sitting with my father, talking about school, about work, as we leisurely had lunch.

When I was nine, my father took a job in Hong Kong, commuting to Singapore for long weekends just once every three weeks. I missed him terribly. This was a man who occasionally chased me around the dining room table with a cane in hand just to get me to practice the piano. But the same man would sometimes wake me up in the mornings by standing quietly at the window, peering out very intently, until I sleepily asked, "What's happening outside?" "OH," he'd reply. "There's an elephant walking down the road," which would always prompt me to jump out of bed and run to the window for a peek. (It took me many years to figure this one out.)

When my father left for Hong Kong, I might have lost my partner in insomnia, but I gained a pen pal. *Dear Cheryl,* he wrote to the ten-year-old me. *Thank you for your two letters. I'm sorry I have not written lately. You can imagine how busy I've been. . . . When I next return to Singapore, can you remind me to order the* Reader's Digest *for you? Meanwhile, I am always dreaming of the beautiful sunshine in Singapore and our swimming pool. Love, Papa.*

September 20, 1984, on hotel letterhead bearing the words "Honey Lake Country Club" and "Shenzhen, China": *Dearest Cheryl, I am now in China for the first time in my life. This evening I spent my time walking around the town to see how people live. The streets are full of bicycles as people here are too poor to afford cars. There are so many bicycles moving in the streets that you worry very much about being knocked down by a bicycle—just imagine that!! Today I visited two towns or cities—Shekou and Shenzhen, both very close to Hong Kong. These two areas are industrial areas— many factories. We are negotiating to buy three factories—a flour mill, biscuit factory, and a feed mill. I hope one day that I can bring all of you to visit China. China is famous for beautiful sceneries, and also it is a chance for you to see how poor people are. With lots of love, Papa.*

Sometime the following year, on stationery from the Prince Hotel in Hong Kong: *Many thanks for your letters and postcards. When I read the letters and cards, I can feel how strongly you love me. Papa is very happy and proud. So proud and happy that I will continue to be a good papa to you and Daffy. . . . I am sad to realise that when I was in Singapore during the Chinese new year holidays I have not heard you play the PIANO ONCE!! What a pity! Especially when Mummy and I struggled so hard to buy you a piano! I'm ashamed. Cheryl, Papa and Mummy love you and want you to enjoy your life and work. Love and good luck, Papa.*

Shortly after that, when my parents had bought me my first computer: *Dearest Cheryl, While the computer may do wonders for you, I still prefer to read your letters in your own handwriting. Your handwriting reflects to some extent your personality. So I hope I will not miss my dearest daughter's handwriting. What do you think of my personality from my writing? Confusing?*

April 15, 1986, a year after my parents bought me a dog, a shih tzu my sister and I named Erny: *Looking back at your letters, you keep mentioning ERNY. Shouldn't we be tired of talking about him now—after more than 1 year? (Or less?) . . . Went to a movie "Out of Africa" last night. Do you know that it won 6 Academy Awards or "Oscars" as they call it in the movie world? The movie's great but I think would be boring for you. It shows or rather teaches us FORTITUDE and DETERMINATION. Love, Papa.*

On religion, and my growing curiosity about Catholicism:

It is not easy to understand or appreciate the Taoist religion that my family has practiced and followed for generations. (To confess, I don't quite understand it either.) But I guess that since Mum and I embraced it when my father passed away in 1976 as a matter of duty to my father and mother . . . the Taoist faith has become a part of our lives. That does not mean that you are bound by tradition to follow the same course. Having a religion is important in life—whether it is Buddhism, Catholic, Islamic etc. We are all children of God and religion helps us to communicate better with God. So feel free to believe in the Catholic faith if it helps you to communicate with God better. . . . Well, this is a rather long letter. I love you, Daphne and Mummy & miss you all. (Ooops. I forgot Erny.) Love, Papa.

September 6, 1987: *Dearest Cheryl, Please forgive if my hand-writing does not look steady. I am having a sore eye and have been applying eye lotion. . . . I have to keep the affected eye closed to allow the lotion to work. . . . Before I go on, I must be frank that I am shocked that you have not mastered the art of "paragraphing" yet—or at least not in the letters you write to me. A good and well written letter deserves at the same time proper paragraphing—it strains the eyes of the reader! Now, I have just found out the reason for my sore eye.*

Each of my father's stories had a point. He was determined not to be the father that he had had. He wanted to show me the world and all its possibilities. And while he had a tremendously successful career—at one point becoming the director of marketing for Vitasoy, one of the largest beverage companies in Asia—he was even more determined that his firstborn would go further than he himself had, having had the advantages of a loving, supportive father that he had so craved. But as I got older, I broke my father's heart and chose journalism over law. Then I broke my mother's heart by insisting on coming to the United States for college. My family protested. I would be too far, I was a girl, and why journalism? But my father had always told me I could be and do anything, and he wasn't going to stop me. He simply asked, "How much will it cost?"

On occasions such as these, my mother often would sigh, shake her head, and blame the fact that I was born in the year of the Tiger. "Why did I have to have a Tiger daughter?" she would lament. "So stubborn and rebellious. If you were born in the olden days in China, you would have been killed at birth!" Sometimes, however, faced with my horrified looks, she would end on a reassuring note: "You know," she once said, "with Tiger girls, they used to pull out one of her teeth so she wouldn't be so fierce and eat up her husband. But don't worry, I didn't do that with you."

Once I moved to the United States, my father visited me at least twice a year. We didn't have the fried shrimp noodles, but we started having a beer after dinner some nights. Now, during my college years, my Singaporean male friends—and even less so my female ones—were hardly ever granted the privilege of bonding with their dads over a beer. (Nice girls didn't drink.) But in my father's eyes, my independence in school, in building my career, had given me the license. Even so, our bar visits often began with "Your mum would kill me if she knew," and "I won't tell her if you won't, Dad." (We also never told her about the cigarettes we would smoke surreptitiously.)

As I built my own career, my father's ambitions became my fuel. And I could never shake the feeling that he was disappointed, somehow. In my early twenties, as I grappled with the guilt I felt over having chosen to stay in the United States, where I saw far greater opportunities in journalism than anywhere in Asia, I looked forward to his trips all the more, for the smallest sign or assurance that I continued to do him proud. The lectures continued—how was my job at the *Baltimore Sun* going? Was I writing stories often enough? Why was I covering something inconsequential (in his eyes) like police or county politics when I could be writing substantial stories about the world of finance? "How come you still don't know how to cook?" he once asked, as he surveyed the suspiciously pristine kitchen of my Odenton, Maryland, apartment. "You cannot just eat *gongzai meen* [ramen] for dinner all the time, you know?" My father knew that while I loved food, I had a checkered past with the act of actually putting it on the table. I'd never cooked as a teenager in Singapore. And when the fourteen-year-old me had persuaded him to let me get a summer job waiting tables at Ponderosa in Singapore (instead of taking summer art classes or studying) because the notion of earning extra pocket money had become fashionable among my friends, my experience had not been entirely stellar. After one too many times in which I'd brought soup to a diner with the tip of my uniform's skinny red tie still making laps around the bowl, and one busy lunch hour in which I successfully delivered a plate of fried chicken to the table . . . only to watch the chicken slide right off onto the customer's lap, I was reassigned to salad bar duty. My father had taken my sister to lunch at Ponderosa shortly after this job change. Silently, they sat at a table near the salad bar, shushing me when I tried to make eye contact or say hello to them—

because it just wouldn't have been professional to chitchat with customers while I was on duty, he believed. I watched my father's pride melt away when he saw that my "job" consisted entirely of refilling tubs of corn and canned beets. And since salad wasn't a popular lunch choice in Singapore at the time, any such action was actually a rare occurrence. Mostly, my father and Daphne just sat there watching me stand in the salad bar island, shifting from foot to foot.

Even so, I couldn't help but feel that I was letting him down in my Maryland apartment. On the last night of that trip, we sat at the rickety IKEA table I had somehow assembled so that one leg was shorter than the other three, my father with his glasses off, sipping a beer and looking back on the days he had just spent, visiting my desk at work—"Why is it so messy?"—and getting to know my life in Maryland—"Make sure you always put the chain on your door when you come home." After a few moments of silence, as I wondered what he was really thinking of this life away from my family that he would never have chosen for me but that he had allowed me to choose, my father finally spoke. "You know, years and years ago, my grandfather left his family in China as a young man to travel to Singapore and seek a better life," he said, squinting hard at the bare white walls of my cheap rental apartment as if looking at something in the distance. "And now, years later, here you are. My daughter left Singapore to travel to America and seek a better life." My father smiled and reached over for his glass, raising it, saying, "Our family's journey continues."

Somewhere in the midst of my American life, I began to heed my father's advice and look beyond ramen in the kitchen.

My initial early obsession with American food was a surprise: meat loaf. The first time I encountered meat loaf, I wasn't sure what to think. It was a loaf. But made of ground beef? How had I not tried this before? This was a revelation amid the cloud of yearning for Singaporean food that set in the moment I entered college, in the mid-1990s. Any Singaporean will tell you that we don't eat to live, we live to eat. Food—or *makan*, as we call it—is a national obsession. My friends and I can spend hours passionately debating where to find the best chicken rice on the island. In a 2007 *New Yorker* piece about Singapore cuisine, Calvin Trillin observed of Singaporeans: "Culinarily, they are among the most homesick people I have ever met." In the fifteen years that I've lived in the United States, I've often said to American friends that, when it comes to Singapore, I miss the food first and then my family. They think I'm joking.

My fondest memories of growing up in Singapore all revolve around eating. On special Sundays, my parents would take the family out for *bak kut teh*, a mouthwatering, peppery pork rib broth that's nearly impossible to find in the United States. And when I was a primary school child, my neighborhood friends and I used to sneak out to a nearby hawker center for ice *kacang*, a dessert of sweet corn, red beans, and jelly topped with shaved ice smothered in evaporated milk and syrup. In fact, food is of such importance to Singaporeans that many restaurants and hawker centers have become landmarks. Even now, people know exactly where my family lives when I tell them it's near the old Long Beach Seafood, a seaside eating hole that hasn't been at that spot in more than twenty years.

The complex flavors of Singaporean food stem from British

colonization in the nineteenth century. The country on the tip of the Malay Peninsula, near Indonesia, was once a quiet island of fishing villages. In 1819, the British discovered the island and established a bustling trading port, attracting settlers from India, Europe, and China. Today, Singapore remains one of the world's busiest ports. However, some might argue that the more significant consequence of this colonization unfolded in the kitchen. As the years passed, Chinese, Malay, Indian, and European cooks took cues from one another, stirring together methods and spices culled from distant homelands such as Gujarat, India, and Xiamen, China, while sprinkling in culinary touches brought over by British and Dutch traders and their families.

The flavors meshed, giving rise to new dishes. A plethora of seafood and a love of spices gave birth to *chilli* crab, a signature Singaporean dish of crab fried in a vermilion, egg-streaked gravy. The influence of the British—whom the locals called Johns when Singapore was a colony—inspired the Malay dish of roti John, which features a baguette topped with beaten eggs, minced mutton, and onions that's then quickly panfried and served with a spicy tomato dip.

As a college freshman in Illinois, I spent many a night dwelling on the long, cold months I'd have to endure before my next taste of roti John or *chilli* crab. In early 1994, when we were all discovering the Internet, an enterprising Singaporean somewhere out in the ether set up a Web site where he posted a handful of pictures of foods like satay and Hainanese chicken rice. Immediately, e-mails with this precious URL raced around the world from one homesick Singaporean to another. I began braving glacial lakeshore temperatures to trek to the computer lab after classes, logging on just to stare with titanic longing at these pictures of dinners far, far away.

At the same time, I was getting a good schooling in a new genre of food. In the heart of my first Chicago winter—and a whopper of one at that, with windchills pushing seventy below one memorable day—I was getting well acquainted with the "classics" of American food. Pancakes, sloppy joes, pizza, buffalo wings—my dorm cafeteria pushed them all. I'd sampled some of these before, of course, Singapore being fairly cosmopolitan. (It even had a Denny's, although I never did find out whether a Singaporean Grand Slam is the same as a Grand Slam in Peoria.)

Meat loaf, however, mystified me. I'd never even heard of it. But from my first bite, I was smitten. Crusty, juicy, moist, and meaty all at once—this brick of red meat was heaven to me. For the first time, I was gripped with the urge to cook something— something that wasn't ramen or instant porridge, that is. I'd hardly eaten beef while growing up in Singapore—pork is generally much more widely used in Chinese home cooking there. So beef held great sex appeal to me. And having never tried meat loaf before, I was hooked.

The meat loaf I began making was basic. After I had dabbled with various mixes, Lawry's became my brand of choice. Jazzed up with an egg, a generous stream of soy sauce, and milk instead of water, this meat loaf mixture remains my go-to recipe even today. In the years since, I've experimented with elaborate meat loaf recipes that have graced the pages of glossy food magazines, perfectly delicious gourmet or ethnic versions conjured up by chefs like Ming Tsai. And yet, this is the one meat loaf that I make when a craving sets in. In fact, it was over this very meat loaf that I fell in love with my husband, Mike.

A rudimentary cook in my twenties who still often made dinners built on the salty shoulders of a can of Campbell's soup, I didn't actually turn a culinary corner until Mike entered my life.

In the summer of 2000, I flew to San Francisco for the Asian American Journalists Association's national convention. I'd been attending the convention since 1995—so had Mike, it turned out. We had many of the same friends in the organization; we'd been to many of the same parties. But somehow, we'd never met—until one evening, when he walked into the lobby of the Hyatt Regency in San Francisco and spotted me talking to one of his colleagues at *The New York Times*. Mike didn't know who I was, but he was pretty sure that if he walked across the lobby to say hello to his colleague, Merrill would introduce us. The next day, Mike and I met at a panel on covering the transgender and gay communities. And coffee. Then drinks. Then dinner. Not long after, he began traveling down to my home in Washington, D.C., to see me on weekends.

A bona fide food lover who'd grown up watching his stepmother make pancakes and pork chops in their rural Iowa kitchen, Mike soon began teaching me little things—how best to melt chocolate, what a food processor actually did, the importance of, oh, lighting the burner before putting the pan on so you don't burn your eyebrows off. For a gal who'd grown up being instructed to stay out of the kitchen, these were key revelations.

We soon began cooking together whenever he hopped on a train from New York City to visit me. One of our earliest collaborations involved making creamed spinach from scratch with a generous sprinkling of freshly grated nutmeg—to go with my Lawry's meat loaf, of course. It was a simple side dish. Nothing special to most cooks, I'm sure. Except that, until that dish, I'm not sure I was fully aware of what nutmeg looked like, much less that it had to be grated. (I'm almost certain I'd not grated anything before then.) Heck, the notion of being able to put creamed spinach on the table without first opening a frozen box had been unfathomable to me until that point.

I fell in love—and not just with the idea of actually being able to make delicious, restaurantlike dishes from scratch.

CHAPTER TWO

There are two New Yorks that coexist twice a year. There is the mad, glittering swirl of models, photographers, fashion editors, movie stars, champagne, thumping sound tracks, silken gowns, five-inch stilettos, and endless air kisses that takes over the city during New York's Fashion Week. And then there's the rest of Manhattan, which tends to fade in a blur of relative grayness during this time.

The pulsating fashion scene, for many years, was my world.

While I was something of a bookworm when I was younger, fashion had barely been on my radar. Then, when I was a young journalist, my head had been filled with romantic notions of covering wars à la Ernest Hemingway, exposing grave human wrongs, and writing lyrical, long narratives that would move readers to tears. At my first journalism job, as a metro-reporting intern at *The Straits Times* in Singapore the summer before I went away to college, I'd gotten a taste of this career I intended to have. A gutsy eighteen-year-old, I had talked my way past the gates of a puppy mill in Singapore, pretending to buy a dog with my "dad," a photographer from the paper. There we found a heartbreaking scene—dozens of dogs, mangy, though with excellent pedigrees, stuffed into the tiniest, filthiest cages, their paws red from padding about on unlined wire mesh, all yapping at a fevered pitch. The story I wrote—"100 Dogs at Breeding Farm Still Living in Misery after SPCA Call"—ran on July 17, 1993. The Singapore government swooped in right away. Investigative journalism became my new obsession.

In Baltimore, however, after a few years on the metro desk writing about murder and politics, I wanted to cover the more enjoyable things in life. Movies, TV, entertainment, food were my new desire. But writing about clothing and shoes? It never crossed my mind—until my boss, Mary, who had been the *Sun*'s fashion critic before becoming an editor, said, in not so many words, "We need someone to cover the fashion shows in New York. You're it." Puppy mills, drive-by shootings, a man who was suspected of pushing his pregnant girlfriend under a moving bus—I knew how to handle all of that. A fashion show? Models? Clothing? I had never so much as read an issue of *Vogue*. I started to panic.

But from the first moment I set my (then rather unfashionably clad) foot in a fashion show (having bought my first *Vogue* just the month before in order to prep for the assignment), I knew I wanted in.

Squeezed into my tiny seat at the Kenneth Cole show in a cavernous hall of Grand Central Terminal in New York City, I watched, slightly shell-shocked, from the eye of a tornado of double kisses and black-clad public relations assistants nervously darting around while barking into headsets. But then the lights dimmed, and a silence, thick with reverence, filled the room. Out of the darkness, the guttural cry for those in the front row to *"uncross your legs!"* came from photographers anxious to have runway shots devoid of heels.

A pounding beat started up. In a single, dramatic flash, the lights came on. Instinctively, we all leaned forward. Models stomped down the runway, a whir of spring's bright colors flashing before us. The air filled with the frenzied staccato clicks of cameras. The clothes were beautiful. My heartbeat crescendoed. I could barely breathe. The energy was intoxicating.

After the finale, I sat in a daze, slowly coming down from the high. I couldn't believe that a mere hour later, at my second of a day's worth of fashion shows, this exhilarating experience would happen again.

One season, I found myself rushing up the steps of the Fashion Week tent in midtown Manhattan, heels clicking, hair flying, palms sweating, as I pondered how exactly I was going to get into a show to which I hadn't been invited but which I desperately needed to include in my fashion roundup for the *Sun*.

At the entrance to the tent, I paused, as I often do, to take a breath and double-check my confidence. And then, the onslaught began. After battling my way through a mob of impossibly fashionable people, I'd made it to the front of the line with my toes miraculously untrodden by the countless pairs of spiky stilettos around me. A tall man with a headset and a crisp German accent gave me the fish eye as I wearily mumbled, *"Baltimore Sun,* Cheryl Tan." "Baltimore," he said slowly, examining me in a way that gave me the distinct feeling he did not approve of my haircut. "What *country* is that?" Before I could respond, a beautiful blonde with a headset next to him butted in. "It's a newspaper," she said, the three syllables of *newspaper* slowly dripping with disdain. "And it's American." With that, Mr. Germany waved me away, and a cashmered elbow emerged from behind to shove me aside.

And then I moved to New York, the fashion mecca. At the ends of days of great fashion-world-inflicted stress, as I nursed the carcass of my self-esteem, the kitchen became my sanctuary. Let others have their ashrams and therapy sessions. I'd come home, pour a glass of sauvignon blanc, then take out two sticks of butter. On weekends and weeknights, I filled the West Village loft that was my newlywed haven with the smells of six-spice oatmeal cookies, apple-cornmeal cakes, chocolate-hazelnut tortes, sugary apricot tarts, lemon-macaroon pies, raspberry-oatmeal bars.

In this cloud of cinnamon-scented zen, the pressures of New York would melt away. Outside the kitchen, life was complicated and meandered in unpredictable and uncontrollable ways. But with my mixer in hand and two sticks of softened butter before me, the possibilities were thrilling and endless— and the outcome was entirely governed by me. There are few things more basic or satisfying than kneading a ball of dough or rolling one out. Having a mind that cannot stay quiet, I've never been able to meditate without going stir-crazy. But give me a ball of dough and the not-so-distant dream of a piping hot cherry tart with a beautiful lattice-weave top and a generous sprinkling of confectioners' sugar, and a feeling of serenity washes over me. My mind instantly hushes.

I began to feel as if I were leading a double life. By day, I was fashion Cheryl, the girl who would follow the unspoken rules by nonchalantly ordering a salad at a business lunch—dressing on the side—but then be so hungry from just grazing on leaves that I had to race to McDonald's for a quick meat fix before heading back to the office. But by night, I went from covering a world that was obsessed with not eating to one that was *all* about eating. Evenings were filled with blissful hours of chopping, searing, boiling, and baking. By the time a pot of homemade tomato sauce was on a delicious simmer and dinner was just minutes away, I would start to feel like myself again. All had been restored.

I tried to make some Singaporean dishes, of course. *Tried* being the key word. And as I faced stir-fry after subpar stir-fry, I found it hard not to resent my mother for not having pressed me harder on this front.

Like me, the women in my mother's family were relatively slow (and reluctant) to enter the kitchen. Mum and her two sisters were a rambunctious lot for whom learning skills that would make them more marriageable (like cooking) was low on the list of priorities. Studying hard, occasionally skipping school, flirting massively with the neighborhood boys—Mum, Auntie Jane, and Auntie Alice did it all. (Well, maybe not Auntie Alice, who, as the eldest, was always the most responsible.) Mum and Auntie Jane still love to tell the story of hiding in their tiny apartment with the lights off on Friday nights if they didn't have dates. "We were pretty girls, you know! We'd lose face if the neighborhood boys knew we didn't have dates!" they would say, giggling.

Their independent streaks would eventually land them successful husbands who could afford maids to do the bulk of the cooking. Although Mum has picked up some recipes from monitoring the maid at the stove over the years, she'll be the first to tell you that her role in the kitchen remains that of the air traffic controller and not the pilot. Feeling that she had nothing to teach, she did not attempt to show me and my younger sister much beyond the go-to brownies she made whenever we were required to bring a dessert to a party and her very own version of banana bread, an oven-toasted snack of white bread topped with gobs of butter, mashed bananas, and sugar that we adored.

Even my sister entered the kitchen in a serious way far earlier than I did. While I was relying on Shake 'n Bake boxes and Campbell's soup cans in my own kitchen, Daphne was light-years ahead of me. Having gone to Cornell University's elite School of Hotel Administration for her undergraduate degree, Daphne had been exposed to glimpses of life in professional kitchens and had begun trying out some of her lessons at home. During a visit that my childhood friend Jeanette and I made to Manhattan one summer in our mid-twenties, Daphne had offered to make dinner for us one night. In my own kitchen in Washington, D.C., I had treated Jeanette to simple grilled steaks and prepackaged creamed spinach. When we sat down to dinner in Daphne's midtown Manhattan apartment, I instantly felt shamed—the younger sister had outdone her elder.

As Jeanette and I watched, Daphne put on oven mitts and pulled roasted squash out of her oven. She dumped it into a blender with cream and a few spices, and presented us with a beautifully smooth roasted squash soup. Then she impressed us even more as she masterfully whipped together an Italian sausage risotto, nonchalantly stirring in cup after cup of broth as she chatted with us over the kitchen counter. This was like nothing I'd even contemplated trying in my own kitchen.

With the help of Southeast Asian blogs and Web sites, however, I managed to piece together some semblances of the dishes I grew up eating.

One of the dishes I desperately wanted to know how to make was *tau yew bak*, a stew of pork belly braised in dark soy sauce, sweet and thick, and a mélange of spices that is a signature dish of the Teochews, the ethnic Chinese group of my paternal ancestors. When done well, the meat is so tender you feel almost as if you're biting into pillows. The gravy is salty, sweet, and gently flecked with traces of ginger, star anise, and cinnamon—just perfect drizzled over rice. And the best versions come filled with hard-boiled eggs and wedges of tofu that have been steeped in the stew for so long that they've turned the color of a good milk chocolate.

My Tanglin ah-ma used to make this dish—often with duck instead of pork belly. You'd smell it the moment you walked into her apartment, and it was always a signal to rev up your appetite for the feast ahead. The idea of making it was daunting— I'd never even *seen* it being made—but with the Internet at hand, few things are difficult to attempt. After some days, I'd cobbled together a recipe from reading several versions online.

It looked simple enough. After slicing the pork loin I'd bought—pork belly being just a little too fatty for me—I fired up the wok until the vegetable oil got nice and crackly. In went the sugar, followed by rapid stirring to keep the sugar moving as it slowly melted and caramelized. Once that happened, I threw in bashed garlic, ginger, a cinnamon stick, and star anise, and fried everything up together until it was an intoxicatingly fragrant goo. Everything after that was simple—dump in the meat, stir it up, add soy sauce, dark soy sauce, water, stir and simmer.

I had been nervous about making this dish, feeling the discerning eyes of my Tanglin ah-ma on me the whole time. But as my very first *tau yew bak* simmered and the smells of dark soy sauce and spices began to fill my apartment, I almost started to tear up.

As much as I'd loved my Tanglin ah-ma and her food, I'd never been able to fully communicate that to her. She spoke only Teochew, which I barely spoke, knowing only how to wish her "Happy New Year" and say "thank you." I'd always wondered what she must have thought of her very *ang moh* granddaughter, who generally preferred to keep her nose in her Enid Blyton books until dinner or pineapple tarts appeared. She probably thought that I never wanted to learn anything from her, that I might never know how to cook. I wondered what she would think of this effort.

The end result wasn't perfect—the meat could have been more tender, and I'd completely forgotten to buy tofu—but it was a first step. As Mike and I slowly chewed on my *tau yew bak* shortly after, I began to wonder how I could learn to make the actual dish I grew up with. My Tanglin ah-ma had died years ago—but when she was alive, she had cooked almost daily with my auntie Khar Imm, who had married my father's brother and played the role of the dutiful daughter-in-law, helping my grand-mother in the kitchen after moving into the family home.

Someday, I thought, I'll ask her.

IN THE FALL OF 2008, AS THE FINANCIAL FRAMEWORK OF the world rapidly dissolved, my employer, *The Wall Street Journal,* was on top of the news. Because I was a fashion and retail writer, fashion label closings and retail bankruptcies became the bread and butter of my work. My days were filled with dev-astating stories, and my evenings were filled with news of friends losing jobs. A twitch under my left eye that I'd had dur-ing a trying relationship in my twenties suddenly returned. My hair started falling out. By early 2009, I'd developed migraines so bad my doctor was briefly worried that I might soon have a stroke. My dad, after all, had had a minor one at age forty.

On that morning in 1985, my father collapsed while brushing his teeth. He'd suffered a stroke that, fortunately, was so mild he was back on his feet within days. His arms were a little weak, and it took months before he stopped feeling tired, but a more signifi-cant change occurred. The man who always had been defined first and foremost as a busy executive—regularly flying from Hong Kong to Shanghai to Taiwan to tour factories or close deals—suddenly wanted to spend more time with his family.

Now it was time for a change for me, too, my body was tell-ing me.

With Chinese New Year approaching, I knew my auntie Khar Imm would be gearing up her baking. On the docket that year were chocolate cookies, almond bites, and of course, pine-apple tarts. I e-mailed my father's family, asking after them and then gently inquiring about this year's tart-making schedule.

And with that, a few weeks later, I was on a plane, heading to Singapore, heading home.

THIS MAY SOUND ODD—AND I ALWAYS HAVE THE DISTINCT sense that I may get struck by lightning each time I think it—but one of my favorite childhood memories was of my Tanglin ah-ma's funeral.

My younger sister, Daphne, and I had led a somewhat shel-tered childhood up until that point. I rarely ventured far from our apartment, except to play soccer or Ping-Pong with the boys in our neighborhood. Instead, I spent most of my time reading, thinking, and penning those Very Important Thoughts in a little journal. I had been shocked when my grandmother died. I had known she was ill but hadn't understood exactly how dire it was. (My parents had thought it best to shield us from the details.)

From the moment we got the news, however, we went from fairly quiet lives centered on homework and boring piano prac-tice to a vortex of nonstop activity pebbled with a motley crew of characters who were loud, boisterous, and filled with life. There was Jessie, my auntie Khar Imm's daughter, who was just a year older than I was but already so commanding a presence that she was somehow able to boss around even those twice our age. There was her father, my uncle Soo Kiat, my father's younger brother, a thinner, louder version of my dad, who always had a glint of mischief in his eyes that hinted at some probably inappropriate joke lingering behind them. Uncle Ah Tuang, a sturdy young man whom my grandmother had taken in as a baby and raised as her own, loved my grandmother and his older "brothers" fiercely and was quick to join in any conversation, peppering it with jovial jokes and laughs, big and deep.

My auntie Leng Eng, my father's older sister, was the serious one who kept everyone in line. A vice principal at one of the most prestigious schools in Singapore, she watched over everything with an eagle eye, directing us in crisp English or Teochew to fetch porridge for a guest or make sure teacups were constantly filled.

And, of course, there was Jessie's mum, my auntie Khar Imm, every bit her daughter's mother in spirit and manner. Auntie Khar Imm had lived with my grandmother since she married into the household—she'd shepherded Tanglin Ah-Ma through her illness and guarded the wake and funeral with the care of a woman who seemed to feel the loss with a silent intensity that the rest of us could only imagine.

I had never spent much time with my father's side of the family, because of a rift that began shortly after my mother married into the family. My parents had met soon after he'd ended a courtship of several years with a woman who would have made an ideal daughter-in-law: She came from a well-off family, she was a schoolteacher, and she was obedient and polite. My mother, on the other hand, was the mouthy nineteen-year-old—nine years younger than my father!—who had taken a job as a receptionist in the company where he worked. "Your mother was a Campari girl, you know," Dad still proudly says of this time. The company they worked for distributed Campari in Singapore, and my mother's job occasionally included holding trays of Campari drinks at events, flirtatiously pressing people to try them. My parents flirted and started dating. Shortly after she took a job as a flight attendant for Singapore Airlines, my mother married into the Tan family.

The Tan household was fraught with tension from the beginning, when my mother refused to quit her job after the wedding. It was something of a beauty contest to get a spot flying for Singapore Airlines at the time, and my pretty mother was at the pinnacle of glamour among her friends. For starters, what she wore to work had been designed for the airline by the French couturier Pierre Balmain: a beautifully regal dark blue batik uniform that was a sexy and form-fitting version of the *sarong kabaya,* a traditional Malay costume consisting of a three-quarter-sleeved blouse paired with a long, pencil-thin wrap skirt. Because the uniform has a scoop neck that dips about as low as it can while still being decent, there is a popular joke in Singapore that involves an SIA flight attendant leaning over to ask a male passenger as she serves the in-flight meal, presumably of spaghetti and meatballs, "Sir—would you like sauce on your balls tonight?" Building on that image, SIA's advertisements from its inception, in 1972, blatantly touted its flight attendants as sex symbols. From the beginning, ads featured dazzling pictures of sarong-clad stewardesses in exotic locales next to the words "This girl's in love with you." The more famous and long-lasting slogan wasn't any less evocative: "Singapore Girl, you're a great way to fly."

Having beaten dozens of hopefuls to win this job that had become a powerful emblem of the new modern and sophisticated Singaporean woman, my mother refused to quit just to cook and be a dutiful daughter-in-law. My grandparents had hoped for an obedient daughter-in-law but instead got my head-strong mother—who had a (in the minds of traditionalists) slutty job, no less. One night, when my dad was out of town, the SIA van arrived at my grandparents' home to pick up Mum for a flight. My grandparents bitterly protested, forbidding her to leave. To pry herself free, my mother slapped my grandfather and ran out the door, so the story goes. When my father returned, he and my mother moved out immediately. For years after that, my sister and I peered at this side of our family over a chasm, politely sipping soda and eating pineapple tarts whenever we visited my Tanglin ah-ma. Undiscussed disagreements from years past had congealed and become impenetrable. Whenever we sat around the coffee table at Chinese New Year or the few other times we visited, the heavy air simply was too difficult to pierce. Small talk about school, health, and business was usually all we could muster.

Tanglin Ah-Ma's funeral, however, brought us all together.

Now, I'm just going to say this. Chinese funerals in Singapore are pretty fun—if you're eleven. And, well, if you're not the deceased.

They're generally drawn-out affairs, grand and long. For my grandmother, the wake took place over seven days. Each morning, my sister and I pinned black squares of fabric onto our right sleeves, the mark that we were mourning for a paternal family member, and headed over to my Tanglin ah-ma's apartment building. In the void deck—the ground floor—of the complex, an imposing display had been set up. A series of large, colorful blankets, which the Chinese in Singapore sometimes send in lieu of flowers to grieving families, cordoned off a space that was filled with dozens of tables for visitors and family. And at the head of the display was a massive altar bearing offerings of food and tea and my grandmother's picture. Behind the picture, my grandmother lay.

My cousins and I had a few tasks, which we attacked with great enthusiasm when we weren't playing gin rummy or poring over issues of *Beano* and *Dandy*, British comic books about a group of rather naughty boys. We had to help with the burning of incense and paper money for my grandmother—until we were permanently relieved of the duty on the second day, when Royston, Jessie's brother, almost set the funeral tent on fire. Our main job, however, was to help Auntie Khar Imm make sure that guests were properly fed when they arrived. By day, we ferried *guay zhee* (dried melon seeds), tea, and bowls of piping hot porridge to the tables on command. But when night fell, our duties changed—we had one task, and it was a significant one.

The Chinese in Singapore believe that if a cat jumps over a coffin, the body inside will awaken as a zombie, rising up to hop around stiffly, as if both feet were tied firmly together. With their arms stretched out washboard straight, these zombies will keep hopping along until they encounter a human. When that happens in Chinese horror movies, death by washboard arms is inevitable.

Naturally, the task of chasing stray cats away from the coffin fell upon us. And boy, did we take it seriously—around and around the void deck we went, keeping our eyes peeled for those little zombie-making buggers, running at them at full speed when we spied one. At the end of each night, when my Tanglin ah-ma's coffin was intact and she remained not a zombie, I couldn't help but feel a sense of accomplishment. It had been a good night's work.

Emboldened by all I was learning, I decided to try picking up some Teochew. I'd learned some Hokkien (or Fukienese), a dialect similar to Teochew that's spoken by my mother's side of the family. The Teochews and Hokkiens are generally proud folks who like to keep their identities separate, even though they hail from the same region of China. I was confident that, since I knew some Hokkien, Teochew couldn't possibly be that hard.

For days, I listened hard to Jessie and my aunts. Little by little, my confidence grew. One day, as I was about to ask Jessie to take a look at something, I paused and then proudly said, "*Le kua!*" thinking I was saying "You look!" Her reaction was instantaneous. "*Aiyoh! Mm see kua, see* toi!" Jessie exclaimed. Of course, I had used the Hokkien word for "look," *kua,* instead of the Teochew *toi*. The ultimate insult.

By the time the seventh day rolled around, I was starting to feel sad that I'd be going back to my regular life, with no older Teochew cousins to school me on the mores and choice words of my people. Before my grandmother's cremation, however, we had to escort her to Heaven.

On the last night, we donned beige hooded robes made of rough gunnysack material—so scratchy that we would be feeling external in addition to internal pain over my grandmother's death. With a great deal of pomp, we set a multistoried paper house, filled with servants, a car, and a driver, aflame; this was an offering for my grandmother, to ensure a good life for her on the Other Side. Then I knelt next to my father, the firstborn son, in the front, trying to follow along as a priest from a Taoist temple chanted.

When my father started crying, I was surprised to discover that my own eyes were wet. I hadn't felt close to my grandmother at all. I'd known her largely through her food. And I wasn't sure why I was crying, except that, over the last week, I had finally felt a sense of connection to her, to my father's side of the family. And as stressful as it had been to be on zombie-fighting duty, I was grateful for that.

As the chanting drew to a close, the priest signaled us to get up. The time had come. My grandmother's spirit was ready to enter Heaven. And we were to escort her. Slowly, he led my Tanglin ah-ma's hooded flock around the void deck, walking in single file in a large circle before we got to a five-foot-long aluminum "bridge" that had been installed earlier that day. Gingerly, we crossed the bridge, having tossed coins into basins of water by its side before stepping on—even heavenly bridges have their tolls, it seems. We circled and crossed the bridge three times, wailing as we went, until finally we reached the gate of Heaven. Outside of this gate we stood, weeping and whispering our private good-byes.

My grandmother entered. Our job was done.

MEMORIES OF GRANDMOTHER'S FUNERAL CAME BACK TO ME as I looked out at the flickering lights of Singapore from my descending airplane from New York. The funeral had been the last chunk of time that I'd spent with my father's side of the family. In the sixteen years that I'd lived in the United States, I had had hardly any contact with them, in fact, beyond a handful of Chinese New Year visits and my wedding, of course. And I often came away from those visits with the feeling that I was seen as too wayward, too different, for pouring my energies into my career and the never-ending climb instead of cooking or bearing children.

Yet here I was, the prodigal niece, heading home to spend two days making cookies and pineapple tarts with my auntie Khar Imm and her sisters, who now assumed my Tanglin ah-ma's baking mantle every Chinese New Year. While I have close relationships with the aunties on my mother's side, I couldn't remember having a one-on-one conversation that lasted longer than a minute with my auntie Khar Imm. An uncertainty started setting in. How would I survive two days? What on earth would we talk about?

But I had asked, and they'd generously invited me over.

I had been too late to learn before. I wasn't going to let that happen again.

CHAPTER THREE

I knew I was in for it when I walked into the room and there were not one, not two, but *seventy* pineapples jammed into tubs.

Stunned, I quickly looked around my auntie Khar Imm's mother's kitchen—there were just five of us there. Exactly how many tarts were we making that weekend?

I started to panic.

I was nervously fumbling for the oranges that I'd bought at the market as a gift, and Auntie Khar Imm stepped forward to welcome me. I hadn't seen her since a visit to her home during Chinese New Year a year or two before. The visit then had been very brief, as all our visits to her home had been since my Tanglin ah-ma died. Somehow, I had always been a little afraid of my auntie Khar Imm—not for any justifiable reason. I'd just always gotten the sense that Khar Imm wasn't the biggest fan of our relatively irresponsible branch of the family. Our visits were often a little stilted and perfunctory.

Now, years later, in her mother's kitchen, where we were to make the pineapple tarts, she stepped forward, kind and warm.

"Ah Lien ah, chi bao le mei you?" she gently said, asking in Mandarin if I'd eaten.

It took me a while to respond—it had been a long time since anyone had called me Ah Lien, my Chinese name. The name sounds so much like Ah Lian, which is a derogatory Singaporean nickname for women who are gauche in both manners and style, that I was relieved when my parents started calling me Cheryl instead as I got older. I get the Ah Lien treatment only from my maternal grandmother and my friends—when they want to embarrass me in public.

"Chi le, chi le," I replied, telling her I'd eaten, as I watched her disappear in a rush to get her guest a glass of water.

There was some clucking over the fact that I'd brought a gift. *"Aiyah, buyong lah!"* Auntie Khar Imm exclaimed, looking pleased nonetheless as she handed the oranges to her mother. She was wrong; a gift was needed, as I was a guest in her mother's home. (I was suddenly thankful that my own mother had reminded her Americanized daughter of the necessity the very day before.)

After introductions were made—I'd never met her mother or sisters—and pleasantries were exchanged, I realized I was already behind. The process had begun without me. At dawn, Auntie Khar Imm's family had gone to the market to pick up the pineapples they'd ordered. The plan that weekend was to make three thousand tarts—more than twenty years after my Tanglin ah-ma's death, dozens of friends and family members still request jars of them every Chinese New Year.

As I entered the kitchen, I marveled at its expanse. The

room itself was large—about the dimensions of a sizable dining room—and it opened out into a white-tiled backyard lined with kitchen cabinets stuffed with cooking utensils, shelves, and a row of burners. In the heat of this big backyard, my aunt's family had spread out in a tart-making production line—each one was hard at work prepping the pineapples for the jam we would make that day. In one corner, Auntie Khar Imm's mother was in a half-sit, half-squat position above a foot-high wooden stool as she hunched over a stack of pineapples, holding a large chopper. With muscular whacks, she worked methodically, chopping off the tops of the pineapples and their tough, thick skins before tossing them into a large red pail. From there, Auntie Khar Imm's two sisters took over. Perched on similarly short stools, they were using small knives to slowly gouge out the eyes from each fruit.

Surveying this hubbub, I wasn't sure what to do. After the obligatory hellos, they immediately bent back over the pineapples, working deftly, silently. They seemed to have it pretty much covered. And it was true, they'd been doing this for decades, since they began helping my Tanglin ah-ma make the tarts, learning the recipe along the way. They certainly didn't need this dilettante around.

But I had come all this way—and I certainly didn't travel 9,500 miles just to *watch* my aunties make pineapple tarts. No, guest or not, I was *making* these tarts.

I asked Auntie Khar Imm for a knife and jumped in—well, sort of. For starters, I was having problems feeling my fingers or getting them to move in the general direction they were supposed to go in the filmy plastic gloves they'd instructed me to put on to keep out the tart pineapple juice. And then there was the issue of maneuvering the knife in said gloves in a way that actually resulted in the eyes getting gouged. Over and over I jabbed, trying not to stab myself as the gloves skidded across my palms like roller skates on ice. The few holes I managed to create were massive and slushy from multiple stab wounds. I could feel the aunties surreptitiously surveying my work—all of them too polite to scold me for wasting chunks of pineapple with my mammoth gouges. The more I stabbed, the more mortified I was. But no matter how hard I tried, I simply couldn't get my fingers to obey.

Finally, one auntie walked over and handed me a Chinese soupspoon. "Try this," she said, gesturing for me to use the handle to scoop out the eyes. With that, my fingers complied. And I started to fit in.

In silence, we worked—my inability to speak much Teochew being a major social hindrance. But as we carefully dug out the hundred or so eyes that were in each pineapple, the stories emerged. Auntie Khar Imm, of course, began by asking the question I'd been getting since I became engaged seven years ago: "When are you having a child?" My clucking answer—that I was just too busy with work, with life, in New York to even fathom producing anything that would depend on me for just about everything—was unacceptable, of course. After a short silence, her sisters nudged me to take a break and eat something, gesturing to a large pot of jet-black liquid on the counter. *"Ter kah dieo,"* Auntie Khar Imm said in Teochew, stopping to explain further in Mandarin when it was clear that I had no comprehension of what she had just said. It turned out the dish was a stew of pigs' trotters braised in black vinegar and ginger. "Good for after giving birth," Auntie Khar Imm said. "Very easy to make."

Point taken.

When the seventy pineapples had been cleaned, prepped, and cut into large chunks, Auntie Khar Imm began running the slices through a juicer, dumping the pulp into a massive wok and preserving the juice in a pot. Into the wok went cinnamon sticks, knotted pandan leaves—from a tropical plant that's similar in scent to vanilla and is used in many Southeast Asian desserts—and a few cups of the juice. And then the truly laborious work began. For the next several hours, we sweated over the stove, stirring the pineapple concoction in several woks, pausing now and then to taste the gradually congealing jam to see if the mixture needed more sugar or juice. Actually, to be more accurate, *Auntie Khar Imm* sweated over the stove. As she did the bulk of the stirring—with me pitching in now and then when she had to take a break—I hovered with my notebook and camera, trying to document every moment, believing that this would be the best way to ensure that I would remember every sliver of this process.

Watching Auntie Khar Imm stir with ease and calm in her mother's sweltering backyard kitchen, I felt increasingly puzzled. She looked nothing like the frazzled bundle of nerves that I was in my own kitchen, where I often found myself glued to a printed-out recipe or instructions on my BlackBerry, not daring to make a move without first rereading the recipe for the twentieth time. Sometimes I would attempt to be bold, but my defi-nition of culinary bravado meant that I would first read the 150 comments on an Epicurious.com recipe for additions that other cooks had made, and after much thought and more Web re-search about the pros and cons of an unorthodox move that hadn't been sanctioned by the mighty editors at *Gourmet* or *Bon Appétit*, I would make the addition, my heart filling with fear laced with the tiniest dash of excitement. Auntie Khar Imm, however, displayed none of this trepidation. Instead, I watched in shock as she would sample the tiniest spoonful of the boiling jam, then cavalierly slit open giant bags of sugar, hoist them over the woks, and give them a hefty jiggle, inspiring landslide amounts to tumble forth. "Wait, wait," I sputtered, "how much are you putting in? How do you know how much to put in?" These questions, at first, confused Auntie Khar Imm, who imme-diately started laughing once she figured out what I was asking. "Aiyah—*buyong* measure *lah!*" she said. "Just taste, taste, taste and then *agak-agak lor*!"

I didn't know it then but *agak-agak*, a Malay phrase mean-ing "guess-guess" that's pronounced "ah-gahk ah-gahk," would be a refrain I would hear over and over during the two days of tart making—usually uttered following some laughter on my aunties' part over my attachment to the preposterous no-tion that cooking should be precise. I wasn't seeing much hu-mor in the kitchen that day, however. I had been hoping to learn a recipe, one that I would be able to replicate back in New York. I had never done the "*agak-agak*" thing in my kitchen. How would I know if I was completely screwing up?

And so I attempted to grill Auntie Khar Imm. "But, really—

how much sugar do I put in?" Patiently, she explained, "You see how sweet your pineapple is lor! Very sweet then add less, not so sweet then add more."

This was patently unhelpful, I thought.

"Um, but how can you tell how sweet your pineapple is? Are pineapples of a certain shade sweeter? Can you tell by their smell? If it's sweet, how much sugar do you add? If it's not so sweet, how much do you add? What *is* your definition of sweet?"

Now it was her turn to look confused for a moment—before erupting once again in laughter. "Aiyah," she finally said when she caught her breath. "Just taste, taste, taste, and then *agak-agak*!"

I was starting to get truly panicked. I had traveled from half a world away in order to learn my Tanglin ah-ma's pineapple tart recipe—but it was starting to look like I'd return to New York with vague instructions built on the nebulous foundation of *agak-agak*. After about the fifth time that we had this exchange, however, Auntie Khar Imm decided to humor me by measuring the sugar she was adding—while giggling at the ludicrousness of the practice.

She had learned to make the tarts—and to cook—from my Tanglin ah-ma not by measuring, taking pictures, or writing things down, of course. She'd learned from watching, from helping, from cooking along with her. There had never been any need for words or lessons. They simply had a job to do—to put food on the table—and they just rolled up their sleeves and did it. If something tasted too sweet or too salty one day, they'd just add less sugar or salt the next. Cooking wasn't a science;

it wasn't meant to be perfect. It was simply a way to feed the people you loved.

No one knew where my Tanglin ah-ma had learned to make pineapple tarts—or any of the other dishes she mastered. But what everyone did know was that she was a formidable woman. From the stories I'd heard, she'd been handed a trying life. Born in rural Singapore to a farming family, she entered into an arranged marriage with a wealthy man who turned out to be as in love with betting on horses as he was with drink. (And, everyone suspected, women.) After watching her husband squander his wealth, she turned to hand washing the neighbors' laundry in order to buy schoolbooks for her three children, my father, my auntie Leng Eng, and their younger brother, my uncle Soo Kiat. But above all, she was devoted to feeding her family. "She would wake up very early to make breakfast," Auntie Khar Imm said, noting that Tanglin Ah-Ma occasionally rose at three or four in the morning to make *bak-zhang*, the pyramid-shaped glutinous rice dumplings that Singaporeans sometimes have for breakfast. I tried to think hard of my childhood and the *bak-zhang* I'd had. Did I remember what my grandmother's dumplings tasted like? But no matter how hard I dug into my recollections of life pre-eleven, I just wasn't sure. I had been so young—and more obsessed with Chicken McNuggets than with these sticky dumplings—that I didn't recall having eaten them very much. Thinking about my grandmother rising in the darkness just to make them for all of us, I felt ashamed.

As we talked and stirred, the jam got denser, darker, turning a woody shade of ocher. It would have to cool overnight before we could bake. As I left that evening, I couldn't stop thinking of my grandmother's *bak-zhang*. I had taken them for granted; now, I desperately wanted to learn how to make them.

THE NEXT MORNING, I ARRIVED BEARING CHOCOLATES.

Once again, there was the clucking, the cries of *"buyong lah!"* and the offering of water to the guest. Auntie Khar Imm and her sisters had already begun by the time I arrived. And once again, they didn't seem quite sure what to do with me. My boisterous cousin Jessie was in the kitchen, too. I'd hardly seen her since we were children, but within minutes of catching up, our banter felt natural. After flitting about, trying to figure out where to fit in, I decided to latch on to my cousin, trailing after her as I'd done as an eleven-year-old at my grandmother's funeral. Jessie, who works in the accounting department of an interior design firm, had missed the jam-making process because she had to work the day before. But now that she was in the fray, Jessie, who as a twelve-year-old had been able to boss adults around, held court once again, brimming with confidence as she dumped butter, flour, and egg yolks in a mixer to prepare the dough for the cookie base.

Having grown up living with my Tanglin ah-ma, Jessie had been roped in to help in the kitchen, learning how to cook along the way. Watching her stride around, mixing and rolling dough with confident authority, I couldn't help but be in awe. Once again, I was the bookish, sheltered eleven-year-old, wanting to be like my fearless older cousin. From Jessie and her auntie Khar Moi, who I was told was the baker of her family, I learned some things—how to mix the buttery dough, create sunflower-shaped rounds with a cookie press, and fill the holes of the rounds with dough. We would then lightly brush the cookie bases with beaten egg yolk, roll up balls of the jam, which by now had hardened a little, place them atop the cookies, and send the cookies off to Auntie Khar Imm, who was squatting on a low stool, manning the oven.

As we kneaded, brushed, and rolled, I gently prodded my aunties to tell me about my ancestors. I'd heard the story of my great-grandfather's immigration from Shantou, in southeastern China, to Singapore in search of a better life. I'd wanted to visit the village for years—here was my chance to find out more. Auntie Khar Moi, who'd actually visited the area, told me about the tiny village called Teo Ann Kim Sar, colloquially referred to as Sar Leng Tan (akin to Village Tan), where my great-grandfather was born. She didn't know much except that it was somewhere between Chaozhou and Shantou, two fairly major industrial cities in Southern China. The more questions I asked—and the more cookies I made—the more they seemed to embrace me, this almost-alien *ang moh,* as one of their own. When a friend of mine stopped by to watch us cook and teased me, saying that I was "very fierce," my auntie Khar Imm immediately leapt in to defend me. "Aiyah," she said, "Sar Leng Tan girls are all very fierce one!"

My Tanglin ah-ma, too, had had this quality, I found out. Among the Chinese New Year cookies she would make was a tiny white cookie called *kueh bangkit.* Now, this sweet, tapioca flour cookie is not easy to execute; when done right, it's supposed to have such an airy consistency that it virtually melts on your tongue. But most versions you buy in stores are so dense that they're not going to disintegrate unless you start chewing.

My Tanglin ah-ma's *kueh bangkit,* of course, was perfect. In the kitchen that day, I learned that each year before Chinese New Year, she would haul her charcoal stove out of her tiny high-rise apartment kitchen and into the corridor. To nail the consistency, Jessie said, you've got to make sure the tapioca flour is super dry. Some bakers spread the flour out on a baking sheet and stick that in a hot oven to dry out. But this easy method was beneath my Tanglin ah-ma. Instead, she did what she'd always done. She'd fill a large wok with tapioca flour, light up her charcoal stove, squat over a low stool, and just start frying, tossing the flour high into the air in the narrow hallway that she shared with her neighbors. "Aiyoh, the neighbors used to get so angry," Jessie said, laughing. "She would get flour all over the place!" The floor, the walls, the doorknobs would be covered with white powder by the time she was done. The neighbors would yell—oh, they would complain. Unfazed, Tanglin Ah-Ma would just keep on frying.

As the evening seeped in, we started packing up. We'd made close to three thousand tarts that weekend. And I had sore arms, still-sticky fingers, and a healthy dollop of pride to show for them. As we said our polite good-byes, my aunties pressed way too many jars of the tarts onto me, insisting that I take them back to my family, back to America.

I left content. I'd emerged with the recipe I'd come for— but I'd also gotten so much more. I thought back to how I'd never given these tarts, the *kueh bangkit,* even the *bak-zhang,* much thought before. I'd enjoyed them while eating them, sure, but I'd never considered making them, having dismissed know-ing how to cook as one of those things that weakened you as a female. And yet there my grandmother had been, cooking with a ferocity that I should be so lucky to have.

I knew now that I'd been wrong all along. And—I really wanted that *bak-zhang* recipe.

CHAPTER FOUR

Back in New York, Mike had his instructions.

He was allowed to try my pineapple tarts—but just one, maybe two. (Three, if he did the laundry.) The rest, after all, had to be my lifeline.

There was snow on the ground. New York Fashion Week was just around the corner. My days and evenings were once again gobbled up by writing, reporting, and haranguing publicists, retailers, and designers for information and fashion show invitations. And, with the retail industry imploding, I was once again chained to my BlackBerry at all hours of the day; when it's 3:00 A.M. in New York, it's daytime somewhere in Europe and Asia, after all. I was sleeping with my BlackBerry by my bed; I was jumping up whenever I heard it buzz, terrified that I was missing some crucial development in the rapidly unraveling economic landscape that I'd need to write about or include in *The Wall Street Journal* fashion blog I was managing. I was barely sleeping. And when I did, I woke up to find alarming amounts of my black hair strewn about my bed. I had never felt more like a hamster on a wheel—a soon-to-be hairless hamster, at that.

At this point, even baking couldn't save my sanity. All I had were my grandmother's tarts. Just opening the fridge and seeing they were there made me feel better. And when I particularly needed a fix, I'd gingerly take one out and slowly nibble, thinking about home.

The home that I knew and loved had recently splintered. Two years before, after thirty-two years of marriage, my parents had suddenly divorced. The signs of marital stress had been evident for a long time. My father's job postings overseas may have drawn us closer as I poured my adolescent thoughts into long letters to him, telling him about the hopes, apprehensions, and dreams that filled me—things I could never tell my mother, who essentially was left to function as a single parent for weeks on end and play the role of the strict enforcer who kept the trains running on time. But his absence thrust a wedge in their relationship. The fracture grew over the years. In the end, however, the tipping point involved a Beijing woman. I did not know much about this woman—just that they had met when she was assigned to be my father's translator and assistant when he went to Suzhou on frequent business trips. She hailed from a rural part of Anhui, China, where she'd grown up on a farm. Eventually, she moved to Beijing, where my father had begun spending half his time in the mid-2000s. There, she continued to help him as a girl Friday of sorts. She spoke very little English but wanted an English name she could use. And so my father named her Ketty. "I don't know why," he said, when I asked. "It just sounds like her."

Watching my family unravel from 9,500 miles away through tear-soaked phone calls in the middle of the night and lengthy e-mails that clearly offered little comfort, I had never felt farther. Divorce is still fairly uncommon in Singapore, even among those in their twenties and thirties. For those in my parents' generation? Virtually unheard of. While I knew of many men my father's age who had mistresses on the side, in the end, they always came home to their wives and families. The feudal Chinese concubine system—in spirit, even if not in law—remained firmly in place in twenty-first-century Singapore. So why deal with the legal hassle of divorce and asset dividing when you didn't have to?

My mother was blindsided. So were Daphne and I. My weekly conversations with Dad became strained. I wasn't sure how to react, what to think. And I felt a little replaced—this new woman turned out to be younger than I was. Was my father now giving her the same pep talks he had always given me? Was I as important? And were my sister and I to blame? I had always felt some guilt over the fissure in my parents' marriage. "We could have gone to Hong Kong with your papa when he went there to work, you know," my mother would often say in low moments during my childhood as she pined for my father. "But your schooling [in Singapore] was more important." I always felt that my parents' marriage might have turned out differently if only they hadn't had me. Now, once again, feelings of guilt began gnawing at me.

The divorce had been largely cordial—my father, who was now running a Singapore-based moving company, still stayed in our family home when he was in town. When he was in Singapore, he and my mother shared a car, had dinner almost every night, and ran errands together. It was just easier—logistically and financially—that way. And they did still get along as friends, after all. Even so, feelings were a little raw all around. And my parents had started avoiding the rambunctious, large dinners my mother's family organized just so they wouldn't face uncomfortable questions—or silences. Of all the developments that had unfolded since my parents' divorce, this struck me as among the saddest.

No one pressured me, but as the firstborn, I felt duty-bound to be there. Daphne now lived in Hong Kong and made the four-hour flight to Singapore to visit my mother whenever she could. Being a good twenty-hour-plus flight away, I wasn't exactly able to head home to see Mum whenever a long weekend presented itself. My mother had given me so much—it was she who had taught me to read, after all, by patiently guiding me through a hefty series of beginning readers' books when I was a toddler. And now, in her time of need, I was far, far away in New York—writing about stilettos. And then, just a few months before my trip home to make pineapple tarts, my father remarried. I didn't know the details—I didn't want to ask. All I knew or cared about was "Is Mummy okay?"

"Wouldn't it be great," I said to Mike one day after much thought (and some pineapple tarts), "if I could just go home for a bit and learn how to cook and also spend time with my family?"

He looked worried. (I suspect the words "Um, what about your job?" flashed across his mind.) But this lasted for only for a moment. (After all, I'd managed to marry a man who is fervent in his belief that I can do anything—which, let me tell you, is a rare and invaluable quality.)

The job, we decided, was an issue. In this economy, it would be impossible to get weeks—much less months—off. To ask for any time away from my desk and BlackBerry at this pivotal moment would likely be construed as a sign of weakness, a lack of dedication to the job. And to ask for time off in order to go to Singapore to *cook*? I suspected my parents would remarry each other before giving me their blessing to commit such career suicide.

And then, just a few days later, my editor summoned our entire fashion bureau to a meeting. When I said I would have to be late because I'd scheduled a hard-to-arrange interview with a chief executive officer at that same time and was immediately told to move the interview, I knew something serious was about to happen. Feeling a little ill, the team of reporters slowly made its way to the conference room. On the other side of the door, a neat stack of crisp envelopes lay on the table. We looked at one another—this was it. We'd spent months covering the massive layoffs and restructuring in the retail industry. Now it was our turn to be "restructured."

What ensued was a blur. I remember only the final words of the human resources woman with any clarity. If we had any questions, she asked us to call, e-mail, or look her up in her office—but only for the next two weeks. It turned out that the person who was laying us off had just been laid off herself.

The first feeling was numbness. Then, panic. The media industry was crumbling as quickly as others were—faster, in fact, than many. Newspaper companies, magazines, broadcasters were laying off people by the dozens, the hundreds. What could possibly be out there for me?

Then, almost instantly, I thought about my grandmother's

bak-zhang. For days I'd been lamenting the fact that I couldn't take a year off, go to Singapore to spend time with my family and learn how to cook, because I had this job that I simply couldn't leave. Now, suddenly, the path was clear.

By the time I got back to my desk, I knew what I wanted to do.

THERE WAS SOME CONFUSION, AT FIRST, OVER WHAT *EX-actly* I was doing back in Singapore.

"Are you opening a restaurant?" my relatives asked.

Well, no.

"Are you writing a cookbook?"

Um, no.

"What about your job?"

I was laid off.

"Oh."

Silence. And then . . .

"But who's cooking for Mike when you're gone?"

The last question, in fact, was the one I would get the most frequently during my time in Singapore. The subtext, of course, was that I was being a bad wife by leaving my husband to fend for himself for weeks at a time while I was off gallivanting in my aunties' kitchens, forcing him to have to buy or, horror among horrors, cook himself something for dinner. At first, I would tell them that he was very happy for me and fully supported my going home to spend time with my family, to learn how to cook. It soon became clear, however, that the only correct answer was "Well, he's very excited that I'm learning how to make these dishes so I finally can cook him good Singaporean dinners."

And it was true, that was a goal—but just part of the goal. I wanted to make delicious Singaporean dinners for my husband, yes. But much greater than that was my desire to learn the cuisine of my people before the chance to learn disappeared. This had been a part of my culture, my heritage, my family, that I'd never known with any intimacy or clarity, thanks to my determination to ignore it as I bulldozed through my career. Also, I had been ambivalent about having children for years, but now that I was in my mid-thirties, it suddenly occurred to me that, if I ever had them, I'd want to be able to make them pineapple tarts, *bak-zhang*, and more. And if they were curious, I'd be honored someday to be able to teach them how to cook, telling them about their great-grandmother, the legendary pineapple tart baker, along the way.

And so the plan was to travel back to Singapore for a few weeks at a time over the lunar calendar year—between the time I'd learned to make my Tanglin ah-ma's pineapple tarts and the next Chinese New Year, the following February. I wasn't sure what I'd learn, but I was eager to find out. The women of my family had fed me well for years. At the end of the year, I hoped I'd know enough. After all this time, it was my turn to feed them.

THE FIRST NIGHT I LANDED IN SINGAPORE, MY MOTHER was waiting. A petite woman, she could be hard to spot in a crowd—except that, well, she's gorgeous. When she's happy, her smile is expansive, infectious, and her eyes are bright and sparkling. When I was a child, she would often bring out mugs of home-brewed hot chrysanthemum tea, nudging grumpy, reluctant me to drink up by dramatically fluttering her eyelids and saying, "This will give you beautiful eyes!" The desire to have my mother's pretty eyes was often more than enough for me to hoist the mug and drink up. (For some years, anyway.)

That May night at the airport, my mother was more tired and grumpy than happy, nonetheless. She didn't fully understand why I was coming home; as always, she didn't want herself to be the priority in our lives. We always came first and were most important, after all. At any dinner table, she would spend most of the meal twirling the lazy Susan about, hovering over the heaping platters, chopsticks poised to pounce and grab the fattest morsels of pork, the duck with the crispiest, brownest skin, and plop them onto the plate of Daphne, me, or my father. Her family came first—and she liked it that way. "Aiyah, don't worry about me—I can take care of myself!" she said and shrugged whenever any of us expressed concern for her. This, too, became her refrain as she went through the dark discomfort of the separation. This wasn't a piece of meat or a plump abalone we were talking about, however. This was her life. And I was happy to give up New York for a while—to come home and see how she was doing, to spend time with my family.

The moment I saw my mother at the airport, her first words, as always, were "Are you hungry?" And our years-long tradition immediately was set in motion. We would hug, park the bags in the car, and then head to a nearby hawker center. Under the bright fluorescent lights, hawkers ran from table to table, delivering sizzling hot plates of chunky radish cakes stir-fried with chili and soy sauce or platters of freshly fried oyster omelets. It wasn't until I tasted my first spoonful of *bak-chor mee*, a bowl of thin egg noodles still simmering in a peppery broth with minced pork and a hefty dose of hot, sliced red chilis, that I felt it—I was home.

Once my mother was done running around to order drinks, food, and tissue paper for cleaning off the table, I asked, "Hey, are you okay or not?"

"Yah, I'm fine—don't worry about me!"

"But . . ."

"Aiyah, you know me, I'm very independent. I'm okay lah. Just worry about yourself!"

I looked at her closely. It was clear she didn't want to talk about it. So I asked her, "How's school?"

My mother had briefly clung to her Singapore Airlines job in the 1970s, keeping her wedding a secret, since SIA stewardesses—the ones in ads who were supposed to be available and "in love with you"—weren't allowed to be married at the time. But her jet-setting dreams were dashed when she became pregnant shortly after getting married. "You were a wedding night baby, you know!" Dad would always proudly say. With my father traveling frequently for business and the arrival of another daughter just three years after me, my mother devoted herself to raising Daphne and me. It was only when I was a teenager that she went back to work as a customer service representative for United Airlines. After more than twenty years with the airline, she'd recently retired to pursue another dream, enrolling in a six-year diploma course in a traditional Chinese medicine school. At the end, our family would have its first true doctor.

"It's tough, you know—all my textbooks are in Chinese!" she complained. Mandarin had never been a forte of my mother's;

she'd been educated at St. Margaret's, an English-language Anglican school in Singapore. And suddenly here she was spending hours in class poring over detailed anatomy charts written entirely in Chinese characters. Having spent twelve years in an English-language Catholic school in which my friends thought it was "cool" not to be good at Mandarin, I couldn't even fathom attempting the same.

I told her about my job, about the freelancing I was starting to do.

"Well, that's good—so you get to try different things lah," she said. "And the money's okay?"

"Yeah, it's actually really interesting. I'm happy, Mummy. Don't worry about me!"

"Okay. As long as you're okay, I'm happy. Don't forget to call your dad when we're home."

Back in the two-story semidetached home near the beach on Singapore's East Coast that my parents had moved into when I was in tenth grade, my bedroom remained almost as it was when I left for college, at age eighteen. The posters of the 1990s soccer stars Roberto Baggio, Marco van Basten, and Jürgen Klinsmann had long since fallen off the walls, but the giant West German flag that the World Cup–obsessed sixteen-year-old me had hung up still fluttered in the gusts of the ice-cold air-conditioning. The now-faded picture of Northwestern University that had inspired me to study harder remained pinned up at my desk. The bouquet of roses my parents had given me on my sixteenth birthday that I'd carefully dried and kept was still propped up in a corner. In my closet, my powder blue Catholic high school uniforms still hung, neatly pressed.

In this room, I'd had fervent dreams of the life I was about to lead. I would go to America, become a journalist, travel to war zones with the bravery of Murphy Brown, and retire from journalism at age thirty to start writing books. I'd win two Pulitzer Prizes—one for journalism and one for fiction. I would live in France, Italy, England—and have season tickets to soccer league matches. I might have a child—with or without a husband, as, really, that bit just wasn't terribly essential—but only one. A girl. And, of course, I'd be so busy being me that I'd have time to marry only when I was forty. (I did plan to make an exception to this last bit, however, if Jürgen Klinsmann ever proposed. In fact, I'd already prepared for this stage of my life by scrawling "Mrs. Cheryl Klinsmann" in Wite-Out on the desks of my tenth-grade classroom.)

Sitting on my sliver of a single bed in my frothy peach and gray–hued room at age thirty-four, however, I realized I'd fallen a little short. The most exciting place I'd been sent for work was not Iraq or Afghanistan but cushy Milan, where the only battle zones I encountered were the ones involving throngs of the Beautiful shoving their way into fashion shows. The closest I came to covering a war zone was when I found myself in Manhattan on September 11, 2001, putting aside my fashion show coverage to race down to Ground Zero as fast as I could in three-inch heels. The Pulitzers? Nonexistent. I'd ended up married ten years ahead of schedule—and not to Jürgen Klinsmann. (Although, I suppose that could still be fixed.) And somehow I'd wound up back here in my teenage bedroom with no job to speak of and an inexplicable quest to learn how to cook—the very thing I'd scorned during my years in Singapore.

I was certain the eighteen-year-old Cheryl would have been terribly unimpressed.

The next morning, however, I was ready to forge ahead with cooking. But first, there was a more pressing matter presented by my mother. "I've started going to this dancing class," she said one day. "Do you want to come?"

I'd loved to dance as a child, having endured ten years of ballet lessons and weekly bouts of wrestling with bandages bound around bloodied toes from point shoes. Ballroom dancing, however, was something I'd never encountered. The main point, though, was to spend time with my mother, to meet the new friends she was making as she started venturing out on her own.

And so, on a Friday night, wearing rubber-soled ballerina flats, the most practical shoes I had brought, I found myself walking into a small, mirrored dance studio, trailing behind my mother. The class was small—and everyone was at least twice my age. Women outnumbered men, which didn't really matter as my mother was obviously the belle of this ball. Patiently, the men waited to take a spin around the room with my mother, who looked radiant in her orange-tinged red lips, chrysanthemum tea–fueled bright eyes, and short, pixie hairdo. (And it was great that she was such a star because it turned out I had two left feet when it came to the waltz. Long after the night was over, I could still feel the frustrated grip of Francis—the slender, affable man in his sixties whom my mother had asked to teach me—around my waist, jerking me back to the right position as he firmly said, "*Concentrate!*")

Watching her glide around the room with the grace of Michelle Kwan, I started to feel like things were going to be okay for her. My mother was happy. Men adored her. It was good to watch the coquettish mother I'd seen glimpses of as a child gradually return.

"You were great out there!" I told her the next day.

"Aiyoh, no lah," she said, waving me away. "I'm just starting."

"No, you were really good!" I insisted. After a silence, I asked. "So, what about that Francis guy? Do you like him?"

"No lah!" she said.

I believed her. But still, it was good to think that someone might be out there for my mother. And at least she was putting herself in that line of fire.

Having failed at the waltz, I started itching to cook. The first person I called was Auntie Alice, my mother's older sister. Of my mother's three siblings, Auntie Alice—whom I call E-Ma because she's also my godmother—was the one who grew up knowing how to cook. She was drafted to cook for her younger siblings when their father had suddenly died and their mother had had to work. I'd told her that I was coming home to learn how to cook, and that I hoped she and my maternal grandmother, whom I called Ah-Ma, could teach me. For starters, I wanted to learn how to make Ah-Ma's *kaya,* a sweet, eggy coconut jam that's just lovely spread over the thinnest veneer of butter on a slice of toasted white bread.

There was one small snag, however. "I told Ah-Ma," Auntie Alice said. "And she said, 'Aiyoh! I don't know if I can remember how to make it!'" It had been more than ten years since my grandmother had made *kaya,* it turned out. And as she was eighty-five, the years were starting to get the better of her memory. Nonetheless, Ah-Ma had some rough sense of the ingredients that went into it, and a few days later, I found myself arriving at my grandmother's home bearing a crate of eggs, grated coconut, sugar, and green pandan leaves, lush and fragrant, freshly snipped from my mother's garden.

"Ah-Lien ah, le deng lai liao ah!" Ah-Ma said in Hokkien, hugging me tightly while kissing me and smoothing down my hair, as she always does, and crooning *"Chao gao kia,"* which means "smelly puppy." (This is a pet name none of her grandchildren have ever understood.) Yes, I'd come home, I said. "Your husband didn't come?" she asked. And I began to brace myself for the next question. "You didn't bring a baby back for Ah-Ma to carry?"

I remained a disappointment to my grandmother in this regard. Month after month, she'd ask: When was I going to give her a great-grandchild? "Ah-Ma is not getting any younger, you know," she'd plead over the phone or whenever she saw me. "I don't want to die until I've seen my great-grandchild." Sometimes, she would simply come right out and say it. "Ah-Ma is dying already—you'd better have a baby soon!" The pressure, which had begun as soon as I got married, in 2004, only intensified as the years passed. Nothing quelled her determination—not protestations that I was too busy, that we didn't have any family in New York to help us, that I had absolutely no idea how to raise a child, that I believed I would be a bad mother. (Her solution to all those problems always was the same—"Move back to Singapore! We'll help you!") Eventually, however, I came up with a way to halt the interrogation. "Ah-Ma ah," I'd say quietly and gravely, "didn't they tell you? I'm infertile!" She would recoil, swatting my hands as she spit out *"Choi! Choi! Choi!"* a refrain meant to ward off any evil or bad luck. My words always worked—she'd stop the questioning. (For a few weeks, at least.)

I always felt a little bad for causing Ah-Ma any further distress. Her life, as related to me when I was a child, had been pockmarked with loss, pain, and poverty. I knew few details, but the black-and-white picture of her wedding day perched in her living room spoke volumes. In the photo, Ah-Ma is a porcelain-skinned twenty-year-old, smiling tentatively while seated next to a older man, tall, dark, and rakish. Gong-Gong had come from Xiamen, China, to find his fortune in Singapore. Although he was a good ten-plus years older than my grandmother, he had won her family over with his chiseled features and high forehead, which the Chinese in Singapore believe is a mark of intelligence and great potential for success. Together, they had four children, and life was blissful—until Ah-Ma learned of her husband's wife and children back in China and decided to take it upon herself to help bring them to Singapore so they could live together as one happy family. The moment Wife No. 1 appeared in Singapore, of course, Family No. 2 was kicked out. Ah-Ma raised her four children in a one-bedroom apartment that was tiny even by New York City standards, always teetering on the brink of complete poverty and seeing my grandfather only when he could sneak away.

I know little of this handsome polygamist from Xiamen except that I probably inherited his great love for soy sauce, which I drizzle over everything—noodles, fried eggs at brunch, hamburgers, you name it. *"Aiyoh, you cannot eat so much soy sauce!"* my mum would frequently yell. "Don't you know that Gong-

Gong died of kidney failure?" In fact, when my grandfather died, my fourteen-year-old mother only found out days later. The family heard from someone who'd heard from someone that he'd passed away in Wife No. 1's home. That night, my mother and her siblings sprinkled flour all over the floors of their kitchen and living room, hoping that they would find footprints in the white mounds, offering proof that their papa's ghost had returned to say good-bye. When they awoke the next day, there were none. And Ah-Ma gave everyone a good spanking for wasting perfectly good flour.

Dreams of my grandfather would haunt my mother for years. In her dreams, her papa would come to her, telling her he had lucky lottery numbers, a gift for his beloved family, for whom he had left nothing. Gong-Gong would try to hand her a piece of paper with the winning numbers, but my mother, generally terrified of ghosts, would squeeze her eyes shut, refusing to look as her father pleaded with her, telling her that even in death, he was the same man she had loved. Just then, a rooster would crow. The sun would start rising. It was time for him to leave for the Other World. My mother would open her eyes and call out to her father, but he'd already be gone.

This story still draws violent reactions from my aunties whenever it's recounted, usually at the dinner table of some family gathering, where talk inevitably returns to the old days. Past regrets and a thousand should-haves are ever-present in my family's life. "Ah-Tin ah, why you never open your eyes?" Auntie Jane, my mother's younger sister, would moan. "We could have been *rich*, you know!" Ah-Ma did go on to have a good life, however—her children all became successful and

also married well. In her twilight years, she was living with my
uncle and his family in a plush house in Singapore's Holland
Village, a neighborhood that's popular with well-paid expats.

That day, in Ah-Ma's comfortable living room filled with a
stylish, modern couch and antiques my uncle had collected in
his travels through Asia, I chose not to invoke any tales of the
past. We had a task at hand, after all. There was no time to
waste on clucking over babies, ghosts, or bad luck. There was
kaya to be made! We began by bundling up the freshly grated
coconut in cheesecloth and wringing out its milk, white and
thick as paint. After squeezing out all we could, we added some
water to the coconut and wrung it out again; the milk from the
second squeezing was thinner than that from the first but
smelled fragrant nonetheless. Ah-Ma perched herself on a bench
by the kitchen, watching us prepare the coconut milk while
loudly lamenting that she didn't fully remember how to make
kaya. "Ah-Ma's old, of no use anymore," she said in Mandarin,
sighing and shaking her head. Just when I started to get worried, however, she switched into the firm, bossy Ah-Ma that I
knew as a child and began barking out instructions.

Making *kaya* was simple, she said. We quickly got to work
in my uncle's modern kitchen, which he'd kitted out with sleek
appliances and a large, gleaming countertop. First, we cracked
ten eggs into a large bowl and whisked them together. Then we
added about a cup of sugar and the coconut milk, mixing it all
up well. Next, Ah-Ma instructed us to place the mixture in a
glass bowl, add a few knotted pandan leaves, perch that bowl
atop a rack in a wok, and just let it steam for forty-five minutes
or so. Auntie Alice and I looked at each other. "Mummy ah, we

don't need to stir it, meh?" Auntie Alice gently asked. Ah-Ma shook her head and hands vigorously. *"Mieng, mieng!"* she said in Hokkien. Auntie Alice and I looked at each other again. This just didn't sound right. *Kaya* is supposed to be smooth, creamy, and easy to spread. I hadn't spent that much time cooking at this point, but I did feel I knew enough to predict how steaming a bunch of eggs, untouched, for forty-five minutes would end up. Just letting the eggs, sugar, and coconut milk steam for forty-five minutes without any stirring was likely to produce a dense, cakelike custard—one that I envisioned us being able to cut up into neat slices, not spread easily over crusty, hot toast. Could Ah-Ma—who had spent the morning telling us that she couldn't quite remember how to make the dishes she had been known for—possibly have misremembered?

I had been afraid of not having enough *kaya* for three households—my mother's, Auntie Alice's, and Ah-Ma's—so I'd brought enough ingredients for two batches. "Well . . . ," Auntie Alice finally said, giving me a meaningful look, "since we have enough for another batch, why don't we just make one batch Ah-Ma's way and one batch that we stir during steaming? Just try lah—experiment!" Ah-Ma shrugged, giving us a distinct "you're wasting your time" look. Auntie Alice and I immediately got to work, whipping together the second batch of *kaya*. Onto the steamer that went, and we started stirring it periodically. Looking at the two *kayas* side by side, we were glad we had decided to try the second batch our way. Ah-Ma's method was yielding a *kaya* that resembled a pudding. The yellow-green custard was puffing up slightly and looked distinctly solid. The *kaya* that Auntie Alice and I were diligently stirring, however, was looking nice and soft. As the smell of coconut and vanilla-like pandan seeped into the air, we were feeling good about our *kaya*. I began to envision the breakfast of *kaya* toast, hot and buttery, that I'd have the next day.

After forty-five minutes, however, our impressions changed. When we removed the two bowls of *kaya*, Auntie Alice and I smiled knowingly at first, as we noticed that Ah-Ma's remained pudding-like while ours looked like a chunky rubble of jam. Then Ah-Ma gestured to us to stir up her *kaya*. It yielded easily to our spoon, forming a creamy, silken mass as we stirred. The version that Auntie Alice and I had concocted, however, remained lumpen and unappetizing no matter how much we tried to whip it into a smooth froth. And when we spread both *kayas* on bread, ours had an alarming grainy texture while Ah-Ma's was perfectly smooth. Just as it should have been.

Ah-Ma didn't say anything. Auntie Alice and I winced. The students had been arrogant enough to second-guess the teacher—someone who had brought decades of experience to the kitchen counter only to be given the fish eye and sidelined. And we had learned a lesson, indeed. Silently, I vowed to listen to my grandmother more.

Quietly, we packed up our *kaya* and hugged Ah-Ma good-bye. Just before letting me go, however, my grandmother gave me one final instruction: "Next time, bring a baby for Ah-Ma."

CHAPTER FIVE

My father was skeptical.

And this was fairly new to me. Now, this was a man who had never been stingy with praise for my grades or Chinese brush paintings, which he'd proudly framed and hung in his office when I was a child. And yet, whenever I produced something I'd slaved over for hours in the kitchen during his visits to the United States, he'd chew quietly and say almost nothing. Knowing that he adored chocolate mousse, I once searched online for days for a recipe that had the largest number of positive comments and spent the better part of an afternoon making the mousse just before he arrived in New York. The mousse was met with silence. When I tried out my *tau yew bak* on him during another dinner in New York, there it was again: silence. (Prompted by Mike's *mmmms* and other effusive and overcompensating grunts of enjoyment, however, my father finally said, "The meat was a little tough.")

It wasn't that my father thought cooking was a waste of time; he'd given me a lecture in my mid-twenties about my inability to make much besides ramen for dinner, after all. It was just that his mother's food was seared on his heart; nothing else could possibly come close. (My mother never even tried to impress him in the kitchen, leaving everything up to her maids.) And I knew that, of all the people who would be sampling my attempts at re-creating her dishes over the following year, he would be my toughest critic. I began bracing myself for the silence.

It was May in Singapore—the days were getting more and more fiery as the hot month of June approached. And I was about to learn a rather difficult dish—*bak-zhang,* the pyramid-shaped dumplings filled with pork and mushrooms and wrapped in bamboo leaves that had been one of Tanglin Ah-Ma's signature dishes. The dumplings were an annual treat for my family, although they can now be found year-round in Singapore. They're traditionally eaten in June around the time of the Dumpling Festival, or *Duan Wu Jie,* which commemorates the death of the Chinese poet and patriot Qu Yuan, who became distraught over the state of his country and committed suicide by throwing himself into a river. When his supporters learned of his death, they threw rice dumplings into the river both as a sacrifice to his spirit and to feed the fish so they wouldn't nibble on Qu Yuan's body. Now, every year, Chinese all over the world celebrate the day by eating *bak-zhang*—which is more commonly known by its Mandarin name, *zongzi*—and having Dragon Boat races. (Those also stem from Chinese lore. As one story goes, Qu Yuan's admirers, after learning of his suicide, immediately hopped into boats and paddled out into the river, hoping to rescue him or find his body.)

In my family, store-bought versions of *bak-zhang* were

taboo, of course. The only dumplings that mattered were my Tanglin ah-ma's. As the years passed and her reputation grew among neighbors, friends, and friends of friends, she began taking orders and selling them. I'd disliked sticky rice as a child and had not really looked forward to eating *bak-zhang* every year. My father, however, had always adored the dumplings, having grown up eating only the best, of course. "Daddo," I said to him one day in May. "Auntie Khar Imm is going to teach me how to make Tanglin Ah-Ma's *bak-zhang*." There it was again: silence.

"Oh?" he said after a moment, looking bemused. "Okay."

THE PORK WAS WHAT GOT ME.

By the time I arrived at Auntie Khar Imm's home in Hougang, a traditional working-class neighborhood in Northern Singapore that has been a Teochew enclave for decades, she'd assembled all the ingredients. Her kitchen was a few times larger than mine in Brooklyn and crammed with appliances, pots, pans, and baskets. This was a kitchen for a serious cook. I had some of the same appliances—the Cuisinart food processor, a large black wok—but mine looked brand-new compared to her weathered pieces. I wondered how many dinners they'd put out. Even though it was mid-morning, the kitchen was fairly dark—being on the third floor of a building surrounded by many other tall apartment towers. What it lacked for in light it had in space, though—enough for two large refrigerators filled with homemade sauces, stews, vegetables, and meats. I imagined both those refrigerators in my own kitchen; there wouldn't be room for anything else. The garlic cloves and shallots had been set out, and the dried Chinese mushrooms were already soaking in water and were well on their way to softening. As Auntie Khar Imm pulled out the slab of pork belly she'd bought, I couldn't help but wince. Although I prided myself on trying to be fearless in the kitchen, I had largely stuck to cooking with meat that didn't resemble an animal in any remote way. I'd make exceptions for fried chicken (my absolute favorite food) and once a year for Thanksgiving, but even then, I delegated any *touching* of the turkey to the heroic Mike. Generally, I like my meat or fish faceless and in the form of a rectangular slab. All the better if there's not a whole lot of blood, which gets me to thinking of the animal that once owned that flesh. On Auntie Khar Imm's kitchen counter, however, lay a large brick of pork belly with a thick layer of fat. And on top of that fat was skin bearing bright pink markings—Chinese characters that had been branded on the poor pig at whatever farm it had spent its relatively short life. I started to feel ill.

I had vowed to be brave, however. Or at least learn how to be brave from my aunties. So I trained my eyes on the pork, readying myself for the inevitable *touching*. For distraction, I asked what time Tanglin Ah-Ma would typically get up to make *bak-zhang*. "See how much she is making lor," Auntie Khar Imm said in Mandarin. "Make more then wake up earlier." Which made perfect sense, of course. I was reminded of the futility of my pineapple tart interrogations. Perhaps I needed to not focus so much on the specifics of time and quantities. Living in New York, in all the jobs that I had had, I had found it hard not to be consumed with minutiae. When exactly was something supposed to happen? What exactly was to happen? What exactly were the details of Every Single Thing? I always needed to know—for work and also for my own sanity—before embarking on anything. Perhaps this had been the wrong approach to cooking all along. Perhaps it was time to start letting go.

With this new determination, the reformed, loosey-goosey me bellied up to the counter, ready to help. At first, this involved a great deal of watching. I watched Auntie Khar Imm mince the garlic cloves. I watched her dice the softened mushrooms. I watched her run the shallots through a food processor. Then I watched her bring a pot of water to boil, placing the pork belly and chunk of pork leg into the water for a quick boiling. After a few minutes, she whipped out a sharp chopstick and gestured for me to look as she jabbed it into the pork to see if it was cooked enough. "If it can go through easily, it's done," she said. I'd always wondered how seasoned cooks gauged how meat was done. In my own kitchen, my eagle-eyed staring at a grilling pork chop or simmering chicken never seemed to work out quite right. As I'd watch my guests start eating, I was never able to shake the feeling that, somehow, my meat had ended up overcooked or undercooked. (Eventually, I started delegating the monitoring of meat doneness to Mike—I just couldn't handle the stress.)

"You don't want it fully cooked," Auntie Khar Imm warned, as she carefully hoisted the pork slabs out of the newly cloudy water. "You just want it cooked enough so it makes it easier to chop." As I watched her chop up the pork belly with grace and ease, it looked simple. So I volunteered to take over and do the rest. Of course, the moment she handed the knife to me, chopping turned out to be anything but easy. Between wrestling with the squishy and slightly slimy pork belly while trying to angle the slender knife to slice the meat and worrying about using too much force and sending the round wooden chopping board flying off the counter, I was managing to cut up about five little cubes of pork a minute. (Or so it felt.) Auntie Khar Imm didn't say anything. I didn't dare look up to meet her eyes. If I had wondered before whether she doubted that I'd ever actually cooked anything in my life, I was pretty sure this display was confirming it all. Patiently, however, she watched. And slowly, I plodded, dicing and slicing until an eternity had passed and a mound of cubed meat lay before me. I'm convinced that process took about three hours—but I was feeling good about my meat. In fact, I was so pleased with myself that I stopped to take a picture.

Next, Auntie Khar Imm grabbed a massive bottle of cooking oil and turned it over, sending large ribbons of yellow into a large wok. I called out, asking her to stop and tell me how much oil she was putting in. And once again, the *a* words tumbled out. *"Aiyah, agak-agak lah!"* she said. "If you use more garlic, then you use more oil." Which, of course, made perfect sense. Sort of. Until I started to think *But how much garlic should I be using? Is ten cloves enough? Not enough?* I was still determined to learn how to make the perfect *bak-zhang*, and my head was nearly exploding from trying to conjure precision from the imprecise. I reminded myself to breathe and let go. But not before staring really hard at the oil in the wok and thinking that the amount looked an awful lot like about a quarter of a cup. Slowly, it seemed, I was learning to *agak-agak*.

Auntie Khar Imm heated the oil and tossed in the minced garlic, gently frying up the sputtering mixture. "You want it to be slightly brown but not too brown or it will be bitter," she said, slowly stirring. When the garlic turned gold, she carefully removed it from the wok, placing it in a bowl. Next, she fried up the shallots in the same oil, adding some more oil—as I watched closely, trying to *agak-agak* along with Auntie Khar Imm— then removed them. Next, the mushrooms went into the oil for about ten minutes of frying. I may not have been measuring out the amounts, but I was studiously watching the clock and scribbling down starting and ending times. Auntie Khar Imm clucked, however, and firmly instructed me to make sure to look into the wok. "You want to fry until the mushrooms are soft and all the water that comes out of them has disappeared," she said. Next, my wonderfully diced pork went in, then the garlic, shallots, some sugar, white pepper, ground coriander, and dark soy sauce, a sweet and thick mixture that looks like molasses and is common in Singaporean Chinese dishes. With the wok almost full now, Auntie Khar Imm summoned up more strength as she fried, swirling the ingredients about the pan as I watched. Finally, she paused to taste a spoonful of the mixture before dumping in more white pepper and sugar. And with just a few more firm stirs, we were done.

The filling looked lovely—it was the shade of bittersweet chocolate and smelled peppery, garlicky, and porky all at once.

The meat would cool overnight; the next day, dumpling wrapping would begin.

THE WRAPPING PHASE OF *BAK-ZHANG* MAKING IS TIME-consuming. For starters, you need to soak the uncooked glutinous rice in cool water for at least five hours. You also need to soak the dried bamboo leaves in water so they're malleable enough for wrapping.

I would be lying if I said I actually did any of this—Auntie Khar Imm woke up at 4:30 A.M. to get all this done before I showed up, mired in a fog of sleepiness, at the (to me) early hour of 10:00 A.M. In fact, by the time I arrived that next morning, Auntie Khar Imm had not only done all of this but had also already set up our *bak-zhang* wrapping station. A long pole was propped horizontally; she had tied two clusters of strings to the pole and arranged a carpet of newspapers beneath it.

I suddenly got the sense that the Ghirardelli chocolates I had brought her the day before were a woefully inadequate gift.

Pulling up two squat wooden stools, Auntie Khar Imm gestured for me to sit. Grabbing a handful of long leaves, she showed me the drill. First, she took two long bamboo leaves and lined them up horizontally. Then she bent them in the middle and twisted one side upward so both ends were pointing north and a triangular hollow had formed at the base. Next, she scooped a tablespoon or two of rice into the hollow and topped that with a layer of the pork filling. Then she filled the rest of the hollow with more rice, patted it down as firmly as she could, grabbed the bottom of the pyramid with one hand, and used her other hand to fold over the leaves so they covered the rice. Finally, she wrapped some string very tightly around the perfect green pyramid and tied a knot to keep everything in place. This entire process took Auntie Khar Imm seconds to do. And then it was my turn.

Now, when I was growing up, origami had its minor moment among elementary school girls in Singapore. Oh, how we would save up our allowances, buy neat little packages of brightly colored square paper imported from Japan, and after consulting a compendium of picture-filled origami books, we'd while away time at home, in school, fashioning frogs, cranes, and intricate little balls that you could actually blow up—and throw at other girls. Well, when I say *we*, actually, I don't mean *me*. I was absolutely ungifted at this paper-folding business. I tried, yes, but cranes, frogs, and (as desperately as I wished to be making them) those tiny paper-ball weapons were completely beyond me. I should have known that I would not be what they call a natural at this *bak-zhang* wrapping deal.

The lining up and folding to create the hollow were mystifying to me. After a few tries, some with Auntie Khar Imm guiding my hands, however, I began to get the hang of it. Holding on to the leaves tight enough and piling on the rice proved a little tricky, though. Clumps of meat and bits of rice rained on my toes and skittered across the newspapers. And no matter how hard I tried, my dumplings looked more like puffy green breast implants than the perfect pyramids Auntie Khar Imm kept making. Probably sensing how mortified I was over my clumsiness, my auntie never said an unkind word. "This is your first time making them," she kept saying. "Don't worry." She did, however, have an issue with my method of packing. *"Mai ah-neh giam siap lah!"* she said, over and over, when she saw how little pork I was putting into each dumpling. *Don't be so stingy.* She was piling four to five heaping tablespoons of filling into each dumpling. I, on the other hand, was putting in two to three. I realized that after all the effort we—well, Auntie Khar

Imm—had put into chopping and frying, I was subconsciously rationing our precious, precious pork. "You want to have a bit of the meat with every bite," she explained. "That's what will make it tasty." Try as I might, however, I couldn't bring myself to stop being *giam siap*. We'd slaved over this pork—if only people knew! They would be lucky to eat this. They should be allowed to appreciate it only in small doses! Like caviar. Or truffles!

And this was how we ended up, two hours and forty-two *bak-zhangs* later, faced with a large bowl of pork filling long after the rice had run out. I wasn't sure what to say. "Oops" didn't quite seem to cut it. Auntie Khar Imm looked disappointed. "Well, we can eat this with rice," she said, packing up the pork.

As I'd wrapped the last of my verdant breast implants, Auntie Khar Imm had set a massive pot of water on the stove to boil, tossing in ten knotted pandan leaves. Carefully, she unhooked the clusters of *bak-zhang* from the pole and immersed them in the water. The dumplings would have to boil for ninety minutes. I looked around the kitchen, the apartment, and wondered, What would we do for ninety minutes? Things were going swimmingly when we had tasks at hand; the concentration I needed to focus on chopping, wrapping, and not pelting myself with pork had greatly limited the idle time we had for conversation. With ninety minutes to kill, however, I wondered what we'd have to say to each other. I needn't have worried.

"When Ah-Ma died, it was very tragic," Auntie Khar Imm began, speaking of Tanglin Ah-Ma, my paternal grandmother. "I didn't really know how to cook. Everything I made, your uncle Soo Kiat said, 'You don't know how to cook. My mother's food is so much better.'" I was surprised—having remembered great dishes that my auntie Khar Imm had made and set out at Chinese New Years past—but I understood perfectly. Decades after her death, my father continued to feel the same fervor about his mother's cooking. *"Wo liu yenlei ah,"* Auntie Khar Imm said. I wasn't sure how to respond—the thought of my auntie crying because the food she made for her family didn't match up to my grandmother's was hard to bear.

My grandmother had shouldered the brunt of the daily cooking, Auntie Khar Imm said, because my auntie had been busy with work and then her two children. She'd helped and watched, sure, but when it came to actually being the mistress of the kitchen, the job was intimidating. "So how did you learn?" I asked. Remembering my Tanglin ah-ma's methods and practice, she said. "And I used to go downstairs and listen to the *san gu liu po* [gossipy aunties]," she added in Mandarin. "Whatever they said about cooking, I would listen, and then I would come home and try it out." And bit by bit, the complaints began disappearing.

Auntie Khar Imm may have silenced her critics, but I knew my toughest one was still waiting to be convinced. I didn't want to watch my father eat one of my *bak-zhang*, and I was grateful that he ate one while I wasn't at breakfast one morning. Not that he said anything all day about it, of course. My *mother* had to tell me that he'd finally tried it.

"Well?" I asked my father, hoping against hope. There was a brief silence, and then "You must tell Auntie Khar Imm that her *bak-zhang* standard has dropped." I was confused. It had tasted perfectly good to me. I couldn't fathom what could possibly have been wrong with those dumplings—apart from the fact that the ones I'd made were entirely the wrong shape. And tiny. And had too little pork. And may have come apart because I didn't tie them up well enough. But apart from *all that*, I thought our *bak-zhang* was fantastic! I started to feel indignant. These Tan men. Would there ever be any way to please them?

"The meat," he finally said. "The chunks are just too big."

And there it was. The one thing I'd volunteered to do was the very thing that had brought down the mighty *bak-zhang* that Auntie Khar Imm and I had slaved over for two days. I immediately confessed that it was my fault; he looked unsurprised.

This "learning to be a Tan woman" quest was starting to look a little bleak.

DURING MY WEEKS IN SINGAPORE, I BEGAN TO FEEL A gaping hole in my heart that only something back in New York could fill.

Just the thought of him would get me itchy—and oh, how I pined. My hands would tremble, my heart would quicken. I spent days thinking about the things I would do with him the moment I got back. I half envisioned our reunion involving a slow-motion running scene, arms outstretched, hair flying in the breeze, my cheeks flushed in anticipation of hand to steel.

Mike understands fully that this object of my pining is not him. It's my oven that I crave—my sturdy little hunk of stainless steel, which has seen me through countless cookies, cakes, and pies in our little Brooklyn home. My mother's Singapore kitchen had no oven to speak of, and in my weeks away from New York, I realized just how much I missed feeling dough between my fingers, the smell of a summer crisp bubbling as it baked. This time, when I arrived back in New York, after a hot and steamy reunion with my oven, I was sated, but still, I wanted more. It was in this fog of longing that it struck me: I am going to conquer bread.

A few summers before, I'd vowed to conquer pies. Over three months, I spent days and nights in my sweltering kitchen mixing, wrestling with dough, peeling and slicing apples, pears, and nectarines, and carefully crimping my way through pie after pie. After finally discovering the wonder of rolling out dough between two sheets of wax paper to achieve a perfect (and easily transferable) crust, I considered pies conquered. Ditto with rhubarb the following summer, when I spent weekend after weekend churning out rhubarb pies, cakes, and crisps. And then there was the summer that I devoted myself to fried chicken. You do not want to know about the extra swath of flesh that appeared around my waist right about then.

Bread, however, had been a force of nature I'd never even contemplated taking on. Yeast? Rising? Kneading? I had absolutely no idea how it all worked. The notion of trying to bake bread was all the more absurd considering that I'd taken cues from the fashion conscious in New York and had all but sworn off eating bread—unless I was in Paris and unless it was amazing bread, that is. And then one day, Nicole, an amateur baker in San Diego, sent out a message on Twitter: "I need a challenge. Am thinking of baking my way through every single recipe in *The Bread Baker's Apprentice*. Anyone want to join me?" A challenge. I was instantly intrigued.

I was beginning to feel the tiniest sprouts of confidence in the kitchen, after having learned pineapple tarts among other lessons from my aunties. And so I signed on, sending away for the bread guru Peter Reinhart's book *The Bread Baker's Apprentice*, a bread-baking bible of sorts. Before long, I was joining more than two hundred bakers across the United States and in locales as far-flung as Berlin and Sri Lanka in this quest to master the art of baking bread. The bakers, male and female, included Internet administrators, stay-at-home moms, an architect, an epidemiologist. The woman from Sri Lanka was a science fiction writer who had moved there from the United States in pursuit of love. (It appeared to be going well.) At the heart of it all was Nicole, an avid baker who flung herself into kitchen projects and blogged about them at www.pinchmysalt.com to get her mind off her husband, who was deployed in Iraq. "This was something for me to jump into to keep me busy," she said. And her deal was simple: Every week, we would all bake a bread in the book. Because the bakers were scattered across the continents, there was no way for us to meet and break our home-made breads. So each of us would simply post an account of baking that week's bread on our own blog. It sounded easy enough. I decided to throw my spatula into the ring (at least during the weeks that I didn't spend in my aunties' kitchens in Singapore).

My first bread was a little redundant for a New Yorker: bagels. Since I live in bagel central, however, I assumed this would be an easy first—something that I, with my newfound confidence in the kitchen, could ace. What could be difficult? A lot, it turned out.

For starters, it was impossible to find high-gluten flour, the ingredient that's essential to making bagels chewy. I called a phalanx of stores that sell hard-to-find ingredients. Nothing. After a day of searching, it became rather ludicrous, given that you can buy bagels on virtually every city block in New York.

I started tearing my hair out; people began questioning the sanity of my quest. "Aiyoh, why did you sign up for something like that?" Simpson, a New York chef friend, said. "Some more, bagels are so cheap!" With my bread-baking deadline looming, my local bagel shop, Montague Street Bagels, galloped to the rescue. After I explained my troubles to the owner with a great deal of whining and gigantic, sad-looking eyes, he disappeared into his kitchen and emerged with a bag of high-gluten flour.

"What else are you going to put in?" he asked, wincing when I mentioned malt syrup and powder. "That's going to give it a bitter taste!" he said, disappearing once again and returning with a little paper bag of brown sugar and very stern instructions to "use this instead." Given that he makes and sells more than two hundred bagels a day using an old family recipe—and that he was now my high-gluten hero—I figured I should listen to him.

Back in my kitchen, I mixed yeast with high-gluten flour and let it sit for two hours to rise. Then I added salt, brown sugar, more instant yeast, and a few more cups of high-gluten flour and really stirred the mix up. This dough was nothing like anything I'd handled before—this was one stiff ball of ecto-plasmic stickiness. I began to understand how victims in aliens movies felt. Then came the kneading—which was supposed to last for ten minutes in order to pass the "windowpane test," in which the dough is so elastic that you can stretch it out to form a semi-sheer "window."

I kneaded. And kneaded. And kneaded. My hands, my arms, my elbows hurt. There was sweat on my brow. I began to think that, even though Michelle Obama has said, "You know, cooking isn't one of my huge things," she might change her mind if she realized how much it could help keep those toned arms of hers in shape. Who needs a gym when you can bake bagels?

After thirty minutes of pressing and pummeling, when the dough felt plenty stretchy even without any windowpaning, I made the executive decision to listen to my aching arms and stop. I rolled up the dough into ten little balls, guesstimating that each one was the 4.5 ounces it was supposed to be. After covering them with a damp towel and letting them rest for twenty minutes, I formed them into bagels by poking holes in the centers and stretching out those holes. Then they sat for twenty minutes at room temperature before going into the fridge to "rest" overnight.

During that time, I made an important discovery. When it comes to baking, guesstimation would be a don't.

Comparing notes with Nicole, the San Diego baker who had started it all, and other Bread Baker's Apprentice challenge bakers on Twitter, I realized that I was supposed to have twelve bagels, not ten. My bagels looked enormous, but it was too late—my bagels had been made. And I had to sleep in them. (Or something like that.) Besides, Mike, a great lover of all breads, had been growing more excited by the hour about homemade bagels for brunch. The next morning, even before his eyes were open, he mumbled, "Don't you have bagels to be making?"

And so the boiling began. I put them in boiling water for five minutes on each side, and then they were ready for coating.

After kicking myself for throwing out the last of the Japanese crushed seaweed, sesame seed, and sea salt mix that I sometimes use on rice, I tossed together some minced garlic, sesame seeds, and poppy seeds. And finally, after two days and two sore arms, the bagels went into the oven. I was edgy with anticipation. (And Mike was edgy with an ever-growing hunger.)

The end result was lovely. I'd never eaten a bagel fresh out of the oven before. The middles were soft and chewy, and they had a lightly sweet taste that made them better than versions I'd bought in stores. When I'd decided to make bagels, even I had questioned the silliness of it. I rarely eat bagels myself—and what would be the point of learning to make something that I probably would never make again?

Watching Mike attack my bagel, however, I began to understand. And when he asked for seconds and then contemplated thirds, the purpose of this endeavor—and of this modern wifery in the kitchen at all—started to dawn on me. In fact, I started to wonder what I had been waiting for all these years.

The next time I return from Bergdorf Goodman with another "sorry honey I just couldn't resist them" pair of Christian Louboutins, I'm making bagels.

CHAPTER SIX

While I didn't have any "aunties" in New York to guide me on the Singapore culinary front, I had recently acquired an "uncle." (Albeit one who shrieked *"Aiyah!"* and squawked quite a bit at the idea of me actually calling him that.)

In Manhattan's West Village, there's a small nook of a restaurant that I race to whenever my stomach gets homesick: Café Asean. The tofu bakar on the menu is a dead ringer for the *tauhu goreng*—a Malay dish of crispy, deep-fried tofu split open and stuffed with julienned carrots and bean sprouts and drowned in a sweet peanut sauce—that I grew up eating. And the *mee goreng*, a spicy Malay fried noodle tossed with shrimp, scrambled egg, and crispy tofu bits, never fails to make me think of my late-night suppers with Dad. After years of eating my way through the Café Asean menu, a friend introduced me to the chef, Simpson Wong, a native of Malaysia whom I instantly admired. He is fearless with food and unafraid to cook, touch, chop, and eat anything. Spleen sandwiches, pigs' organs—you name it, he's devoured it. In the few years that we've known each other, Simpson has very patiently tried to teach me some things about making the dishes of our motherlands. Soon after I got to know him, we began to get together every few weeks to cook—usually in his modern, spacious home kitchen, which opens out into a large, airy living room. (My own Brooklyn Heights kitchen, alas, is the size of a closet. I have a New York friend with a purse closet that's about the size of my kitchen.) Helping Simpson put together meals for our friends, I've learned a few things about Southeast Asian cooking.

Catching a glimpse of stacks of sardine cans during a recent trip to Chinatown, Simpson was suddenly transported to his days as a child growing up in the small logging town of Tanjung Malim, Malaysia, where his family was so poor that sardine sandwiches were a treat. I'd grimaced slightly when I walked into Simpson's apartment, ready to help him in the kitchen, and he mentioned the word *sardines*. I'd never liked sardine sandwiches myself, even though they were popular in my primary school tuckshop. They were too fishy, my breath would stink for hours afterward, and I loathed the fact that bone fragments were a more than occasional feature. But Simpson, who's always experimenting with Malaysian and Singaporean dishes that he might introduce in his restaurant, was making a finger-food version that he hoped would appeal to New Yorkers.

The Singaporean recipe for the mashed sardine filling calls for minced red onion, lime juice, ketchup, and some chili sauce. Simpson had thought about this and come up with a strategy for the fishiness that I've been wrinkling my nose at for years. "It's simple," he said. "You just put some Asian sesame oil to cut the flavor lor!" He took out a bottle and generously drizzled the sardine mixture with the sweet, honey-hued oil. He was right. With the sardine mix mashed, along with slender slivers of onion, cucumber, and tomato between slices of toasted bread, the sandwich was heavenly. If only the sandwich uncle in my primary school had experimented a little more.

One day, I told Simpson that I missed *popiah*. The Singaporean-Chinese version of the summer roll came filled with a mélange of ingredients like minced shrimp and jicama. Ah-Ma had made fantastic *popiah*, but it had been years since she'd done it, so I hadn't had a homemade version in ages. Once I mentioned this, of course, Simpson was on a mission. A few days later, we found ourselves in Chinatown, feeling up jicama and poking at carrots before racing off to his kitchen with our loot of ingredients.

Cooking with Simpson isn't easy. For starters, I am the sous chef. Not only that—I am the sous chef to a man who's used to bossing around *professional* sous chefs. Combine that with my limited knife skills and general anxiety around peelers—which, hello, can easily take the polish off your well-manicured nails—and you have an almost surefire friendship breaker. (In my own kitchen, Mike is the designated sous chef. I find that if I keep myself very busy taking a nap while the ingredients get prepped, more love gets put into the food, the end product is better. Forget kissing the cook. Sous chefing for the cook—now *that's* pure love.) In Simpson's kitchen, however, no naps are allowed. He desperately wants me to learn—and he believes the only way to learn, of course, is by actually chopping and peeling. Quaint idea, that.

And so I found myself at his kitchen counter, sipping a flute of Veuve as I peeled and chopped jicama as best I could to the repetitive chorus of a rather disdainful teacher. "Aiyoh! Why you chop so big?" Simpson would say, grabbing the knife and showing me how to slice the jicama into straw-thin slices. As hard as I tried, however, my fingers once again didn't cooperate. We ended up with a mountain of chunks that looked more like cigarettes. I shuffled the slices around, positioning the thinner ones on top, hoping he wouldn't notice—mind, rather. But Simpson stared hard at the mound. "Ai*yoh*," he said. I wondered where I could find an actual cigarette.

Sighing, he decided to carry on anyway. First, he drizzled some oil into a pan and started frying up the shrimp. Then shallots, then jicama.

Finally, he set out *popiah* wrappers on the counter, showing me how to assemble the rolls. First, he spread a leaf of lettuce on the wrapper so the wet ingredients don't rip through the thin wrapper—then he piled on the stir-fried shrimp, jicama, and shallots. Finally, he drizzled Southeast Asian bottled sweet sauce and chili sauce on the edges of the ingredients and deftly rolled up everything. After slicing the *popiah* into three-quarter-inch bits, we dunked them into more sweet sauce before eating.

The rolls were delicious—a combination of crunchy, savory, and slightly sweet. As we chewed, I tried to think back to my grandmother's *popiah*. But I couldn't quite remember how they tasted. Were they better? Different? It had been so long I genuinely couldn't tell. As I was thinking, Simpson watched me carefully. "It's good," I finally said. He rolled his eyes.

For months afterward, when anyone mentioned cooking with me, he'd immediately squawk: "I worked so hard to make

popiah like your grandmother's, and you said it was only okay—
cheh!"

Getting my maternal grandmother to teach me her recipe
for *popiah* a few months later in Singapore would prove to be
difficult. Once again, she didn't quite remember what went into
it. And once again, Auntie Alice and I were left guessing. "Well,
we definitely need *mang guang* [jicama], . . . right?" I said, adding the one piece of knowledge I remembered from my *popiah*-
making episode with Simpson. "And shrimp?" Over e-mails
and phone calls, we hashed out a rough ingredients list, and
once again, I was in my grandmother's kitchen.

This time, I brought a sous chef—Erlinda, my mother's
uncomplaining maid. Auntie Alice and I were instantly relieved
she was there, because the bossy fussiness that Simpson had,
my grandmother had in spades. And more. The kindly and
sweet smelly puppy–crooning ah-ma I knew vanished the moment the peeling started. "Not like that!" "Thinner!" "Smaller!"
"Where's the dried shrimp?" Auntie Alice, my sister, and I
trembled in a corner, watching the orders fly out of her mouth
as Erlinda valiantly chopped on. (My mother, still avoiding the
kitchen, had reluctantly joined us but very wisely decided to
take a nap while all this went down.)

"Ah-Ma wants to teach you the best recipe so you know
how to do it on your own in America," Ah-Ma finally explained
quietly. Coming from a woman who had cried bitterly when I
first announced that I was going to college in America and then
cried more each time I left Singapore for the United States in the
following sixteen years, this was significant. She had never
wanted me to be away from her. But now that I was, and now

that I might have a family of my own there someday soon, she wanted me to listen up and learn.

Once the ingredients were fried up, the wrapping began. Before we knew it, we had a mound of *popiah* on the table. It was time to see how we'd fared.

The *popiah* was tasty—not better, not worse than Simpson's. Watching my sister, my mother, my auntie Alice, and my grandmother gathered around the kitchen counter, wrapping *popiah*, I couldn't remember the last time we had all spent an entire afternoon together. And with my active avoidance of anything culinary, when we had gotten together, cooking certainly had never happened.

Whether the rolls were delicious or as we remembered, of course, had been immaterial all along.

I HADN'T SPENT MUCH TIME BACK IN SINGAPORE BEFORE another substitute uncle appeared in my life.

We had first met in New York, at a Singaporean cooking demonstration the year before. One night I'd entered a cavernous space near Manhattan's trendy Meatpacking District, flustered, flushed from the cold, horrendously late because of work, and hungry for the spicy Singaporean food I could already smell in the air. The moment I got there, I was immediately instructed: "Try the *laksa*—it's amazing." Now, *laksa*—a dish of noodles with tofu and shrimp in a creamy, curried soup—isn't my favorite Singaporean dish. I'd hardly eaten it as a child; it is so rich and thick that I find it impossible to swallow in ninety-degree weather. But a chilly October night in New York felt like the perfect time to be having some. And so I sauntered up to the *laksa* table and waited for a minute. The young server in a white cook's uniform was off in some corner idly chitchatting. I waited, and waited, then I tapped the server on the shoulder, asking him with immense irritation if he could just please dish out a serving for me. "Of course," he said, rushing over to scoop soup into a bowl for me swiftly and politely.

The *laksa*, as billed, was delicious. Thick, creamy, incredibly spicy, and heavy with the scent of coconut milk and curry, the broth was heavenly. I downed it in a flash and went back for more. In my *laksa*-induced coma, I asked, "Who is the chef? I *must* meet him." The answer? The obsequious server who'd borne the brunt of my impatience, of course. His name was Willin Low, and he was the chef at Wild Rocket, one of the most highly regarded restaurants in Singapore. He was so well respected, in fact, that the Singapore government had flown him to New York to be a gastronomic ambassador at this event. I was mortified.

A few nights later, however, I was dining with a friend at Per Se, the incredibly high-end and famous Thomas Keller restaurant that's something of a shrine to fine dining in New York City, when in walked Willin. After he was seated at a table near us, we exchanged quick and perfunctory pleasantries. And our meals began. My dining companion that evening happened to be K.F. Seetoh, the founder of Makansutra, a Zagat-style guide to restaurants and hawkers in Singapore, a fact that our waiter had duly noted and conveyed to the chef. As our meal progressed, we rapidly learned what that meant—instead of just ten courses, our meal would unfold over fifteen, compliments of the chef. A perfect-looking eggshell arrived in a lovely cup, cracked open just so and flanked with the tiniest spoon for us to scoop out a delicate truffle oil–infused egg custard. A foie gras terrine came paired with juicy Oregon huckleberries.

As each course surfaced, I looked over at Willin. His (by comparison) measly ten-course meal was speeding by a lot more quickly than ours, and as dish after dish that wasn't on the pre-planned menu appeared at our table, he looked increasingly crestfallen. I began gesturing to the openmouthed, flabbergasted Willin to watch as I licked my truffled egg custard off the shiny silver spoon with gusto. After a waiter appeared with a heavy, velvet-lined wooden box, opening it with great flair and asking me to take a deep whiff of the pricey truffle the size of a fist that lay within before he lightly grated it over spinach rigatoni, I wandered over to Willin's table to ask, "And where are *your* truffles?" With some fist shaking, he quietly shrieked, "I have *none!*"

Willin's meal, however, had a happy ending after the waiters discovered that he was a fine-dining chef from Singapore. Truffled egg custard and more appeared on his table as well. But our friendship had been sealed long before that. There we'd been at Per Se, one of the toniest and most impossible to get into restaurants in New York City, and we'd filled the evening with snotty playground taunts, uncouth, Hokkien-splattered diatribes, and much jealous pointing—a display that had entirely been fueled by a shared love for food. In an instant, I knew we'd be dear friends. What my friendship with Simpson had taught me, after all, was that boys may come and go, but if you find a person who loves food and loves to cook as much as you do, you'd better hang on.

Whenever I touched down in Singapore for more cooking lessons, I began texting Willin as soon as I could turn on my phone. "Welcome back, my friend!" he'd always say, almost instantly. And then: "When are we eating?"

Together, we began eating our way through Singapore. We ventured to a hole-in-the-wall Cantonese restaurant in search of shark's fin scrambled eggs, which neither of us had had for years and which we were beginning to believe had been a figment of our imaginations. We nibbled on squid ink and Parmesan breadsticks at Jaan, a high-end restaurant at the top of the tallest hotel in Singapore, marveling at the throbbing cityscape seventy floors beneath us as we giggled over much too much wine. On a particularly decadent evening, we visited Fifty Three, a new restaurant opened by a law student turned Heston Blumenthal *stagiaire,* and inhaled Japanese tomatoes, impossibly tiny and so incredibly sweet, paired with creamy burrata and a fiery and icy horseradish granita, chased with crunchy ducks' tongues and lobster in a rich, brown butter sauce.

Over these meals, I shared my enormous fears with Willin. "My aunties are really hard-core in the kitchen—scary," I'd say. "I'm not sure that I'll ever be able to cook like they do." Or "I don't even really remember what real Teochew food tastes like sometimes."

Patiently, Willin would listen. And his answer, just like Mike's, always was "Of course you can do it." Like all my aunties and my uncle Simpson, Willin wanted me to learn. He himself wasn't Teochew, but he'd grown up in Singapore's Teochew enclave, the Hougang neighborhood. He'd been raised by a Teochew auntie who'd plied him with the porridges and soups of my people. Years later, after ditching a lucrative law career to open Wild Rocket, he'd even incorporated Teochew elements into his modern fusion menu, introducing a pasta with a duck ragù that had been slow-cooked with spices like star anise and cinnamon, which the Teochews use in braised duck dishes.

After he'd listened to me whine, Willin and I came up with a solution for my insecurities. To fully understand my quest and divorce myself from the fear of my aunties' Teochew cooking abilities, I should see how the professionals do it. Wherever we ate, Willin and I would dissect each dish with the enthusiasm and confidence of scientists splitting the atom: What were the ingredients? How could we re-create this dish? What would we add or change to make it better? Always, always, we came away with the fervent—if sometimes misguided, especially on my part—belief that we could do it. Or that we could come somewhat close trying.

For me, however, this bravado was still hard to summon when it came to Teochew food. These dishes had long ceased to be just food, having been wrapped up for years in the tangled mysticism of my family, of its history. After all, I tended to eat Teochew food only at family gatherings, for which it had been painstakingly cooked by my aunties or late grandmother, my impulse when I eat out being to seek Western food or spicy Szechuan or Indian dishes, which are far more oomphy than the relatively subtle Teochew cuisine.

I decided that perhaps Willin was right—I needed to start thinking of Teochew food as just food. And before I knew it, we were in a tiny restaurant in a working-class neighborhood of Singapore, sipping tea impatiently as we waited for dishes to appear. We had asked a well-regarded Singaporean chef who happens to be Teochew, Ignatius Chan, where he went when he craved Teochew food. And as soon as Iggy was free, we invited him to join us at Swa Garden, his Teochew restaurant of choice.

A bowl of porridge—a hallmark of traditional Teochew cuisine—appeared. The water was just slightly milky, the grains of rice soft, yet still separate and not so soft that they were mushed together, as they often can be in lesser versions. The porridge was simple and clean—a lovely canvas for the subtle dishes that would follow. A giant steamed fish came peppered with slivers of ginger and swimming in a slightly sweet broth with tinges of the tomatoes and sour plums that had been steeped in it. A crunchy beggar's purse erupted in an avalanche of diced chicken when sliced open. Perfectly fried prawn balls were crunchy outside and hot and juicy inside. Goose legs and wings came braised in sweet soy sauce to such softness that the meat was like cotton puffs on our tongues.

Willin and I were speechless after. "You don't have so many flavors fighting for your attention," Willin said. "It's very *cheng*," he added, using a Chinese word for "clear."

The dishes had been unfussy and plain. Delicious, yes, but, in my mind, doable. Willin was right—things had become a little more clear.

CHAPTER SEVEN

In my quest to retrace my grandmothers' footsteps in the kitchen, I had known, of course, that there were compulsories I'd have to nail.

Bak-zhang and pineapple tarts were two. But these were special occasion items made just once a year. Twice, if we were lucky. When it came to everyday food, however, the single Teochew dish that my relatives and friends continually asked about was one that had me genuinely afraid: *giam chye ar tng,* or salted vegetable and duck soup.

This soup had been a hallmark of Tanglin Ah-Ma's repertoire. Every year, at the big family reunion dinner, she would make a feast on the eve of the Chinese New Year—and this was the dish that I always looked forward to. Salty and sour with a delicate layer of meaty umami, this clear soup was simple and light, yet complex. It wasn't easy to pull off—the balance of salty, sour, and sweet had to be just right. When done well, it was lovely on its own but also scooped over a bowl of plain rice to lend the grains a subtle sour flavor. My father spoke longingly of it for years after his mother died. In our own home, although my mother is an absolute ace at making Chinese soups, she never once tried this. Why bother, after all? It would just be futile—nothing would come close to the memory of my Tanglin ah-ma's salted vegetable and duck soup.

So when Auntie Khar Imm invited me over to help her make it for a weekday family dinner, I jumped at the chance.

As I barreled along with my quest, my mother seemed increasingly uncomfortable. She had never enjoyed cooking, seeing it as a chore that should be left to the maid, if you could afford one. And having always been cordial at best with my father's side of the family, she wondered why I suddenly wanted to spend so much time with these people whom she'd much rather forget, given the divorce.

"You don't have to do this, you know," she said one day.

"But it's the only way I'm going to learn," I protested.

"Why don't you just ask your e-ma to teach you things?"

"I am. But I also want to learn the dishes that Tanglin Ah-Ma made!"

After a silence, she would finally say, "Okay lah, just tell me what time you're going. I'll fetch you there."

We began to have a ritual. My mother would drive me to my auntie Khar Imm's apartment in Hougang and leave me with firm instructions to "*text me* when you're done—I'll come fetch you!" As I waited in my aunt's apartment for her to return, Auntie Khar Imm would always say, "Ask your mummy to come up and sit down for a while, say hello." But my mother could never bring herself to leave the car.

"You know why that is," my mother said. "Your father invited them to his second wedding. How can I face them?"

And so I would make an excuse. "Oh, my mum has to rush to class, so she can't come up for tea." "She's not feeling well." "Maybe next time."

I felt increasingly torn between the two sides of the family. I wasn't sure if I'd ever be able to bring them together, even over food. I wasn't going to let that stand in my way, however. The olive branch had been extended; there were many more dishes to be learned.

The moment I got to Auntie Khar Imm's kitchen for our salted vegetable and duck soup lesson, I saw problems ahead. When I'd balked at dicing the somewhat piglike pork belly, I'd sensed that more animal-like meats would be in my very near future. No amount of preparing for the moment, however, could have diminished my horror at seeing a pale, cold duck in a large red basin, its neck gently curled around its body, its beady eyes fixed on me. I wasn't sure what to do.

Fortunately, Auntie Khar Imm took the lead, grabbing the duck, giving it a quick rinse, and then hacking at it with a cleaver, chopping it into large chunks. We would be making dinner for her family tonight—for Uncle Soo Kiat, my cousins Jessie and Royston, and Royston's wife and toddler. I'd never met two-year-old Giselle or her mother, Kat; in fact, I'd never been invited to a small family dinner at their home without my parents or sister before. I fervently hoped that my "helping" wouldn't ruin the meal the way my chopping skills had ruined the *bak-zhang*.

Working quickly, Auntie Khar Imm brought a small pot of water to boil for blanching the duck chunks. "If you don't do this, the soup will have a very smelly, meaty taste," she said. I barely heard her. I was too stunned after seeing her dip the duck's head into the water and swirl it around. I wondered how a duck skull, eyes, and beak could possibly enhance the flavor of soup. (I also wondered if it would be impolite to refuse the soup at dinner that night.) But hey, I'd rarely made soup before—and the best soup I'd made thus far involved heavy cream, corn, potatoes, and bacon—so what did I know about Chinese soups, really? I watched her place the blanched duck in another pot, toss in sour plums, ginger, and tamarind leaves, and bring that to a boil before starting on the rest of dinner.

Also on the menu that night were sweet and sour pork and steamed egg custard. The egg custard was fairly straightforward. Auntie Khar Imm carefully cracked three eggs into a bowl, filled an eggshell six times with water, and added it to the mixture. (At this point, I had given up trying to guess at the amounts and dutifully wrote "six shells of water" in my notebook.) She rapidly beat the egg mixture with a teaspoon of salt and strained it. "This will make the eggs very smooth," she said. Onto the steaming rack it went, and we moved on to the next dish.

I had been surprised to hear her mention sweet and sour pork, a dish that's definitely not Teochew or even, really, Singaporean. "I learned it from the gossipy aunties" chattering about cooking to while away hours in the neighborhood, she explained. While I wasn't crazy about sweet and sour pork, I had a rather lonely—and, often, hungry—husband who adored the dish. Mike had been very patient with me—never grumbling about my cooking trips or having to get up at four in the morning to take me to the airport for my insanely early flights to

Singapore. Always, always, he'd send me off with a pep talk: "You can do it," he'd say. "Don't let anyone get you down." And as the plane took off and the sadness subsided, I'd still feel the rosy glow of his confidence as I thought of the weeks ahead without him. Mike liked pineapple tarts well enough, although he'd once confessed that they weren't his "favorite." *Kaya* wasn't his thing either. But sweet and sour pork—now, here was something he truly adored. When Auntie Khar Imm brought out the pork, I started paying very close attention.

Once again, this pork was slimy. "You want something with some fat on it," Auntie Khar Imm said, as she swiftly chopped the white-speckled pink meat into slender strips. (I noticed she was not offering to let me help with the slicing this time; perhaps she'd gotten the same complaints about the *bak-zhang* we'd made as I had.) As she mixed beaten eggs, tapioca flour, salt, pepper, plum sauce, ketchup, and sugar in with the pork, I asked her about Giselle, her grandchild. Her life had changed since Giselle was born. Although Royston and Kat didn't live with his parents, they stopped by every morning before heading to work to drop off Giselle for Auntie Khar Imm to watch. This is a fairly common arrangement in Singapore. (My father has made it clear for years now that, if I have a child, he'll happily babysit, as long as he can do it at his golf club.) My auntie Khar Imm's arrangement was a little more traditional, however. She now spent mornings and afternoons looking after Giselle, who, she kept telling me, was an unceasing jumping bean who sang and chattered away nonstop and ate like a maniac. After work each day, Royston and Kat would come over for dinner and take Giselle home for the evening.

"Lu-Lien ah, you don't want to give your mother a grand-child?" she gently asked. I wasn't sure what to say. None of my earlier excuses had really mattered—family was family after all. Living all by myself in New York, I should want to have a child. For the firstborn in my family, who'd been married for five years by now, it really was time. And besides, who was going to take care of me when I was older? "Maybe later," I finally said. It occurred to me that this was the first time I'd uttered those words. Fortunately, the conversation didn't go much further. There were vegetables to be fried, there was rice to be made.

Auntie Khar Imm paused only to tell me quickly how my cousin Jessie had made the *gway neng gou* (egg cake) that she was sending home with me. "Just whisk six eggs with sugar, a bit of flour, and pour in three quarters of a can of Sprite," she said. "Your sister likes it, right?" It was a detail that even I had forgotten, after many years of not having this steamed egg cake.

Soon enough, dinner was on the table. As I watched the tiny Giselle shovel down a bowl of rice swimming in salted vegetable soup with bits of steamed egg aloft in it and then chase that with jumping and singing, I found myself thinking for a moment, *Perhaps I could do this*. And then half an hour later, when the jumping and singing continued, I thought, *Hmm, maybe not*. I hadn't done much that day besides watch Auntie Khar Imm cook, but I was exhausted. I had no idea how Auntie Khar Imm and generations of housewives before her had pulled this off without dropping dead from exhaustion. Suddenly, motherhood seemed like a very noble calling, one far nobler than anything I'd ever endeavored.

Calling it a night, I said my good-byes. It wasn't until I was almost home that I realized what had been missing. I'd been in Auntie Khar Imm's home for the better part of the day—and not once had she offered to get me water or tea. I'd been there enough times by now; I was family. Not a guest anymore.

MEANWHILE, ON MY MOTHER'S SIDE OF THE FAMILY, THERE was hardly any cooking going on. Everyone was consumed with one thing: a big family wedding.

When a man loves a woman, in Singapore, the courtship ritual often ends something like this: the man and his entourage pounding on his loved one's door, waving red packets of money as bribes, demanding to "buy the bride." Once they're inside, a number of the dishes are set out, ranging from the sickeningly sweet to the downright vile.

The groom and groomsmen's task is to consume what's set before them with as much gusto as they can muster. Only then have they earned the right to claim the bride for the wedding to proceed. While it sounds like a prank, the practice actually is a legitimate part of Singaporean Chinese wedding tradition. By eating items that are *suan, tian, ku, la* (sour, sweet, bitter, and spicy), the groom is symbolically acknowledging that he expects to go through these phases with his bride in the years ahead. (Think of it as something of a literal take on the "for better or for worse" contract of Western marriages.)

I could say that the women involved in these proceedings often feel sorry for the poor sods—but I'd be lying. Any bridesmaid helping out with the *suan, tian, ku, la* bit relishes the opportunity to really stick it to the boys.

It had been years since I'd thought of this ritual. I'd been married for five years, and my marrying friends in New York certainly didn't indulge in anything this masochistic. In our courtship, however, Mike had been informed of these Chinese wedding proceedings should he pop the question. Bravely, he decided to take the plunge anyway. The night Mike had proposed, I'd had an inkling that something was up. Before my trip to New York for the weekend, he informed me that he had made a reservation at One If by Land, Two If by Sea, a starched-tablecloth, candlelit restaurant in lower Manhattan that I discovered through a quick Google search was noteworthy at one point for being the setting for an average of twenty-four marriage proposals a week, so the story goes. We hadn't been dating long, and I wasn't sure what my answer would be.

In our short time together, Mike had become my best friend, my first true love, and a trusty older brother to my sister, who lived in New York, working as a hotel industry consultant. With no family in Manhattan, Daphne was regularly calling or e-mailing Mike, leaning on him with an easy comfort that had been there from the very start. On 9/11, as I raced around lower Manhattan reporting my front-page story for the *Baltimore Sun* and, when I could get a signal on my cell phone, calling only the paper's rewrite desk to file dispatches—or Mike to ask for directions to Saint Vincent's Hospital or where I might find a store to buy sneakers so I could ditch my heels—my sister and family had been beside themselves. They had no idea if I was alive or hurt. Even though Mike had just met me, he took it upon himself to handle my family—calling my sister to let her know I was okay. I was simply working. From that day, Daphne treated him like a brother.

I thought about 9/11 as my Amtrak train raced up the Atlantic to New York. I thought about how I knew Mike had already asked my sister if she was free later that night for after-dinner drinks. And I thought about how he had always treated my friends, my family, and me with such intense love and care. By the time I was seated at One If by Land, Two If by Sea, sipping the flute of champagne Mike had ordered for me, I was nervous.

The meal flew by uneventfully, however. I was so antsy, carefully inspecting every move Mike made, steeling myself each time he reached into his pocket for something, that I barely remember anything I ate. (If I have no recollection of a beef Wellington that's passed my plate, you know that something is up.) When the bill had come and gone and still no velvet box had surfaced, I felt relieved. And then worried. What if I had been too presumptuous? What if he didn't actually want to marry me?

We decided to take a walk along the water in Battery Park City. "The last time I was in this area, it was 9/11 and I was so scared," I recalled as we strolled in the cool darkness, pausing to look out at the water and the Statue of Liberty glowing in the distance. "But you were there for me. It made me feel better." Mike was silent. Slowly, he went down on one knee and pulled out a little black box. Nestled in the velvet pillow was a twinkling diamond ring. We hadn't discussed rings at all before—yet somehow he had known that I was a solitaire (large, if you please) kind of girl. Of course, I said "Yes."

Sixteen months later, on a sunny Valentine's Day in 2004, Mike and I had the first of our two weddings. Against the canvas of a brilliantly clear blue sky with Diamond Head in the background, we proceeded to have what Jim, one of Mike's best friends from college, called "the gayest straight wedding" he'd ever been to. My dear friend Victor, who had been with his partner Charles for more than a decade, draped a long, regal garland of orchids around his neck and officiated. Smitty and Rachelle, two women who loved each other with a gentle ferocity that made anyone around them feel privileged just to be in the presence of such intense devotion, read at the ceremony. Mike's friend Jim, a Hollywood screenwriter who had recently come out, stood by his side as he watched me come down the orchid-lined grassy aisle. On my side of the wedding, next to Daphne and a phalanx of bridesmaids, stood my bridesman, Greg, who had been one of my dearest friends and confidants since he happened to sit beside me at my very first fashion show. After that fateful day, we would spend way too many evenings over the following years sitting at the Oak Room bar in Manhattan's posh Plaza Hotel, huddled over sauvignon blancs, whispering as we pointed out which men at the bar we might consider "going with"—a term Greg prefers because, as he always says, "I'm a lady."

My parents had flown to Honolulu from Singapore for the wedding—I wasn't sure what they would make of the occasion. The modern Narciso Rodriguez dress I had chosen wasn't a bridal gown—it just happened to be a white dress he had designed for his collection that season. And with its spaghetti-strapped halter top and revealing cut-out design that from the back made it look as if I might be wearing a bikini top paired with a long flowing skirt, the gown, though elegant, was a little racier than ones that most Singaporean brides wear. Mike and I had decided against a formal ceremony, choosing to write our own ceremony and vows—slipping in a line about believing in the basic right for everyone to marry, but also making it a brief affair that ended with Victor announcing, "I now present to you Mr. and Mrs. Cheryl Tan!" While there had been laughter all around, my parents' faces had been grim. "How can you be so disrespectful?" my mother had quietly said, the first moment she could get me alone. "Mike is a man, you know. You must give him face." And then there were our guests, a motley group of colleagues past and present and friends plucked from different stages of each of our lives. They had arrived from New York, Switzerland, Detroit, Phoenix. It was the first time my parents were meeting some of them, and I worried about how they would take to them. Although gay culture has become more mainstream in Singapore in recent years, it's still not widely embraced, especially among those of my parents' generation.

I had taken great care to include my Singaporean identity in my American wedding, however. Even though the Moana Surfrider Hotel, a grand colonial building that is the oldest hotel on Waikiki Beach, didn't do Chinese meals for weddings at the time, I had insisted that the chef specially create a nine-course Chinese banquet for us. Midway through our banquet, I disappeared into the bridal suite to change into a scarlet dress, a nod to the lucky red cheongsams that Chinese-Singaporean brides wear. After the first course, I had gathered my Singaporean friends together to deliver the traditional toast of Chinese weddings in our homeland. Forming a circle, we raised our glasses high as we bellowed "*YUM SENG!*" (which means "drink all" in Cantonese) as loud as we could, dragging out the *yum* bit so it extended well over a minute, with people occasionally pausing to take a quick breath before jumping right back into the yelling. And knowing that my mother loved to sing old Chinese ballads by the Taiwanese pop singer Teresa Teng, I had made sure to give our deejay a disc of her songs, instructing him to not only play them but also encourage any singing that might erupt. Sure enough, the moment my mother heard the first notes of "The Moon Represents My Heart," a gently lilting Teresa Teng song that she and I used to sing in her little gold Mazda as she shuttled me around Singapore from ballet classes to after-school Chinese tuition, she grabbed my hand and made for the deejay, gesturing for the mike.

"*Ni wen wo ai ni you duo shen, wo ai ni you ji fen,*" she softly sang, firmly holding my hand and looking at me. "*Wo de qing ye zhen, wo de ai ye zhen. Yue liang dai biao wo de xing.*"

You ask me how deeply I love you,
    how much I really love you.
My feelings are true, my love is true.
The moon represents my heart.

I had had my concerns about the wedding in Honolulu—when my parents visited me in New York or Washington, D.C., they had met and spent time with my American friends. But they certainly hadn't shared entire days and evenings with them as they were doing in Honolulu, where Mike and I had planned group trips to essential stops like Diamond Head or Lanikai Beach, a somewhat secluded tranquil spot that's often largely devoid of tourists. Through these excursions and meals, my parents were learning about my life and how I interacted with my friends—the fact that I occasionally swore like a pirate; that I tend to use the word "like" a little too often. While I still spoke to my parents in the British-inflected English that I had grown up using, in the United States, my American accent was flawless— I had frequently been told I sounded like a California girl.

How would my parents feel about the life I had chosen— who their daughter had turned into on this foreign shore? Holding my mother's hand as she sang to me with my smiling father and sister looking on, however, my anxieties faded. They were happy—and they were happy for me. And that was all the reassurance I needed.

> You ask me how deep my love is for you,
>   how much I really love you.
> My feelings will not waver,
>   my love will not change.
> The moon represents my heart.

The following Saturday, we were scheduled to do it all over again in Singapore—this time with a traditional Chinese tea ceremony at which I wore a red cheongsam. And a traditional Chinese banquet, albeit one that turned out to be not so traditional, since my father planned it. (The first indication of this was that he had taken a cue from our Hawaiian wedding and planned a first dance. When we sat down with the Grand Hyatt's wedding planner to go over the schedule for the evening, she had asked which song Mike and I would like for our first dance. In Honolulu, it had been "Twilight Time" by The Platters, which had figured prominently in a rather romantic episode of *The X-Files* we had watched together over the phone one night while dating long-distance. Before we could say anything, however, my father jumped in. " 'Endless Love'! That's one of my favorite songs," he said. So "Endless Love" it was.)

As Mike and I walked into the banquet hall, my father had arranged for dry ice to fog our pathway as the theme song from *Hawaii Five-0* blared. After the meal, when dancing began, I noticed that my father and his secondary school mates had disappeared, one by one. In fact, some of my male childhood friends were out of sight, too. I heard strange screams and yells coming from the conference room next door, the one my father had insisted the hotel wedding planner provide free of charge because "my daughter needs a place to change—come on." I had thought it a strange request at the time, given that I had a room upstairs I could just as easily have used for quick changes. Once I followed the screams, however, all became clear. I opened the door to find the long conference table filled with playing cards. In the center was a large pool of money. And around this table were my father, his friends, my childhood friends, and a former editor of mine who had flown in from Tokyo—all of them drunk as sailors and louder than pirates. They were playing Polish (also known as In Between), a card game that my father's friends and mine spend hours playing over the Chinese New Year holidays. We started playing the game as adolescents, choosing to see if we could double our lucky money from the New Year. Everyone gets two cards, and you bet against the pot of money on whether the third card you get will be between the numbers of the two cards you already have. If you are feeling lucky, you yell "polish!", indicating that you think your cards are strong enough to polish off the whole pile of money.

My father had transformed my wedding into an illegal casino. Watching his friends and my friends, sharing cigarettes and slapping one another on the back and occasionally breaking out in the anthem of Saint Joseph's Institution, the all-boys school most of them had attended, Mike and I smiled. This had somehow turned into the coolest wedding we'd ever been to— and it was our own!

Just then, the wife of one of my father's schoolmates came over, feeling sorry for the bride. "This is what happens after you get married lah," she said, sighing and shaking her head. "Boys will always be boys." "Well," I said immediately, "I certainly hope so."

The only thing I feel sorry about when I think of our wedding is that when Mike had to buy his bride, the worst thing that he and his Singaporean groomsman, Eudon, had to do was down a large spoonful of wasabi (spicy) and immediately chase it with a pint of Guinness (bitter). What made me even more bitter was the fact that, as the bride, I was locked in a bedroom and unable to watch how green they got. So, when we found out that my dear cousin Valerie, my auntie Jane's daughter, was getting married in Singapore, I knew we had to pull out all the stops. Valerie and I had played together often as children, after all—she was practically a sister to Daphne and me. In the years since I'd left Singapore, we had written each other regular letters and postcards to keep in touch. I knew that before we let her dashing French fiancé whisk her away into his family, we had to make him earn his bride.

As soon as morning broke on her wedding day, Valerie's gaggle of bridesmaids—also known as hens or aunties—descended on her father's apartment in the Pasir Ris neighborhood of Singapore, near the country's East Coast. There was Gen, the chief hen, who supervised the proceedings with the calm cruise director air of a recent mother; Nat, the sophisticated traveler who spoke fluent French and had a weakness for Chanel; a second Gen, the effervescent journalist who spoke a mile a minute, a verbal force of nature; and my sister, Daphne, and me, representing the family. We'd not spent much time with Valerie's friends before that day, but intimacy was of little importance. We were united in our crucial mission—to make the boys suffer.

We got to work as soon as we arrived, divvying up items we'd each purchased as Gen the Number One Hen gave out orders. For starters, we created a *suan* concoction of freshly squeezed lemon juice and dropped in preserved plums, which are generally so sour they induce wincing all on their own. For *ku*, we sliced up a big bitter gourd, whose name is pretty much self-explanatory. It's widely regarded as the most bitter of vegetables. Next, we prepared a real *la* treat for the boys: white bread generously buttered with wasabi on one half and super-spicy *sambal belacan* (a Singaporean shrimp-chili sauce) on the other and then folded over to form a sandwich. (Because we did feel slightly bad for the boys as we were preparing these, we decided to slice them up into finger sandwiches for easier consumption and sharing.)

Now, you might think that the "sweet" part would be a welcome respite. Not so in Chinese weddings, where bridesmaids never let up—unless the groom wants to fork over more money in bribes, of course. Although, all things considered, gobs of pancake syrup and honey stirred into soda probably weren't too hard to down after wasabi sandwiches and bitter gourd.

Once all the dishes were prepared, we carefully set them out on the table and waited for the knocking.

A gleaming black car arrived; well-scrubbed young men in dark suits emerged. And soon enough, there was a rattling at the metal gate. Gen the Journalist sprang into action, racing to the gate, immediately barking out demands for lucky money. Cramming ourselves around Gen and pressing our faces against the gate, we screamed, "At least three zeros!" knowing full well that most modern brides in Singapore command well below that. (When Mike bought me in 2004, he got away with forking over just $288, a lucky number since the word for the number eight sounds like "prosperity" in Mandarin and Cantonese.) After a short huddle, David, the groom, approached the gate, handing over a fat red packet—which was promising. Gen quickly opened it—it was filled with Vietnamese currency. More screaming, one more huddle, one more red packet—this one filled with Thai baht. We'd gotten many zeros all right, but not in the right currency.

After much back-and-forth, they finally produced a red packet that was somewhat satisfactory—a well-rounded $500—and the gate was opened.

Getting through the gate was only the first step, however. There was the battalion of humiliating tasks we'd dreamt up: making the groomsmen bend over and spell out "Valerie" using their butts; requiring David to sniff a bunch of perfumed cotton balls and identify the scent that his bride regularly used. And when all that was done, there was the tasting. The relief on David's face rapidly disappeared as he spotted the trays of glasses and bowls containing mysterious liquids and solids that we'd carefully arranged on the dining table. He may have grown up in France, but after years of dating Valerie and attending numerous Singaporean weddings, he knew the drill. Rallying his groomsmen, David unflinchingly went through the bitter gourd, the honey and pancake syrup cocktail, the lemony sour plum drink, and even the wasabi-chili finger sandwiches as Valerie's increasingly impressed elderly aunts looked on.

Having breezed through the four rounds of food, David thought he was done. Not so, however. Before he was allowed to open the bedroom door to claim his bride, he had one more hurdle—a particularly potent finale.

The hens had been having so much fun planning the menu that we didn't want it to end. Weeks before, as we were discussing our plan of action, Daphne had visited a traditional Chinese medicine shop in Hong Kong—the kind that reeks so much of earth and fungus that you carry that smell in your hair for a long time after. My mother and grandmother adore these shops, often stopping in to pick up wizened bits and bobs to brew in Chinese soups and drinks; it was never clear what exactly was in these soups. They said only "Drink it—it's good for you."

As a result, I'd generally avoided these shops as an adult, quickly walking by as soon as I caught a whiff of them in New York's Chinatown.

This was a special occasion, however. And once Daphne had perused the stock and explained to the owner what she was doing, he immediately began plucking items out of jars with tweezers and carefully wrapping them in crisp white paper. The sight, when we unwrapped the packages, was unforgettable. Our treasure trove included starfish; dried sea horses; a long, dried, black object that was a dead ringer for a calcified horse dropping . . . and a package of salted bugs.

We boiled them all together in water for an hour, as per the medicine man's instructions. When the soup was done and the pot was uncovered, the name of the concoction was obvious: smelly.

As we ladled the yellowish soup into shallow bowls, we made sure each dish came with a sea horse and a couple of bugs for garnish. And the look on David's face when we unveiled the bowl was priceless. "No!" *"No!"* "You are kidding!" came the wails.

Unfortunately for these suddenly green groomsmen, we were most definitely not.

"It's good for virility!" we volunteered. They, of course, looked skeptical. "It might even be good for sore throats!" we coaxed. (Which may not have been too far from the truth. These items are actually used in soups to cure sore throats—or enhance virility—the medicine man had said. At least this was what my sister gleaned with her limited grasp of Cantonese.)

When it became clear that we were not budging—except on

the point of actually making them eat the sea horses and bugs—David rallied his men for the final push. Steeling themselves, one by one, they quickly downed the soup, letting out a chorus of giant *Ughs* at the end.

And then the groom's battle was over—he had earned his prize. Stepping aside, the hens cleared a path. David strode to the bedroom door and opened it. Inside, Valerie sat, big-eyed and demure in a bright red cheongsam, her hair swept back and piled high on her head, looking every bit the lady in a Wong Kar-wai movie. (In fact, she had flown to Hong Kong to have her dress made at a tailor who had supposedly done work for *In the Mood for Love*, but that's another story.) There was a hug, and a kiss. And a small bowl of soup was brought out—this one made with sweet dates, a blessing for the sugary life we all wished for them in the long years ahead. In the bowl were two *tangyuan*, plump, round balls made with glutinous rice flour—a symbol of their new family unit. David clutched the bowl and took a moment to gaze at his bride. The ever-impatient Valerie pouted and started pointing toward her mouth. Knowingly, patiently, David grabbed a spoon, scooping out one *tangyuan* and gently feeding his bride. The deal was complete.

The ritual of eating the sour, the sweet, the bitter, the spicy, and even the smelly had served its purpose. All those steps make the reward at the end all the more prized.

That day, there had been much laughter and merriment. (And only one groomsman had suffered a close encounter with the wasabi coming right back up.) I'd like to think that David, having faced a wall of bridesmaids and survived the food, burst through the bedroom door that day to claim his bride feeling triumphant and exhilarated. After the sour plums, the chili sandwiches, and the salted insect soup, perhaps, just perhaps, it was true that there was little out there they couldn't face together.

CHAPTER EIGHT

Back in New York, I was starting to get cocky.

Barely off the plane, I once again threw myself into baking bread. The first big project—challah, which looked impossibly complicated, with its twisted braids and perfect honey coloring—terrified me. I was convinced that I'd never pull off braiding gooey logs of dough, and yet I did. Easily, too. When Brian, one of my best friends, who happens to be Jewish, proclaimed it "just beautiful" and rapidly devoured the half a loaf I'd given him, I almost teared up.

Heartened, I took a moment to reflect and admit to myself: *I am the bread-baking bomb*.

And then I almost burned down my kitchen.

In the back of my mind, even as I had sailed through bagels, brioche, and challah, I'd known that one day it would come to this: me sitting on the floor of my smoke-filled apartment, staring at three rock-hard, blackened loaves and thinking, *I am a failure*.

Having never baked bread before, I'd known it was a little insane to sign up for the weekly Bread Baker's Apprentice challenge with bakers who had years of practice. But the successes had gone to my head. My breads were turning out well; the lessons my Singaporean aunties were sharing were giving me a confidence that I'd never had.

So when Simpson mentioned that there would be some Italian friends at his Fourth of July party, I thought it was a sign. The next bread on the challenge list was ciabatta—and who would be better at judging the quality of an Italian bread than Italians themselves?

Mike looked skeptical, but only briefly. And he most certainly didn't say anything. After all, he generally likes to leave it up to me to get in the way of myself. Brief as it was, however, I'd seen his look of doubt. Never mind, I figured. I would show *him* as well.

It all began promisingly enough. On the first day, I prepared the *poolish,* a sponge that's meant to give a bread more complexity of flavor. I took some bread flour and a bit of instant yeast, and mixed in some room-temperature water to create a watery dough. After that sat for a few hours at room temperature, I stuck it in the refrigerator to rest overnight so the flavors could deepen. I was feeling good about myself—I even envisioned Simpson's Italian friends grabbing me, madly kissing me on both cheeks as they murmured "Brava! Brava!" A Singaporean gal acing ciabatta, who would have thought?

The next day, however, things got a little insane. In addition to ciabatta, I'd volunteered to bring desserts. I'd made my lemon thumbprint cookies the night before and was planning to whip together a strawberry rhubarb pie using a recipe that Haley, a fellow Bread Baker's Apprentice challenge cook, had suggested. When Simpson's guest list grew a little, I decided to add a coconut-lime cake to the lineup. Two desserts *and* ciabatta? I'd churned out far more on Thanksgivings and Christmases past. This would be nothing—I thought.

I mixed together more bread flour, salt, and instant yeast, and removed the *poolish* from the fridge. It had gotten nice and stretchy. All was good. After letting the *poolish* warm up for an hour, I added it, together with a bit of water and extra-virgin olive oil, to the bread-flour mix to create a dense dough. I then took the dough out for some stretching and folding to form a rectangle.

Now, ciabatta, whose name means "carpet slipper" in Italian, is supposed to look like a slipper. I wasn't seeing the resemblance yet. (I confess, despite my years covering fashion, I wasn't entirely sure what an Italian carpet slipper really looked like.) But, ever positive, I took this rectangle to be a promising beginning. After letting it rest for a while, I stretched and folded it and let it rest again. Then I divided the dough into three portions, letting it rest for a bit longer on a handy kitchen towel that had to stand in for the canvas couche cloths that hard-core bread bakers use to create crusty breads.

Then, things started to go awry.

Between the chopping of rhubarb, the grating of limes, and the baking of shredded coconut for the desserts I'd promised, I'd skimmed over the last bit of the ciabatta recipe. I'd believed the hard parts of ciabatta making were over. I'd stretched, I'd folded, I'd stretched, folded, and then cut. The rest, really, should be a piece of cake. (Or bread, I suppose.) All I had to do was lay the loaves on a bed of cornmeal, stick them into the oven, and wait for the amazing smell of baked bread to wash over me.

It turned out, first, I had to transform my oven into a make-shift hearth, setting it to a whopping 500 degrees and creating a steam bath for my bread. There was also some business in the recipe about opening the oven door periodically to squirt water in to generate more steam.

I began to be afraid.

I'd come this far, however; I wasn't turning back. I still could hear the faint words "Brava! Brava!" in my head—that could happen only if I soldiered on.

The moment my loaves entered the oven, I sprang into action. A pan of hot water was set at the bottom of the oven, and steam began billowing forth. I couldn't see a thing. Precious seconds were ticking away. I panicked. Filling a turkey baster with hot water, I blindly stabbed at the oven's dark, misty air, shooting water all over my bread and cornmeal. The smell and awful, awful sound of cornmeal starting to sizzle filled the air. Smoke began filling my apartment, gradually getting denser. Mike was coughing and looking grumpy. At one point, a plastic tub of turmeric I had perched on the top of my stove backguard actually *popped* and began to melt. It was that hot. Mike grabbed the gooey mess of marigold plastic and waved it at me, sighing. This ciabatta making was getting dangerous, I knew. And yet I wasn't sure what to do—keep it baking as the recipe specified or just give up and take it out?

At thirty minutes, my bread looked well baked. But I'd thought the recipe said to let it go longer. I was torn and confused. I'd been instructed by my Singaporean aunties to live by *agak-agak* and have faith in my own eyeballing. But baking was a completely different thing—precision and following the rules were crucial.

And so I went on Twitter and sent out an SOS signal to my bread-baking friends. Somewhere in Ontario, a baker sent these sage words: "Don't go by clock, go by the loaf!" I ran to the smoking oven to grab my loaves and take them out.

The word *coal* immediately came to mind. The loaves were hard, completely blackened—and still emitting wispy tendrils of white smoke. Mike coughed a little more. Then he picked up the recipe and said, "Hey, did you lower the temperature to 450 degrees after the last thirty-second stretch?"

Lower? Seconds? *What* was he talking about?

First, I'd completely skimmed over the lowering part. Second, in my rhubarb-chopping fog, I'd registered one of the baking times as thirty minutes instead of thirty seconds.

There was a long silence. Well, unless you count the words *COLOSSAL FAILURE* that kept ringing through my head. I had to sit down. On the floor. Next to my blackened, smoky loaves.

After many more silent minutes, I decided to cut one loaf open. Actually, from the sound of my bread knife on the stony ciabatta, it was more like *madly chisel* it open.

On the inside, there wasn't any of the holey perfection that ciabatta usually has. But it wasn't horrible, all things considered. In fact, except for the crust, it was edible—well, if you like bad bread—which was amazing considering I'd baked it for more than four times longer than I should have. (I know, I do like making excuses for myself.)

"You take on too much," Mike said. And he was right. One dessert and ciabatta would have been fine. Beyond that, I was just being delusional.

When I thought of what my Tanglin ah-ma would have done, however, I stopped feeling sorry for myself. Here was a woman who had never complained about cooking or having a fear of cooking. From everything Auntie Khar Imm had told me, I gathered that if something didn't work out so well the first time around, she would have just gotten back on that horse and tried again. If you wanted to put food on the table for your family, you had to stop whining and worrying and get in the kitchen and do it.

I decided to set aside my self-pity—and back into the kitchen I went.

Love, too, can be a powerful motivator. In this case, that would be Mike's profound love for cinnamon buns, which happened to be the next bread on the Bread Baker's Apprentice challenge list.

In fact, since I'd joined the bread bakers' challenge, Mike had been waiting impatiently for cinnamon bun week. And by the time cinnamon buns came up, I had begun to see a greater purpose to baking them. I thought they might help assuage my lingering guilt over a not-so-little visit I'd made to Stella Mc-Cartney during a recent Paris trip. (Hey, 50 percent off is pretty good, even in euros.)

The buns began easily enough. First, I took some sugar, salt, and shortening, and mixed it all together, adding lemon extract and an egg. Once that had been beaten to a smooth consistency, I added bread flour, yeast, and milk, and mixed it all up. Then came the kneading—for about ten minutes. How to tell when it's done? The recipe specifies that's when the dough is "silky and supple, tacky but not sticky."

This created momentary anxiety. Tacky but not sticky? My powers of comprehension still went only so far when it came to bread. But that's the thing about baking along with two hundred people—someone out in the ether always has an answer. In this case, that would be Phyl, a fellow Bread Baker's Apprentice baker who writes the blog *Of Cabbages & King Cakes*. According-ing to the very informative Phyl, an amateur baker in Ohio, you press your hand into the dough and pull it away; if dough sticks to your hand but then detaches itself, so your hand is clean, the dough is tacky. If it sticks to your hand and won't come off, it's sticky.

I was doubtful of dough's ability to feel silky, but once I touched mine, I knew what the recipe was talking about. It reminded me of a particular washed-silk Lanvin dress I once fondled that instantly inspired a great hunger in me. *This feels like warm butter*, I remember thinking. *I want to eat it.* I might not have been able to eat the Lanvin number, but lucky for me, that could actually happen with this silken blob before me. First, though, it had to rest for more than an hour so it could rise.

Then came the tricky part—you're supposed to roll it out into a rectangle of a certain size. Having lost my tape measure, I grabbed the only ruler I possess—a naughty one I'd gotten from the Betsey Johnson Spring 2004 fashion show with the words GUYS ♥ B.J. emblazoned across it. I'm certain my Tanglin ah-ma would have approved. Once the dough was rolled out, I sprinkled a fairly thick layer of cinnamon sugar all over the top, then took the ends of one side and started rolling it inward to create a cinnamon log of sorts.

When I sat back and looked at it, a slight alarm washed over me—this log was looking mighty lewd. And I was pretty sure it wasn't just because I was using a rule with the giant letters B.J. to measure it. *Delicious* did not immediately come to mind. (*Uncircumcised*, maybe.) When I shared a picture of the log, wondering if it looked right, my online friends had plenty to say. Dave, a former editor from Baltimore, helpfully noted, "I guess if the recipe fell flat, you could use the adjective 'flaccid'—which is not often found in cooking tales."

These buns were getting made, regardless. I decided to soldier on. Next came the fun part: The log had to be sliced up to form little buns. (Mike noted that I seemed to enjoy this slicing of the lewd log bit a little more than was becoming.) But the end product looked promising. As the dough rested on a pan, they rose again, so the buns filled out and began pressing into one another. This was looking a lot more like a Cinnabon creation. I started to get hopeful.

Once they went into the oven, the scent of cinnamon and caramelized sugar began filling my apartment—which was a vast improvement over the smoke and burned-cornmeal aromas that my ciabatta had produced. After I drizzled some lemon fondant across the buns when they came out of the oven, we were good to go. And within minutes of them hitting the cooling rack, four had disappeared.

"Better than Cinnabon," Mike mumbled midbite.

Relief, instantly, came over me. I had tried, failed. Tried again—then succeeded. I had overcome my insecurities, and made my sweet-toothed husband happy. In the process, I'd gained some confidence while committing some wickedly good wifery.

Somewhere out there, I imagine my grandmother must have been proud.

CHAPTER NINE

Every August in Singapore, we would wait for the white moth.

Some years, it would take a few days to show up; sometimes it would be right on time. But always, at some point, it would flutter into our house, park itself on a chair, watching us as we had dinner, keeping an eye on me as I did my homework, so it seemed. Always, my mother would say, "That's your grandmother." Or "your grandfather," followed by "You'd better behave." The thought would always petrify me. Was I practicing the piano hard enough? Were these moths watching when I was in bed reading way past my bedtime? I never could tell.

The gates of Hell open in August, you see, and your loved ones are supposed to return to you in the forms of white moths. As a child, I'd never thought of anything so terrifying as my dead grandfather whom I'd never met giving me the fish eye while I plotted a new way to make my sister's life hell.

Of all the holidays I've celebrated, the Festival of the Hungry Ghosts remained the trickiest. The Chinese in Singapore believe that August—the seventh month in the Chinese calendar—is when ghosts are released from Hell and allowed to roam the earth. (Who knew the Other World was so generous with vacation time?) Think of it as Halloween—on steroids—celebrated over an entire month. And completely unironically. This is a month when many Singaporeans avoid swimming in pools—where ghosts can pull you down and drown you—or walking in dark spots—where ghosts can attack and kill you. This isn't just teenage horror-movie speak; people in Singapore talk of ghosts as they would their parents, friends, colleagues, the celebrities they see on TV. That ghosts exist is not something anyone debates; the only question is, who has the better story to tell? In the French convent primary school I attended, even the teachers knew the stories of the girl, many years ago, who fainted and came down with a fever after seeing the ghost of a nun perched on the wall of the school garden, cackling away.

In my own family, ghosts are taken seriously. When I was a baby, my dad was posted to Taiwan and moved us into a posh apartment in a high-rise building in Taipei. The first time Mum walked into the apartment, she immediately declared that she could not live there. "It's dirty," she said. "There's a ghost here. A very unhappy one." Dad pooh-poohed the notion. A few days later, he returned from work, calling out to Mum the moment he took his shoes off. No answer. He walked through the living room and spotted her standing on the balcony. "Tin? Are you okay?" he asked, unease setting in as he walked toward her. Mum was standing on the balcony in a daze, holding me over the railing. If her fingers had relaxed just a little, a death drop would have been certain. Dad grabbed me and shook Mum, whose eyes were rolled back in her head, so the story—which they now often tell with great laughter—goes. The next day, they moved out.

Perhaps because of this, my mother now sees ghosts every-where. And I mean everywhere. "I saw a ghost right by that tree," she once tossed out while pulling into a parking spot near our old apartment. "She had long hair and was just standing there. I asked her what she wanted, but she didn't say anything. Sad . . ." Daphne and I weren't quite sure what to do with the information. But before we could fully process it, Mum was bundling up our school things from the backseat and chastising us for moving slowly. And the moment passed.

Fortunately, there's a very simple way to appease Singapor-ean ghosts. Unlike their Western counterparts, Singaporean ghosts aren't obsessed with eating humans or general carnage. (Unless their corpses have been turned into zombies by jumping cats, that is.) It's food that they crave. They're hungry the mo-ment they leave Hell, and it's only if they remain hungry that they'll turn on people. So as a very practical matter, you'll see massive feasts of fruit and home-cooked dishes set out along streets at this time. Even families who don't have much food to put on their own tables will shell out for tea and overflowing platters of food in order to get these hungry spirits off their backs.

Getting between a ghost and its food has its consequences— as any kid who's been warned will tell you. My aunties still regularly tell the story about my kuku (uncle), who was walk-ing home from school one day and kicked over a roadside of-fering of food and incense. "That night, he had a very high fever, and he kept saying that he was this man, a man we did not know," my mum will say, as my aunties quietly nod, re-membering. "And he kept saying, 'My mouth is full of dirt, my mouth is full of dirt!' This ghost had been buried, you see . . ."

The fever subsided only when my ah-ma called in a monk to pray over Kuku.

I hadn't thought about this festival in years. August certainly is far enough from Halloween that no one is thinking of spirits in America. Landing in Singapore in August, however, I had one hungry grandmother to be thinking about.

"You can come to the temple on Saturday" said the text from my cousin Jessie. My grandmother would definitely be hungry that first weekend of the Festival of the Hungry Ghosts. And if her family wouldn't feed her, who would?

I wasn't sure what to bring for my Tanglin ah-ma. Auntie Khar Imm and Auntie Leng Eng would probably come laden with sweets, tea, noodles, and spring rolls for her. My parents had not gone with the family to visit my grandmother during the Hungry Ghosts month for years, preferring simply to give Auntie Khar Imm money for offerings. This was a big moment. I would be representing my own family at this feast for my grandmother. What could I possibly bring that would be a worthy addition? The answer became obvious after very little thought.

And so that Saturday morning, at the temple in Singapore's Hougang neighborhood where my grandparents' ashes are kept, I arrived teetering under the weight of a massive pineapple, the largest I'd been able to find. Auntie Khar Imm looked amused.

The temple was packed the moment my family arrived. Amid the hum of activity, dozens of people bustled about, setting out food and drink for their dead loved ones with great care. Swirling, slender plumes of smoke from incense filled the air, seeping into our hair. All along the walls were little rectangles of yellow paper, each crammed with Chinese characters—names of those whose ashes were housed in the temple—and serial numbers that were almost like apartment numbers indicating where those ashes could be found. Addresses for urns within a columbarium—it was almost too precious.

We found the spot bearing the serial number of my Tanglin ah-ma's urn and started putting out the feast. We'd brought noodles, spring rolls, a vegetarian tofu stir-fry. There were little sweet cakes, capped with tea served in three thimble-size, delicate cups. And, of course, there was my giant pineapple, which suddenly seemed more than a little out of place. I looked around at the spreads of cookies, cakes, and noodles that everyone else was setting out; no other pineapples were evident. I wondered if I was being gauche. But then I thought, *Screw it. The queen of pineapple tarts really deserves to be having a pineapple.*

When we were done, we took turns lighting joss sticks as an offering to my grandmother. And the waiting began. The dead had to eat, after all—we couldn't rush them. A procession of chanting monks passed through the grounds. I wasn't sure what they were chanting—Teochew not being my forte—so I found myself pressed into a corner, trying to avoid the general hubbub, along with Auntie Leng Eng.

"So your auntie Khar Imm is teaching you how to cook?" asked Auntie Leng Eng, generally a woman of few words. I hadn't seen her since my quest began, and I'd been a little nervous about it. As the vice principal of one of the top girls' schools in Singapore for many years, Auntie Leng Eng prized education and professional success. Her school, Singapore Chinese Girls' School, had churned out many female leaders in the country, after all. Auntie Leng Eng herself did not cook, having spent her time on her career instead of in the kitchen. I knew she had been proud of my success in journalism, and I wasn't sure what she would think of my cashing that all in to learn how to cook.

"Well, yah," I said. "I've always wanted to learn how to make Tanglin Ah-Ma's dishes. I always regretted that I never did." She nodded, silent for a moment. I told her about the dishes that I'd learned and wanted to learn—pineapple tarts, salted vegetable duck soup, braised duck—noting that I'd brought the pineapple because I thought Tanglin Ah-Ma would have liked it. "Anything very sweet or very salty, she just loved," she simply said. "Your ah-ma had a *very* sweet tooth," she added, smiling at the thought. I was relieved to think of my grandmother enjoying my pineapple, even though it was unlike any other offering. As we spoke, it was a little disconcerting to imagine us standing there casually talking about soup and cookies when spirits were supposedly all around us, gathered at tables, stuffing their faces.

Soon enough, it was time to pack up and head home. Auntie Leng Eng gave me a big hug. "Stop by and visit sometime," she said. "If you have time."

A FEW DAYS LATER, I GOT MORE MARCHING ORDERS. AN e-mail from Jessie arrived: "U can come by 29 Aug Sat early we are making the pink rice cake and braised duck." The e-mail warmed my heart. Niceties in our communication had been dispelled—I was truly beginning to be treated like family.

Soon enough, I was back in Auntie Khar Imm's kitchen.

This time, another aunt was there as well, Auntie Sophia, the wife of my father's adopted brother. I'd met Auntie Sophia only a few times before—at Chinese New Year, during cursory visits her family made to my house, and at my Singapore wedding, which had been a blur of food, way too many toasts, and 250 guests, most of them friends and associates of my parents whom I absolutely didn't know.

"Hello, Auntie!" I said brightly when Auntie Sophia arrived.

"Not Auntie lah!" Auntie Khar Imm said. "You must call her Ah-Sim." Even as a child, I'd been mystified by the very specific Chinese names assigned to relatives. Auntie and Uncle were too simple to be acceptable; each person had a specific title based on gender and birth order. My mother's younger brother, for example, is Kuku to me, a name that indicates very specifically that he's my mother's younger brother. Beyond that, I had no idea how to address everyone—and Auntie Khar Imm was determined to school me on that.

"Ah-Sim," I echoed. And Auntie Sophia smiled.

We got to work right away. On the menu that day was *beng gway*, which means "rice cake" in Teochew. The bright pink cakes are basically squishy glutinous rice flour shell in the shape of teardrops filled with glutinous rice that has been stir-fried with shallots, pork belly, mushrooms, and dried prawns. (Sometimes peanuts are mixed in for added crunch.) These are usually eaten for breakfast or a daytime snack—with generous dollops of fiery red chili sauce. And they're often presented as offerings to the gods or to loved ones on the other side—the festive pink color making them lucky food.

I hadn't had *beng gway* since I was a child, largely because they're fairly hard to find in the United States, even in New York City. And since I'd never been a big glutinous rice fan, these cakes had never been a favorite of mine anyhow. But with the Hungry Ghosts Festival still on, make them we must. Auntie Khar Imm was the teacher in this instance, Auntie Sophia having a busy job with the government's housing agency that generally prevents her from spending much time in the kitchen. She'd heard that Auntie Khar Imm was giving me cooking lessons and asked to tag along, however. So there we were. Auntie Sophia and I rolled up our sleeves and tried hard to follow along as Auntie Khar Imm demonstrated.

Auntie Khar Imm had chopped up the shallots, the pork belly, mushrooms, and dried prawns, and had boiled the peanuts in water for three hours to soften them a little. Standing beside her, we watched as she fired up the wok, pouring in gobs of cooking oil and then frying the shallots until golden brown. Removing the shallots, she preserved the oil, adding the mushrooms, shrimp, pork, then peanuts and frying it all up with a little salt, white pepper, and a dash of monosodium glutamate. Once that was all mixed up, she added the glutinous rice she'd soaked for hours and then drained and steamed, stirring it all together. When that was done, she set the mixture aside to cool as she prepared the dough, mixing several cups of rice flour and tapioca flour with nine rice bowls of hot water and generous dashes of bright pink powdered coloring to form a paste. Once that cooled, she placed the dough in a stand mixer for several minutes of kneading.

When the dough was done, our assembly line began. Auntie

Khar Imm showed us how to make the cakes using the one neon pink plastic teardrop mold she had. First, she took a small ball of dough, rolled it out into a flat square, and covered it with glutinous rice filling, then folded over the extra dough to cover the top, and sealed it, forming a small pink purse. Then the person in charge of the mold took this ball and pressed it into the mold, smoothing it out at the top before giving the mold one solid *whap* on the side to dislodge the cake. And there you had it, a perfect pink teardrop filled with rice and pork. Auntie Sophia and I got to work mimicking Auntie Khar Imm. Because I had already learned to make *bak-zhang*, *beng gway* was easy for me. Auntie Sophia was struggling a little. "You want to learn," Auntie Khar Imm said at one point, "you must come more often, like Lu-Lien." I felt my cheeks flush with pride as I tried to quicken my hands to make her even more proud.

When the pink dough ran out, Auntie Khar Imm made more dough, this time choosing not to add pink coloring and instead showing me how to dot the plain *beng gway* with liquid red food coloring so the cakes wouldn't be just white, the color of death. "Luckier for praying," she said. And when the rice filling ran out, she thought for a moment before rummaging through her fridge and chopping up some cabbage, lightly salting it, and adding a few dashes of minced dried shrimp for more flavor. "You can use the dough to make dumplings," she said, pressing a small amount into a circle, filling it with cabbage and shrimp, and then folding over the dough and crimping it deftly and beautifully to form a perfect half-moon.

Try as I might, however, I couldn't get the crimping down. Auntie Khar Imm's creases were tiny and perfect, far prettier than those of any dumplings I'd seen at the best dim sum restaurants. And she did them in a flash. I had to ask her to slow down several times so I could actually see what she was doing. Mine, on the other hand, were clumsy and fat, and I probably made one dumpling for every four she was turning out. I was that slow.

I was beginning to feel that perhaps I hadn't been deserving of Auntie Khar Imm's recent praise. "Aiyah," she clucked after watching my brow furrow ever more with frustration. "I've been doing this for so many years already. You just started." And so I kept going. I didn't get discernibly better, but I did get a little faster. I was starting to feel better.

As the day came to an end, we packed up the rice cakes and the dumplings for steaming. Auntie Khar Imm picked up one of my later dumplings, inspecting it. "This one's not bad leh," she said, smiling. "Just practice."

I began to feel like I was getting somewhere.

WHEN I THINK OF THE FAMILY FEASTS OF MY SINGAPORE girlhood, there's always a duck in the picture.

To say that my people—the Teochews—adore duck would be to make a major understatement. In Shantou (also known as Swatow, which is its Teochew name), the area in Southern China where my great-grandfather lived as a boy, duck and goose are inescapable at many dinner tables.

So it's more than slightly sacrilegious to say that duck simply isn't one of my favorites. I do make an exception for some versions, however, and Teochew-style braised duck is one of them.

While I'm really good at eating it, making it is another mat-ter altogether. But this was something Auntie Alice was intent on fixing right away. "Cheryl ah, do you want to learn how to make *lor ar* [braised duck]?" she called one day to ask. My mother's side of the family is Hockchew, not Teochew, but Auntie Alice's husband, Uncle Yong Hai, was one of my *kaki-nang* (own people). "Your uncle Yong Hai's sis taught me how to make it. I can teach you if you want," Auntie Alice said.

If I want? "How soon?" was the more appropriate question.

A few days later, Auntie Alice arrived at my Singapore home armed with two ducks and a bag of ingredients, and the tutorial began. First, we peeled and sliced galangal, peeled and bashed several garlic cloves, and measured out some sugar and dark soy sauce. (This sauce is thicker, much sweeter, and has a more intense flavor than regular soy sauce.) Then we cleaned the duck, which entailed chopping off its behind and head, carefully washing it inside and out, and snipping off as much loose skin as we could get to. (Duck skin is incredibly fatty and will make the sauce very greasy.)

For a moment of full disclosure, when I say *we*, in some in-stances this would actually mean my mother's maid, Erlinda. Auntie Alice was whizzing through the steps so fast that she was directing Erlinda to chop off the duck's skin, behind, and head, knowing that she would be much quicker at it than I would likely be. Auntie Alice had arrived with her one-year-old granddaughter, Bernice, in tow, after all. She had little time to spare.

Next, "we" mixed together some five-spice powder and salt and rubbed it all over the outside and inside of the duck. Then we stuck the duck in the fridge to let it marinate for at least two hours.

Once the duck was marinated and ready to go, we heated up the wok over low heat and added some sugar, stirring until it melted. Then we tossed in the sliced galangal and bashed garlic and stir-fried it until the mixture turned brown. Next, in went the dark soy sauce. Then we lightly rinsed off the duck and slid it into the wok. Using a metal spatula, Auntie Alice carefully coated the duck with sauce, turned it over, and poured enough water into the wok so that the liquid covered half the duck. Once the liquid came to a boil, we covered the wok.

Every fifteen minutes, we uncovered the wok and turned the duck over before covering it up again. As we waited for the duck to cook, Auntie Alice and I watched over Bernice, who had an endless curiosity about her surroundings, picking at invisible objects on the carpet, slipping her tiny feet into the massive wooden clogs my parents had bought in Holland decades ago.

Inevitably, of course, the question came. "You don't want one yourself, meh?" Auntie Alice asked. Immediately, I launched into the same litany of excuses—I was too busy, Mike was too busy, I didn't have family near me in New York, I was traveling too much. She didn't want to press the issue, so instead she just let me watch Bernice play. It wasn't as tiring as watching Giselle jump and sing ceaselessly, but I felt a tremendous responsibility nonetheless. If we looked away for just one second, who knew what Bernice would pick up off the floor and put into her mouth? I still wasn't convinced I was up for this. No, I decided, at the moment, the freedom to go out to dinner—or Rome—on a whim and be able to stay up all night playing Scrabble was far more important. I understood my family's concerns that, being so far away, I'd have no one to look after me when I was older, especially if Mike passed on first. Yet having a child remained far too abstract an idea for me still.

After fifty minutes to an hour, Auntie Alice pulled out a chopstick, showing me how to poke it into the fattest part of the duck to see how easily it would go through. The meat had been simmering so long that the chopstick pierced it with great ease; the duck was finally done. We let it rest for ten more minutes, and it was ready to serve. As Auntie Alice hoisted the duck out of the wok, it struck me: The whole procedure was so easy I started to feel cheated that I'd gone all these years without making Teochew braised duck.

But I needn't have fretted, because just a few days later, when I was in my auntie Khar Imm's kitchen, she hauled out two ducks and announced that *she'd* be teaching me how to make *lor ar*. Her method, which she'd learned from my Tanglin ah-ma, was a little different. Instead of using five-spice powder, Auntie Khar Imm used actual spices—whole star anise and cinnamon sticks, to be precise. And she used those only in the braising part, choosing to rub the duck inside and out with salt instead and letting it marinate—at room temperature—for a few hours.

Once the duck was sufficiently marinated, she carefully washed it inside and out—twice—to get rid of excess salt. Then she rubbed the inside of the duck with salt, stuffed it with four thick slices of blue ginger, and slid it into the wok, already bearing a simmering liquid of dark soy sauce, several rice bowls of water, star anise, cinnamon, and more blue ginger. While the duck simmered, Auntie Khar Imm prepared several hard-boiled eggs. "You can also put tofu into the gravy," she said. As the simmering neared an end, Auntie Khar Imm pulled out a chopstick. She'd shown me her method of gauging the doneness of meat so many times that no explanations were necessary.

Hearing Auntie Khar Imm mention the eggs and the tofu immediately brought me back to the special meals of my childhood. Back then, I'd avoided eating the duck, but I'd loved drenching bowls plump with rice with the rich, dark gravy and devouring the rice with a hard-boiled egg and tofu that had been steeped so long in the sauce that it had turned the color of milk chocolate. My mother had never known how to make it—so it was a dish that I looked forward to whenever we visited my Tanglin ah-ma's home.

And here I was, decades later, with not one but two braised duck recipes. Both were equally delicious; both were made and handed down to me with equal love and care.

Someday, perhaps, I might have someone to hand these recipes down to. The thought suddenly didn't seem so terribly unappealing after all.

CHAPTER TEN

It was around this time I discovered my maternal grandmother is a liar. Well, it's not that she *lies*, per se. It's just that she has developed a selective memory.

Auntie Alice and I had decided to get to the bottom of our collective family history. One afternoon, we took a break from cooking and met in my grandmother's bedroom, sitting on the floor at her feet as we plied her with questions.

That she'd lived a hard life was indisputable. All my life, though, I'd wondered why she'd made the decisions she had. Why marry my grandfather? Why bring his first wife and family over from China?

This much we had known: My grandmother had come of age during World War II. Just as she was blossoming into a young woman, the Japanese occupied Singapore, renaming it Syonanto and beginning a reign of terror that poisoned daily life. "I was afraid to go out," Ah-Ma says in Hokkien. "We were always afraid that Japanese soldiers would rape us."

It was around this time that a handsome man began calling. He worked in a coffee shop across the street and had befriended

Ah-Ma's brother. Soon he began coming by after work to play cards. Almost as soon, he began expressing interest in my grandmother's hand in marriage. Fearing for her safety as a young, single woman during the occupation, my grandmother consented. "I was so afraid—just anyhow get married is safer lor," she says, sighing. "Aiyah, I was so silly, everything also didn't know."

Fast-forward to the picture of my grandmother on her wedding day, dressed in white, wide-eyed and tentative, with the faintest of smiles; a tall, dark, older man, fourteen years her senior, the protector she had sought, towering next to her. Then fast-forward yet again to the moment of discovery—that the man she'd married had another wife, another family back in China. Instead of anger, instead of frustration, Ah-Ma felt only pity. "People in China," she says, "they were suffering at the time." Besides, her own father in Xiamen had had four wives, she says. She understood how love, or something like it, could be sometimes. And so she cleared out a room in their home for this other wife, sewed together new pillowcases for her, implored her husband to bring over his first wife. "I thought we could all live together," she says. "I was so, so stupid."

From the beginning, things were difficult. "I cooked for her to eat," Ah-Ma says. The first wife, of course, only complained ceaselessly. Ah-Ma became an outsider in her own newlywed home. Finally, Ah-Ma moved out, and the first wife proceeded to lord over the home that once was hers. "Your marriage was so messy!" Auntie Alice suddenly exclaims. Her face is wrinkled in disgust at the hardships her mother had to endure. "If it were me, I wouldn't have stood for it, you know," she whispers to me, putting her hand to her face to shield her mouth.

But times, of course, were different. In 1940s Singapore, a young married woman with children had few options—especially if she was the second wife, even if she hadn't known it at the start.

My grandfather started sporadically coming by to drop off provisions and cash for Ah-Ma and their growing family. Auntie Alice was born, then my mother. Then Auntie Jane and my kuku. It was difficult to determine when Gong-Gong would come. This is when the selective memory starts to kick in. *"Wah mana eh gi!"* Ah-Ma says of this time, saying she doesn't remember much of what her new life as the exiled second wife was like. "My memory is that Papa rarely came back—right?" Auntie Alice asks softly. "He worked seven days a week. He didn't have Saturday and Sunday off." (Leaning over, Auntie Alice whispers to me, "I think she remembers—she doesn't want to say.")

"Aiyah," Ah-Ma finally says. "If he wants to come, he comes. If he doesn't want to come, he doesn't come. I was very stupid before," she adds quietly, sighing again. "But did I have a choice?"

Years went by, and Ah-Ma's little family grew up. Auntie Alice suddenly remembers the one family outing her father took them on. "He came on a bicycle to fetch us. We went to have dim sum," she says. "That's the only outing I remember, you know. As a father figure, I don't think there was much communication. But it was really a nice feeling, a once-in-a-lifetime outing with your parents." Shuat Giau, the first wife, too, stopped by to see Ah-Ma. "I was in Primary Six, and she came to the house. I remember I opened the door and I didn't even know what she was saying. But next thing I knew, I got slapped," Auntie Alice says.

And then one day, my grandfather fell in the bathroom and hit his head. A few days later, he was dead. "People came to notify us, but Shuat Giau didn't want us to attend the funeral," Auntie Alice, then a teenager, says as her own memories return.

Privately, the second family mourned. And then Ah-Ma went to work; the neighbors' laundry became her business. Auntie Alice began taking care of the household, cooking for her younger siblings, watching them after school. Instantly, this teenager became a young mother. "And then you started having gambling in the house, right, Ma?" Auntie Alice says. The selective memory kicks in again. "No lah, I don't remember that," Ah-Ma says. "Don't write that down," she adds, pushing my pen away. (Once again, Auntie Alice leans over and quietly says, "There *was* a gambling den in our house—but only for a few years.")

The hardships this man had brought on Ah-Ma didn't diminish her desire to see if he was okay, however. She missed him; she was curious. Shortly after Gong-Gong died, she went to a psychic with a reputation for being able to call up the souls of dead loved ones so the living could see how they were doing. The message was one that Ah-Ma would remember for decades. "Gong-Gong said, 'Right now you are suffering, but your life ahead will only become better and better. I know you had a hard life, but don't worry, you will have good days ahead. And this woman who made your life difficult, within three years, I will take her with me to the Other World.'"

Ah-Ma wasn't sure what to make of it. But within three years of my grandfather's death, his first wife died. And as for her own life, my grandfather had been right—it only got better and better. Her children all grew up and became successful professionals, making them all the more able to grant her the comfortable life she'd craved and had always, always deserved.

Ah-Ma was tired, the trip through a thicket of unwanted memories having exhausted this spry eighty-six-year-old.

"People need to have ups and downs," Auntie Alice finally says, as we hug our good-byes. "It's only if you have downs that you'll get to have the ups."

AT THIS POINT, I WAS BEGINNING TO FEEL A CHANGE whenever I stepped back into my New York kitchen.

I'd approached meals, cookies, and certainly, breads with some degree of confidence before, but it was always laced with the unshakable fear that something was not going to work out. Or explode. Or perhaps even both. Each time I returned from Singapore, however, I was feeling this fear dissipate. The attitude from the first egg cracked, the very first stirrings, was gradually becoming one devoid of doubt. Things were likely to work out, I started believing—and even if they didn't, well, so what? I could always try again. My looser approach was freeing, and amid the lack of fretting, I discovered that I was truly starting to enjoy cooking.

I was still making my way through the Bread Baker's Apprentice challenge. On the docket this time, however, was a bread that was anything but titillating. The last time I'd baked a bread, what emerged from the oven was a loaf of casatiello, a gorgeous hunk of Italian bread studded with salami and oozing with hot cheese. I'd started priding myself on being able to tackle focaccia, beautifully braided challah, breads that I'd never even contemplated making, much less producing versions people marveled at and couldn't keep themselves from clawing.

So you might understand why I wasn't exactly looking forward to the next challenge loaf: light wheat bread. After the sexy Italian, wheat bread seemed like the yawner of a boy next door. (You know, the ugly one.)

But after having spent several weeks in Singapore without an oven at my disposal, I was itching to bake something. Anything. And as it turned out, this plain boy next door had his surprises.

This bread began as several others do. First, I mixed together the dry ingredients, which in this case were bread flour, whole wheat flour, powdered milk, and yeast. Now, in this recipe by Peter Reinhart, the wheat flour accounts for only 33 percent of the total flour, so it's not as hard-core as whole-grain loafs. If you're more of a white-bread kind of person, this loaf's for you. Next, I added in some shortening, honey, and room-temperature water. And after mixing and kneading, it was time to let the ball of dough ferment at room temperature for ninety minutes. (This bread turned out to be a real riser—it more than doubled in size during that time.)

Next, it was time to press that dough ball out into a rectangle and then roll up the rectangle into a loaf and let it sit for another ninety minutes or however long it took until the dough "crest[ed] above the lip of the pan." I set the timer and, of course, proceeded to forget to check on whatever cresting activity might be happening. So when the timer went off, this was what had happened: My dough had grown so much it was on the verge of *sprouting hands and lifting itself out of my loaf pan.* Into the oven it went, and less than an hour later, this gorgeous, caramel-hued loaf came out.

Now, when it had been baking, I wasn't quite sure what to expect of this bread.

Unlike the casatiello or the impressive-looking double-decker braided cranberry-walnut celebration bread that I'd made in previous weeks, this loaf did not fill my apartment with any discernible smell during baking. There was no provolone fog or clouds of cranberry mixed with lemon. When I sliced it open, however, there it was—the simple, sweet smell of freshly baked bread.

Toasted and slathered with blueberry jam, this bread was just divine. And it was even better buttered with Dijon mustard and a little mayonnaise, and topped with cheddar and thickly sliced bone-in ham from the fancyish store down the street. And for the next few days, Mike and I would be reminded over and over, as we pulled it out to savor with breakfast or lunch, that sometimes it's important to nail the basic as well as the fancy—a lesson whose importance extends far beyond any kitchen, really.

As bread goes, this light wheat bread may not have been my first choice. Oh, how I'd sneered at it! But in the end, it turned out to be basic, yes, but also versatile and surprisingly satisfying— the sort of bread that really grows on you.

You know, just like that boy next door often does.

CHAPTER ELEVEN

When I was a child in Singapore, my mind would inevitably turn to butterflies, dragons, phoenixes, and horses as each September approached.

With the Mid-Autumn Festival coming, the neighborhood provision shops, already crammed with an array of colorfully packaged candy and snacks, would start taking on a crimson tinge from the dozens of red lanterns shopkeepers would hang from the eaves. The blazing tropical sun would pierce through these lanterns, made of red cellophane fashioned into festive dragons or butterflies, bathing everything in a fiery warmth that was both titillating and comforting.

What we looked forward to each year was getting to pick out a lantern to take for a spin on the night of the festival, which occurs on the fifteenth day of the eighth lunar calendar month. It celebrates the autumnal equinox, the time when the moon is at its fullest and roundest—the reason the day is also known as the Moon Festival.

After carefully perching a toothpick of a birthday candle in the middle of my lantern, I'd race through dinner and wait impatiently for it to get dark so my sister and I could head down to the playground to join the impromptu lantern parade, a giggling procession of bobbing red lights in a river of black. I never had a dragon—those always seemed more for boys than girls. But a horse, a butterfly, a puppy. Those seemed perfectly acceptable. As I got older, however, lanterns became passé, too uncool for teenagers, to be sure. I stopped making trips to the playground—going there being a little unseemly if you were not, say, between the ages of six and ten or in possession of a child within that age range.

However, there was still one thing to enjoy about the Moon Festival, and that was mooncakes, round cakes of lotus-seed or red bean paste wrapped in either a soft, biscuitlike crust or a pliant pandan-scented wrapper made with mochi rice flour.

Now, there are a few old stories that explain the reason for eating these little cakes. My favorite is the one of Ming revolutionaries planning to overthrow the Mongolian rulers of China during the Yuan dynasty and spreading word via letters baked into mooncakes. (Julia Child, with her intrepid intelligence service background, would've been so proud!)

During my Singaporean girlhood, I'd known the stories, I'd eaten the cakes. As for making them? That seemed so laughably difficult it never once crossed my mind. I was perfectly content buying them from Chinatown every year—that is, until I found out that my aunties knew how to make them.

It turns out, they're incredibly easy—you just need the right teachers. In my case, that was Auntie Khar Imm's sisters, who make a massive production of mooncakes every year. With the list of family members and friends requesting mooncakes getting longer by the year, Auntie Khar Imm and her sisters have a serious production line going.

As usual, when I arrived at Auntie Khar Imm's mother's house, the activity was already well under way. You know you're walking into a hard-core kitchen when the first things you see are stacks upon stacks of boxes filled with gorgeous, homemade mooncakes. Now, the last time I'd seen these aunties had been just before the Chinese New Year, when I'd tried my best to keep up as I watched them make my Tanglin ah-ma's pineapple tarts. It wasn't until I saw their mooncakes, however, that I truly realized: These women are fearless in the kitchen.

When I walked into the kitchen that day, a sour and deeply spicy aroma hit me. Having prepped myself for making sweet mooncakes, I was completely unprepared for this scent. It turned out there was *mee siam* simmering on the stove. The sour, chili-based Malay noodle soup with shrimp and tofu is not by any means a regular dish for a Chinese family to be making. First of all, it's not Chinese. And second of all, it's incredibly labor-intensive—most people just buy it. I was perplexed about where this was coming from. "Orh, this is your ah-ma's *mee siam*," Auntie Khar Imm casually explained. "She took in this elderly Indonesian cook who was in poor health and had nowhere to go later in life. This cook taught her all her recipes." I was surprised, but realized I shouldn't have been. Of course my Tanglin ah-ma had been selfless enough to take in another mouth to feed even when she might not have had enough for her own family. And in return, she'd gotten a prized *mee siam* recipe that my family apparently now just whips together as simply as, say, tossing an egg in a frying pan for breakfast. Years later, here I was, standing in my auntie's mother's kitchen, taking in these incredible smells, making a major mental note to ask Auntie Khar Imm—no, *beg* her—to teach me.

But first, I had some mooncakes to learn. For my daylong apprenticeship, I was attached to Auntie Khar Moi, Auntie Khar Imm's younger sister, who is a true pro and a stickler for detail. (Luckily for me, she also possessed the infinite amount of patience required to endure the many ugly mooncakes I made before I started to get the hang of it.)

First, you take a bunch of lotus-seed paste. (In Singapore and other Asian countries, this can be pretty widely found in the weeks leading up to the Mid-Autumn Festival.) Then, you mix in a bunch of melon seeds for added crunch. (This is optional.) Next, I watched as Auntie Khar Moi formed them into little balls, each weighing just under an ounce. You can make these cakes with several kinds of fillings—in Singapore, green tea paste has become popular in recent years—so Auntie Khar Moi took some of the fir-hued paste out to show me what it looked like. Once the filling is done, you set it aside and move on to the dough.

I watched as Auntie Khar Moi mixed together confectioners' sugar; a few kinds of flour, including Japanese mochi flour; shortening; and pandan water. Now, many cooks use pandan essence added to water for the "pandan water" bit, but that just will not do for my aunts. Instead, Auntie Khar Moi showed me how to boil several knots of fresh pandan leaves in water. "Boil it until you can smell it," she said, as I began to ask her how long it needed to be on the stove. Soon enough, the liquid started to smell deliciously grassy and vanilla-like. I realized I hadn't even noted the time. (I also realized that I was starting to be perfectly fine with not trying to write down exact timings for Every Single Bit of the process.)

Once the dough was all mixed together, Auntie Khar Moi showed me how it needed to feel. "Stiff but also soft," she said, nudging me to touch it. I thought back to the breads I'd been making, and immediately I understood. It was similar to tacky but not sticky—as Phyl, my bread-baking friend in Ohio, had explained. I marveled at how that consistency was as desirable in Chinese baking as in Western bread baking. When the dough was tacky but not sticky, in went a few dots of green food coloring. "Just a little bit," Auntie Khar Moi cautioned. "You don't want it too green." From eyeballing, it appeared that you wanted it to be more sea foam than Incredible Hulk.

Then Auntie Khar Moi rolled out a little circle of dough and placed a lotus-seed paste ball in the center, turned it over, and stretched the skin to cover the ball, sealing it at the bottom. Next, she grabbed a crucial piece of equipment—a mooncake mold. These fluorescent pink plastic molds make cakes of two sizes; my family prefers the smaller ones, which you can devour in about three bites. Deftly, Auntie Khar Moi placed the dough ball she'd made into the mold with the sealed side up and smoothed the dough with the palm of her hand, making sure the cake filled all of the mold. After rapping the mold on the counter a few times to loosen the dough . . . voilà! A perfect little mooncake.

Now, some people like salted ducks' egg yolks in their mooncakes, because the salty taste cuts the sweetness of the lotus-seed paste. For those, Auntie Khar Moi made a slightly lighter ball of paste, hollowed it out, and filled it with yolk. (Regular mooncakes—which are about the size of a hockey puck— typically feature one or two yolks. For the small ones, it's best to use just a quarter of a yolk each. After filling the ball with yolk and rolling it back up, you want to weigh the ball again. It should weigh just under an ounce, including the yolk.) It was simple enough. Before long, I was rolling bits of dough with crumbly yolks and whapping out little green mooncakes along with Auntie Khar Moi.

I was definitely feeling proud of myself. Unlike making pineapple tarts, this process had been straightforward—rolling, wrapping . . . It was so easy I felt silly for having been nervous about helping out. This being my super-chef family, however, we didn't stop there.

My aunties had prepared a large bowl of sweetened mashed yam that morning. And when that was pulled out, I started to get nervous again. What lay ahead? I had absolutely no idea.

It turned out that, while regular mooncakes were fine and good, there was another kind of mooncake that was more "traditional" for our family. "This is the mooncake that Teochews eat," Auntie Khar Moi said. I suddenly felt like a very bad Teochew, given that I had absolutely no idea what she was talking about. Patiently, she explained that they were yam-filled balls wrapped in a deep-fried, flaky, crumbly crust. I'd seen those in stores and had always avoided them, starchy yam never really being my favorite thing. Intently, I watched as Auntie Khar Moi took bits of white dough from two different piles, laying them side by side, and rolled them out together into a flat, round circle. Then she took a ball of yam, placed it in the center of the circle, and wrapped it up, sealing it at the top. The wrapped spheres were then placed on a tray bound for the deep fryer that had been set up in a corner.

It all looked terribly easy. Eagerly, I jumped in, trying to copy Auntie Khar Moi's actions as I meshed the two doughs together, wrapping the yam. After a while, the activity became mindless, and we began idly chitchatting. Somehow, the conversation turned to learning and schools and the difficulty of the Singapore school system, the intense pressure that can be placed on children.

As a six-year-old, I remember being so overbooked I sometimes felt too busy to think. My after-school hours were spent endlessly shuttling from watercolor classes to ballet to Chinese brush painting lessons and swimming. Once I entered first grade, there were the tuition teachers my parents hired to give me additional lessons in Mandarin, math, and science so I could ace all my classes.

Auntie Khar Moi recounted how my cousin Royston had had a fierce tuition teacher who reduced him to tears with her sharp words, diminishing any desire to learn. "We're better off being oxen!" she said, anger spiking her voice. Better to work the fields than be bullied into studying hard for an intellectual life, that is. I marveled at the pride I could hear in her words, wishing that my parents had had the same understanding when I'd come home in tears after yet another piano lesson in which my teacher had whacked me on the knuckles with a ruler because I was such an ungifted—and lazy—student. Instead, I'd plodded along, trying to keep up, until many years later my parents finally accepted the fact that I probably wasn't a prodigy and allowed me to stop. My piano remains in my parents' living room to this day, gathering dust—an enduring symbol of my childhood shortcomings. Talent is immaterial in my family; it's the trying that matters. Considering that I often sat down to practice only after my father or mother had spent some time chasing me around the dining table with a cane in hand, I would say it was widely thought that I simply did not try hard enough when it came to the piano.

Mired in my memories of not trying hard enough, I was soon to be reminded of those feelings all over again. Our little Teochew mooncake balls were done and the fryer was revved up. We popped them in, several at a time, watching as they slowly turned a golden brown color. Most of them looked lovely: The crust turned out perfectly, with a slender spiral of dough that flared out as it circled each ball. Some, however, were just flat and smooth, resembling Ping-Pong balls as opposed to beautiful spheres with decorative crusts.

What went wrong?

I retraced my steps, mentally walking through the various things I'd done. At some point, I suddenly realized, I'd been so busy listening and chatting that I must have stopped mixing the two doughs together, using just one kind instead. "Um, what is the purpose of using two doughs?" I asked Auntie Khar Moi, more than a little ashamed that I'd not asked her this question, say, *as* we were making the mooncakes. "One has oil in it, and one doesn't, so when you fry it up, the dough with the oil explodes," she said, noting that this was how you got the spiral effect.

Somehow, I had done it again.

Quickly, I assessed the situation. There weren't actually

that many Ping-Pong mooncakes coming out of the fryer. I must have been paying *some* attention—or perhaps I just had not made that many mooncakes. Either way, I was relieved that the damage was limited. And once I bit into one, the exterior didn't really matter. Crunchy outside and just lightly sweet on the inside, they were a pleasure simple and true, especially with a hot cup of Chinese tea.

As I ate one, and then another, I wondered how it was possible that I'd never had one of these Teochew mooncakes before. But all these years later, it certainly wasn't too late to start.

AFTER SOME MONTHS IN SINGAPORE, I BEGAN TO WONDER: Is my mum ever going to teach me how to cook something?

Oh, how she'd protested when I first mentioned wanting to learn to cook from her. "Aiyah, don't ask me lah. I'm not a good cook!" she squawked. "Your e-ma or ah-ma can teach you better!" Having had a maid handle the cooking in her home for more than three decades, my mother knew she was rusty at the stove. In fact, she seemed genuinely embarrassed by the idea of imparting recipes, seeming to feel that she didn't know how to make anything special. "It's so easy," she'd say whenever I asked her how to make a tofu and pork lunch dish or the carrot and corn soup we had at least once a week with lunch or dinner. "Just throw everything in and boil, boil, boil!" This was a refrain that I'd heard for years, never questioning it. I wasn't about to let it go this time, however.

"Mommo," I said one day, using the name that my sister and I had, for reasons we can't remember anymore, been calling her for years. "You make really good soups. I *really* want to learn how to make them." She paused, looking doubtful. "It's so easy—" she started to say again. "But, Mommo," I said, cutting her off, "don't you want me to learn how to make them so I can be healthier?" This, apparently, did the trick.

My mother would do anything to protect Daphne and me. This was especially evident when I was sixteen and was stricken with dengue hemorrhagic fever, a potentially life-threatening disease in tropical countries that is spread by a certain breed of mosquito. My mother and I both were felled by dengue fever and found ourselves hospitalized for a week, watching an alarming rash spread across our bodies that turned out to be tiny blotches of blood just under our skin. Once we were back at home, my mother was livid. She became convinced that our next-door neighbor, who had numerous potted plants, had turned her yard into a breeding ground for the dengue-carrying mosquito.

For days, my mother fumed, peering across the fence that separated our home from the neighbor's, squinting at her plants, staring venomously at the neighbor whenever she surfaced. Finally, my mother decided something needed to be done. She made an anonymous phone call to the health department, tipping them off to my neighbor's deadly garden. This being hyperefficient Singapore, inspectors were next door in a flash. After a thorough inspection, they found nothing. Since they were in the neighborhood, they decided to go door to door to see if they could find the source of the mosquito. My mother welcomed the inspectors with a litany of complaints about our neighbor. She was aghast that her nemesis had been innocent and would not have to pay a hefty fine. Just then, however, the inspectors found something. The larvae of dengue mosquitoes did exist—in my mother's own potted plants.

This would be what Singaporeans call *kenah bang*—or, you've been slammed.

When it came to soups, however, my mother was on surer footing. Ever since I was a child, my mother had religiously made soups for my sister and me not because they tasted good—which, frankly, is not the case with some of them—or because they went well with dinner or lunch. Rather, her sole purpose for making them was to *bu shenti*—restore your body. My mother has always been a firm believer in the restorative powers of herbs and vegetables. Home-brewed chrysanthemum tea, after all, had been dangled in front of me as a way to help improve my vision and give me sparkly, pretty eyes. And the various mélanges of red dates and gnarly-looking, mossy-smelling Chinese herbs that she tossed into massive pots of water along with chicken or pork and daikon, carrots, or watercress were all meant to help keep her family's yin and yang energies in balance.

The Singaporean satirist Colin Goh once noted in a column that "if Harry Potter went to school in Singapore he'd learn in potions class that there are two kinds of potions: heaty and cooling." Colin's take may be funny, but my mother, along with many Chinese, has a deep—and very serious—belief in foods having properties that can heat your body up or cool it down. The key is to figure out whether you have too much yin or yang and adjust those fires accordingly. When she heard my sister or me so much as clear our throats, much less cough, we instantly knew what was coming. There would be cups of barley water, milky and sweet, strewn about our house, perched right by our beds. The concoction was meant as a cooling agent, to help bring the fires within us, the yang energy, down a few notches.

In fact, my mother believes in the healing properties of herbs and various foods so much that she decided a few years ago to turn this conviction into a career. Several nights a week, she began schlepping massive, heavy books imprinted with endless mazes of characters and instructions on anatomy, acupuncture, and of course, the Eastern belief in the healing properties of herbal concoctions, all in a bid to wrap her head around the ancient remedies of our people. In the last few years, the Chinese medicine class had become her lifeline—a welcome distraction from the family turmoil. And the more she learned, the prouder I was of her.

I had been doubtful of this process at first, gently and then more firmly refusing whenever she offered to cup me. (This ancient Chinese process of healing involves fire, smoke, and little glass cups being suctioned onto one's back to release energy in key parts of one's body. Gwyneth Paltrow did it several years ago, bravely showing off the round bruise marks the cups left in a backless dress she wore to an awards show. Somehow, I lacked Gwyneth's courage.) When my mother started learning acupuncture and began fishing about for practice subjects, I made myself even more scarce in the house.

Herbal remedies, however—this was something that I could get behind. My mum, too, was immediately for this idea. For years she'd been trying to convince me of the powers of heaty or cooling soups, and now, finally, I was embracing them. Her lessons, however, fell a little short at first. With her class schedule and her six mornings a week in a traditional Chinese healer's clinic for practical experience, my mother was busier than any of my retired or generally not-working aunties. So when I mentioned I'd like to learn how to make her green carrot–red carrot soup (which is what we called the soup she regularly made by boiling carrots and daikon with chicken or pork), the ingredients magically appeared on the kitchen table with instructions from my mother to watch as Erlinda taught me how to make it. (It was true that the basic strategy in many of the soups I learned from Erlinda did involve tossing everything in a pot to "boil, boil, boil," as my mother had insisted.)

One day, however, I implored my mother to spend some time in the kitchen with me. "The point is to spend time learning from you!" I said. She looked a little guilty. Despite my forays into the kitchen in recent years, we'd not really cooked together. When she'd visit me in the United States, she would take over the kitchen sometimes, making her soups and some basic stir-fries or steamed fish to be served with rice for a simple dinner. The few times she'd been in New York for Christmas, I'd pretty much kept her out of the kitchen as I undertook my traditional two- to three-day whirlwind of cooking just to set appetizers, entrées, side dishes, and a hefty lineup of cookies and festive cakes out for Christmas dinner. We had hardly ever cooked together, but I was eager to change that.

And my mother finally relented when I explained to her that I wanted to learn how to make the sweet green bean soup she'd made for me when I was a child, because I wanted to share it with a group of food bloggers spread from Paris to San Diego who had started a monthly virtual lunch date. We had decided to swap recipes for chilled soups in September, and I'd immediately thought of my mother's green bean soup.

The soup—which is just lightly sweet and basically made with green mung beans and water—was a dish that I had looked forward to as a child. In Singapore, this soup is generally eaten either chilled or piping hot, as a dessert or a snack. However, I often had bowls of it for breakfast and sometimes lunch. Whenever I had schoolmates over, my mother would whip out green bean soup and fried chicken wings—a snack combination that was both delicious (fried chicken wings) and healthy (green bean soup). (This is also supposed to be a "cooling" soup that helps prevent and get rid of acne. Perhaps Mum was just trying to save us all from pockmarked skin.) In any case, on those sweltering tropical days when we'd spent hours running around in the sun or, later, having a marathon mah-jongg session, what I truly looked forward to at the end of it all was a bowl of my mother's green bean soup and some garlicky chicken wings.

Despite my love for this sweet soup, I've never known how to make it. So when my Let's Lunch bunch suggested that we make a chilled soup for our next virtual lunch, I jumped at the excuse to learn my mother's recipe. I knew I could count on my mother's deep-seated desire for me to have friends, which goes back to the time she tried bribing my fellow preschoolers with chocolate to get them to talk to me. I don't think it worked.

One afternoon, she carved out some time, and our tutorial began. We started with green beans (mung beans), pearl sago, tropical pandan leaves, and a sweet potato, which is optional. Now, this is a pretty basic soup. But my mum usually adds sweet potato to the mix if she wants it to be a little heartier. (I think she thinks it also makes the soup look a little fancier.) So, to impress my Let's Lunch friends, we peeled and cut the sweet potato into small, bite-size cubes.

Then we put some water into a pot, knotted a few pandan leaves, threw them in, and brought the liquid to a boil.

After a while, my mother tossed in the green beans, then the sweet potato, and finally the sago and sugar. After just a little more boiling—when the beans had split and softened—the soup was done. So, yes, Mum wasn't just being humble when she said the recipe consists of tossing everything into a pot and boiling.

But the fact that something is easy to make doesn't mean it isn't good.

After a bowl of our soup, I wasn't sure if I felt "cooler" or if my skin felt less oily. But another word for how I felt did come to mind: content.

CHAPTER TWELVE

The first time my Tanglin ah-ma was hospitalized for the mysterious pains that would lead to her death, she had one thing on her mind.

Summoning my uncle Soo Kiat to her bedside, she said, "I've made the chili paste for *otah*," referring to a creamy and spicy fish paste wrapped in banana leaves that was one of her many signature dishes. "The fish has been bought; the *otah* must be made."

She whispered the recipe to my uncle. Her mind, then, was at rest.

Now, *otah*, a Malay dish, would not be an expected notch in a traditional Chinese home cook's kitchen post. The paste—also known as *otak* or *otak-otak*—is a spicy mousse, usually made with mackerel, that is wrapped in banana leaves and then steamed or grilled. It can be eaten on its own, mashed into rice, or slathered on bread for a savory lunch or breakfast.

Simply thinking about it is often all it takes to get my mouth watering. I'd never known where my grandmother got her recipe, but after some digging, it became obvious—the ailing Indonesian cook she had taken in later in life. In addition to sharing her *mee siam* recipe, this cook had given Tanglin Ah-Ma her *otah* recipe. Now, decades later, this would be passed to me—a product of my grandmother's selfless generosity.

The *otah* process takes two days. On the first, Auntie Khar Imm and I began by chopping up lemongrass, shallots, galangal, turmeric, and lightly toasted, crumbled belacan (fermented, ground dried shrimp), and blending them in a food processor with candlenuts and a little water to make a paste. By now, Auntie Khar Imm was letting me chop along with her or take over some basic slicing tasks as she moved on to other steps. When it came to fresh turmeric, however, she protested. "No need lah!" she said, gesturing to my pale pink nails, which I'd had manicured just the day before. "You'll stain your nails!" I had come this far, however; I was determined not to be pampered. So, fifteen-dollar manicure or not, I waved off her protests and jumped in. She was right, of course. Before long, the juices spurting out of the bright orange turmeric were turning my fingers, my nails, bits of my wrist an alarming, electric yellow. Hoping it would wash off—but not really caring—I kept chopping.

Next, we started frying this paste over medium heat in a large wok. While it was frying, we tossed sun-dried chilis that had been softened in boiling water and tiny, flaming-hot bird's-eye chilis into the processor and blended them together. We then added this paste to the wok, mixing it all up well.

We wanted the chili paste to get really dry. The best way to tell whether there's still water in the paste is to add oil (which we did periodically during the frying) and then inspect the oil to see if white, wispy strands appear. If we saw the wisps, there was still water in the mixture.

About an hour and a half later, the paste was dry enough. We scooped it out into a bowl to cool overnight on the kitchen table.

When I showed up at Auntie Khar Imm's the next day, I was presented with a massive gray fish. *Beh gah he,* she called it, as I tried to jot down what those Teochew words sounded like. With my grasp of Teochew being tenuous at best, I quickly took a picture of the fish, desperately hoping that its face or sheen had enough identifying characteristics that I might be able to find it back in New York.

As we chopped, squeezed shredded coconut for its thick milk, and added that together with eggs, sugar, coriander, tapioca flour, salt, and a dash of monosodium glutamate to the fish-and-cooled-chili-paste mixture, Auntie Khar Imm began to share the story of my Tanglin ah-ma and the cook who had taught her this dish. "She had one eye!" she said of the cook. "And she cooked for this really rich family." I began to think: Every family history really is enhanced by the appearance of a one-eyed Indonesian cook. This was pretty cool.

And now, decades later, there I sat in Auntie Khar Imm's kitchen, carefully scooping fish paste into banana leaves, sealing them up, and steaming them while marveling at the generosity of my Tanglin ah-ma, and the *otah* recipe that it had earned.

On the way home, I noticed massive neon-yellow splotches still covering my very newly manicured nails. The marks of my grandmother's recipe, however, felt oddly satisfying.

A few days later, I bundled up a few sticks of *otah* and brought them to Gunther, the head chef of one of Singapore's most expensive French restaurants, who had heard about my *otah* lesson and asked for a taste. With no small amount of anxiety, I wondered what this Belgian import who adored spicy Singaporean food and had spent years mastering local techniques would think.

"You don't have to try it right now," I said in the coolness of his restaurant, just before dinner service started, hoping that I wouldn't have to watch him eat it, possibly loathe it, and then say something polite. Instead, he opened the Tupperware container right away, picking up an *otah* with his fingers and popping it into his mouth. Carefully, I watched his face. His eyes widened. He smiled. "It's spicy—*very* good!" he said, reaching back in to grab another *otah*. His face had brightened visibly. He didn't seem to be lying.

"What's in it? How did you make it?" he asked. I was so taken aback, I wasn't sure what to say. I'd always thought my Tanglin ah-ma's cooking was amazing, of course. But to hear one of Singapore's top chefs marvel over something she had passed down, something I had made with my bare, yellow-splotched hands, made me momentarily speechless. After a few seconds, I sputtered out the steps that we'd taken just the day before in my auntie Khar Imm's little kitchen. Gunther nodded and thanked me, while calling over his waiters to "try this— it's excellent."

Gunther broke out some gin, and we had a toast. As I sat there sipping expensive gin in a posh French restaurant that my Tanglin ah-ma never would have even thought to enter, where the chef had devoured her *otah* and been incredibly impressed, I couldn't help but think, just perhaps, she would have been so, so proud.

LONG BEFORE I HAD MY UNCLES WILLIN AND SIMPSON, I had another set of intrepid-eating *kaki* (people).

There was Kevin, who attacked his food with such vengeance that he once had a girlfriend who barely ate at meals with him because—she confessed when they broke up—watching him eat literally made her feel ill. There was Regina, the skinny captain of our high school girls' tennis team, who had a bottomless pit of a stomach. And Jeanette, who was as constantly hungry as she was pretty, with not a spare ounce of fat on her body to reflect the seemingly endless snacking that we saw her do. We had met in Catholic Junior College, where we plowed through the Singapore equivalent of American eleventh and twelfth grades under the somewhat watchful eyes of nuns and Catholic teachers. Together, we were united in our love for food. The eating of it, that is. Being a man, Kevin never had to worry about cooking. And Regina and I only started dabbling in it when we came to the United States for college and suddenly had to fend for ourselves. As for Jeanette, she was lucky to have married Eudon, a man whose father was a chef and had instilled in him a love for the kitchen. With a husband who would go on fishing trips to net squid and then come back home to make squid-ink risotto from scratch, all Jeanette had to worry about in the kitchen was cleaning up. For years, the rest of us wanted to kill her.

Kitchen pangs struck her as they did me, however. I had been sharing my stories of cooking with my aunties—as well as the spoils of those lessons—with Nette, as we call her. Her curiosity was piqued; soon we began plotting the adventures we could concoct together. One evening over cocktails, Nette spent several minutes spinning a long, mouthwatering tale of the *ayam masak merah* that our friend Aisah's mother makes for the annual feast she prepares to mark the end of Ramadan, the Muslim holy month of fasting. The dish, one that I often seek out at Malay restaurants and food stalls, consists of fried chicken that's cooked in a dense, crimson chili gravy, which is both spicy and sweet. It's often served as part of *nasi padang*, a meal of rice accompanied with a variety of dishes that first originated in Indonesia. (In Bahasa Indonesia, the Indonesian language, *nasi padang* literally means "rice from Padang," a city in Sumatra.) The dishes you'll typically find in a *nasi padang* restaurant include fried or grilled fish in curried sauces, *achar* (super-sour Indian-style pickles), and spicy beef *rendang*, a delicious dish of beef slow-cooked in a rich, coconut milk–based curry. The Dutch also have a version of this meal, transported back from their days as colonialists in Southeast Asia, known as *rijsttafel*, or "rice table."

I'd never considered trying to make *ayam masak merah* before, having relegated it to the category of foods you have to buy. It seemed like such a difficult dish that I could never have even fathomed knowing anyone who would know how to make it and could teach me. "Aisah's mum's *ayam masak merah* is so good," Nette said over and over. After some thought, I began texting Nette to ask, "When are we learning?" A few weeks later, Nette and I found ourselves hauling a gift of chocolates up the steps to an airy apartment in Ang Mo Kio—a neighborhood in central Singapore whose name means "red hair bridge" in Hokkien and was either named after a British Royal Army engineer, who built a bridge in the area when Singapore was still a colony, or a British expatriate, Lady Jennifer Windsor, who owned an estate there in the 1920s, depending on which story you believe.

"Hello, hello!" Aisah said brightly, welcoming us into her mother's home and looking stylish as usual, even in basic shorts and a casual blouse. In the years after our Catholic Junior College days, Aisah had gone on to earn a coveted job as a Singapore Airlines flight attendant. She spent several years jetting to Europe and all over Asia before settling down to run a clothing boutique on Haji Lane, a recently fashionable shopping spot in Singapore. Even though she no longer flies with SIA, Aisah still carries herself with the grace and fluid elegance of the airline's flight attendants—and is always as put together.

At lunchtime, Aisah's mother's apartment, on a high floor in a tall building, was sunny and had a lovely breeze drifting through it. We peeked into the kitchen to greet Aisah's mum, Auntie Jianab, who was already hard at work at the stove. Standing by a big wok filled with bubbling hot oil, she was methodically frying up pieces of chicken that she had lightly salted before carefully sliding them into the oil. As soon as they turned golden, she fished them out and set them aside on paper towels. "She doesn't speak English," Aisah whispered to me. While I spoke Malay excellently enough to order "*mee siam*, one" I could hardly be relied on to learn how to cook in Malay. Aisah had that taken care of, though. "I'll translate as she cooks," she said.

As Auntie Jianab fried her chicken, she instructed Aisah to

ready the *rempah* (spice paste). Using a blender, Aisah chopped up shallots, dried chilies, and garlic to form the paste. Next, Auntie Jianab stir-fried the spice paste together with tomato puree, liquid *gula melaka* (palm sugar), salt, a chicken bouillon cube, and *kecap manis* (an Indonesian sweet soy sauce), and then added the chicken to the mix and stirred. "You have to make sure to strain the *gula melaka*," Aisah cautioned, wrinkling her slender nose. "Sometimes you'll find bugs in them." There apparently was no escaping insects in Southeast Asian cooking.

Auntie Jianab made the whole process look terribly simple, gliding with lightning-quick ease through the motions while Aisah, Nette, and I watched nervously, trying to keep up and make sure every step was carefully committed to both notepad and memory, while also jumping in to measure a liquid or open a can wherever we could. Before long, the chicken was done and we were sitting down to eat. Auntie Jianab's *ayam masak merah* was a little darker—and sweeter—than versions you'll typically find in *nasi padang* stalls. And it was far superior, I thought—many versions I've tried are too heavy on the spiciness or so bland that the sweet notes are barely detectable.

As we dug into the chicken, also padding up our rice plates with gobs of stir-fried garlicky green beans, Auntie Jianab emerged from the kitchen with a tiny bowl of crackling deep-fried *ikan bilis* (anchovies). I loved this inch-long, slender salty fish that is delicious mixed with some chili sauce and hot rice but also a lovely counterpoint to an ice-cold beer on a summery evening. But I'd never once fried it at home. "Is there anything special to frying it up?" I asked. Aisah, after conferring with her mother, said, "You just have to look for the lighter-colored *ikan bilis*. Those taste better. Then you just deep-fry it in oil until it becomes crispy."

Watching us eat, Auntie Jianab began to share her kitchen tales. She had learned to cook when she was a girl, she said, growing up in Singapore. For years, she made mostly basics like simple Malay curries and soups—it wasn't until Aisah turned four that she had more time to learn more complex dishes. Her *ayam masak merah* recipe was gleaned from watching women cook at Malay wedding festivities over the years, she explained. "Wow," Aisah said. "I never knew all this about my mum!"

As our eating slowed and we finally, regretfully, put down our forks, Auntie Jianab shared one more story. One day, in the village where she grew up, Auntie Jianab spotted a handsome man who instantly caught her attention. Since he was new to the village, her family began inviting him over for dinner—and this turned out to be a chance for the shy, young Jianab to impress him with her cooking skills. Over the course of several dinners, she plied him with delicious curries and rice dishes.

Her cooking worked its magic. And the rest, as they say, is history.

Back in her own kitchen, Nette had become inspired. "*Allo allo*," an e-mail from her one day read. "to baptize our pizza stone . . . we have decided to throw a pizza party next Sat. you guys will prob be the guinea pigs." While I'd cooked for Nette before, making a simple breakfast and a steak dinner for her once when she'd visited me in New York, I'd never actually cooked *with* her. (I didn't think we could count our watching of Auntie Jianab in the kitchen as "cooking.") Instantly, I volunteered to come up with the toppings for one of the pizzas.

In recent years, I had become obsessed with clam pizza. The first time I had it was unforgettable—my friend Greg, who worked in Hartford, Connecticut, where he wrote about food and fashion for the *Courant*, had been astounded that I had never tried the famous clam pizza at Frank Pepe Pizzeria in New Haven, Connecticut. Finally, after years of raving about it, he made a date. Mike and I got in a car and headed to New Haven. After waiting in line for more than thirty minutes, we slid into a booth where Greg proceeded to order a large clam pie with bacon. The salty, cheesy, and crispy combination had me mesmerized right away. Bacon or no bacon, this clam pizza was phenomenal. I began swinging by Pepe's whenever I was remotely close to New Haven.

"Do you like clams?" I asked Nette. "If so, I may make a clam pizza topping." Nette looked a little skeptical—pizza places in Singapore tend to err on the traditional side. When menus offer adventurous toppings they tend to be Asian-inspired, such as tandoori chicken, for example. I had never seen a clam pizza on a Singaporean menu and it sounded like Nette hadn't either. But as always, she was game to try anything. I had shared Peter Reinhart's pizza dough recipe—which my bread-baking friends had unanimously adored—with Nette, and Eudon was hard at work tossing pizza dough into the air by the time I arrived in the large kitchen of her fourth-floor walk-up apartment in Singapore's centrally located Tiong Bahru neighborhood. While much of densely populated Singapore is crammed with tall buildings—both residential and commercial—a small section of Tiong Bahru remains a quaint little pocket of relatively squat apartment buildings, some of which date back to the 1930s, when this government-created housing estate was developed. (An estimated 80 percent of Singaporeans live in comfortable, affordable apartments built by the government.) Some of these white, boxy buildings, which go up to five stories high, have a modern art deco feel to them. Before World War II, the neighborhood apparently was a place where the rich kept their mistresses, which earned it the name *Mei Ren Wuo* or "den of beauties." In modern-day Singapore, however, the neighborhood is more like a den of yuppies. The relatively young and professional have been attracted to Tiong Bahru's streamlined structures, which are modern yet also conjure a bygone era in Singapore—a time when buildings didn't all loom dozens of stories high.

At Nette's that night, Eudon twirled large disks of pizza dough in the air, readying them for the oven. The first few were delicious standards—basic pepperoni and a margherita pizza, dotted with mozzarella, basil, and fresh tomatoes. Then Nette cleared a spot for me in her kitchen for my clam pizza. Eudon had spread the dough out onto the stone; I sprinkled it with minced garlic, Italian parsley, canned, chopped clams, red pepper flakes, and grated Parmesan cheese, before drizzling olive oil on top of the mound of ingredients. (Since it was Nette's first clam pizza, I figured I should make a pure version and left off the bacon.) After twelve minutes in the oven, the pie came out smelling delicious. It stood little chance of surviving more than five minutes outside of the oven, disappearing almost instantly.

As we capped the night with whiskey and homemade chocolate cake and surveyed the crumbs of our dinner scattered about, Nette and I felt pleased with ourselves. Guests had arrived ravenous and they'd been well fed—not with food purchased from the many great hawker stands that fill Tiong Bahru, but with pizzas produced in Nette's own kitchen. In all our teenage years of daydreaming about the lives that lay before us, we had never contemplated cooking together or throwing a dinner party. We had never considered the act of making food for people as anything less than a chore, a necessity—something we were intent on avoiding as much as possible.

Looking at the satisfied smiles around the dinner table, I realized what silly schoolgirls we had been.

CHAPTER THIRTEEN

There are numerous things to love about my auntie Alice. The bottomless well of warmth and pure, well-intentioned kindness that she possesses. Her fervent love for her family—the thing that nudges her to try, regularly, repeatedly, to bring us all together for dinner or afternoon tea. The no-nonsense approach that enabled her to raise three handsome and close-to-perfect young men, each one more gentle and well behaved than the last. The infectiousness of her humor, her body starting to rock as she titters, one hand coyly reaching up to cover her mouth while the other reaches down to slap her knee when it's a laugh that's really worth enjoying.

The one thing I truly admire in her, however, is how practical she is, a problem solver to a fault. In her longtime job as a public relations manager for a big hotel in Singapore, this quality was, of course, handy. In the kitchen, it has proved essential. If Auntie Alice doesn't know how to make something, it doesn't matter—she'll figure it out. Which is why she knows how to make a whole host of dishes that are so labor-intensive and easy to buy at hawker stands that most Singaporeans never even bother to attempt them at home.

"Cheryl ah," she said one day on the phone. "What else do you want to learn?"

"*Kueh lapis?*" I said, hopefully. Auntie Alice had always been a wonderful baker—and my mouth still watered when I thought of her buttery slabs of *kueh lapis*, a pandan-scented, spiced, striped cake comprising multiple one-eighth-inch layers of dough baked atop one another.

"Um, I don't really bake anymore leh," she said, sheepishly confessing that her oven had been turned into storage space for pots and utensils years ago. "I don't know if I remember how to make *kueh lapis*!"

Before I could start feeling sad, however, Auntie Alice volunteered: "What about chicken rice?"

Ah, *chicken rice*—two words that tug at the hearts of many Singaporeans who live overseas. Widely considered Singapore's national dish, chicken rice—also known as Hainanese chicken rice because Hainanese immigrants first started making the dish—basically consists of boiled chicken and rice. When done well, the chicken is so tender that its juices practically spurt out, coating your tongue as you bite into it. (Boon Tong Kee, a hallowed chicken rice joint in Singapore, is known for steaming it and then cooling it in such a way that a hefty layer of gelatinized juices and fat sits between the meat of the chicken and its chewy, fatty skin.) But for many, the best part of this dish is the rice itself—ever so slightly pandan scented and oily, and made so that each grain of rice is slick with chicken fat and juices.

I'd eaten chicken rice and dreamt of it more times than I

could count. But I had never once thought of making it. I'd had it made for me from scratch just once, fifteen years before, and the occasion had so impressed me that it's been seared in my memory. During my sophomore year in college, a group of Singaporean friends and I traveled to Bloomington, Indiana, to attend a national conference of Singaporean students living in the United States. Sure, it was going to be an honor to meet S. R. Nathan, Singapore's ambassador to the United States at the time. But the main reason any of us was going, really, was the remote chance that we might get to eat some semblance of Singaporean food.

On our very first day there, things looked promising. I met Andre, an eager young Singaporean student who was hosting me and my group of friends: Francis, Leonard, and Kevin, three guys I'd known since I was eleven, back when we were a rambunctious lot who spent hours playing Ping-Pong, skateboarding, and kickboxing in the swimming pool. As we sat around Andre's living room lamenting the fact that it had been ages since we'd eaten chicken rice, he said the words: "I can make chicken rice, you know."

There were audible gasps; our hearts started racing. Francis and Leonard quietly wondered aloud if I should take one for the team and make out with Andre to grease the wheels. Fortunately, no making out was in order. Andre the affable was instantly enthusiastic about making his chicken rice for us. Immediately, we drove to the grocery store to purchase the ingredients, and Andre set about working his magic.

I'd like to say that I helped—or that we helped—but really, none of us cooked or was even vaguely interested in the cooking.

Instead, the four of us simply sat in the living room and waited for the smells to hit us. The result was okay—not as delicious as professionally cooked chicken rice. But it truly was amazing. Biting into the chicken and chasing it with garlicky, greasy rice, this group of loudmouths was reduced to a long stretch of silence. It was fall, and there we were in cold, cold Bloomington, Indiana—right smack in the middle of America's heartland—and we were huddled around a table eating homemade chicken rice! I briefly considered making out with Andre after all, just because I was so grateful. The four of us began bickering bitterly over who would eat the last piece of chicken. *"Jie,"* Leonard said, calling me "older sister" as he had since we were eleven. "Eat it lah." "No, you eat it," I replied. And Kevin jumped in, too, urging someone—anyone—else to eat the last piece. It was only polite, after all; we'd all gone so long without chicken rice. One of your loved ones, not you, should really have the last piece. After several minutes of this, Francis, who had been watching mostly silently, jumped up from his corner of the table, holding his fork just so. "Aiyah, *I'll* eat it," he said, leaning over to spear the final piece and dump it on his plate. We watched, stunned, as he devoured the last of our precious chicken rice with great gusto, then laughed. It wasn't until I was back in my dorm room at Northwestern that I started to feel the pangs of regret. I couldn't believe that even in my fog of greed I hadn't bothered to learn or even watch how to make Andre's Singaporean chicken rice.

So this time, faster than you could say "chicken," I was in Auntie Alice's sunny kitchen with my notebook and pen in hand.

Auntie Alice moved quickly, washing two cups of rice and

rinsing the chicken. I'd dealt with so much raw duck at this point that I didn't even wince when I saw the cold, white chicken sitting in her sink. Auntie Alice saved me from touching it, however, grabbing it and deftly cutting off its head and trimming off its backside. "Make sure to cut off the extra skin ah," she said. "Otherwise it will be too fatty." Instead of tossing out the skin, however, Auntie Alice placed it in a bowl, gesturing for me to note that the skin should be saved. Next, she grabbed some salt, waving me off as I started to ask her how much. "I just use my hand to *agak-agak* lor," she said, taking what looked to be about a teaspoon of salt and rubbing it all over the inside of the chicken. Then, she bashed up nine garlic cloves and a two-inch piece of ginger—"You want to bring the smell out," she noted—placing them inside the chicken together with two stalks of scallions. With that, she pinched together the skin around the chicken's behind and sealed it with a sharp toothpick.

Taking out a large pot, Auntie Alice brought some water— "enough to cover the chicken," she said—to a rolling boil. Once the water had boiled, she placed the chicken in the pot, breast side down, covered it, and let it simmer over medium heat for twenty minutes.

As much as I love the chicken and the rice aspect of chicken rice, I also adore the little bowl of salty soup that usually comes with it. At hawker stands and restaurants, this soup is often flavored with monosodium glutamate, which I try not to use in my own kitchen. So I was curious to see how Auntie Alice would flavor her chicken rice soup. Shiitake mushrooms, apparently, were her secret. And so was *dong cai*, which are briny, brownish flecks of preserved Chinese cabbage. I'd never cooked with *dong cai* before. In fact, I'd never given it much thought beyond *Hey, this salty stuff tastes awesome* when I encountered it in soups. Auntie Alice pulled out a little bit to show me how it looked. "No need to use too much of it, just enough to add some flavor," she said.

While the chicken simmered, we sat for a moment, putting our feet up and enjoying a light breeze in her large living room, which opened out into a little garden, as she kept one eye on her granddaughter, Bernice. Now, Auntie Alice had learned to cook as a teenager out of sheer necessity. With my grandmother having to work to put food on the table, Auntie Alice simply had to become the person making the food. Her repertoire then, of course, included nothing near as fancy as chicken rice. "I remember when I learned to fry fish for the first time," Auntie Alice said, scrunching up her face and hunching over the table as she often did when she was getting to the meaty part of a story. "I was fourteen or fifteen years old, and when I slid the fish into the oil, all this oil splattered everywhere. I had blisters so big I had to go to the doctor, you know," she added, pointing at me as if reminding me to always be careful when frying fish. (Being a big red-meat eater myself, I'd not attempted any fish frying before. I supposed it was good that I'd not attempted it without first hearing this sage advice.)

My mother and her younger sister, Auntie Jane, had always joked about Auntie Alice being "fierce" as a teenager. "We used to call her the dowager!" my mother had told me that very week. "She was so strict!" My mother's recollection of those days largely involves Auntie Alice being a tyrant with a broom, yelling at her three siblings to keep their feet off the floor as she raced through the house, trying to sweep it clean.

Auntie Alice laughed when I mentioned the word *dowager*. "Aiyoh, your mummy ah," she said, shaking her head. "In those days, your mum and Auntie Jane were younger, they didn't do much housework, and they were so naughty! I was the one who had to learn how to keep the house clean, you know. If I'm cleaning the house, whoever stepped on something, I would just scream at them!" Housework was just one of her worries at the time. "Your ah-ma had a little gambling den on the weekends," she said. "We were living in Selegie House," a building in a neighborhood that currently is dotted with karaoke and KTV lounges, where everyone knows the girls usually can be paid to do more than just sing. Well, into just a microphone anyway. "We used to have gamblers come over and play *seesek*," Hokkien for "four colors," which is a popular Chinese card game involving slender, long cards of four colors. With gamblers filling the house on weekends, Auntie Alice and her sisters were relegated to being girl Fridays who fetched tea or noodles from the nearby coffee shops when anyone got hungry.

"Did you ever get upset over having to do this?" I asked, thinking about my pretty auntie Alice and her sisters having to deal with hungry, sketchy, sometimes angry men in their own living room. Auntie Alice's large, bright eyes widened, which often happens when she's really thinking about something, giving her face the look of an innocent girl on the cusp of some amazing discovery. "It didn't occur to me at that time, you know!" she finally said, erupting in soft laughter again.

And that was that. Being the tea girls for strange men in their mother's illegal gambling den on weekends was just something practical. You didn't question it. If you wanted to be able to put food on the table, you just did it. I started thinking about my question and how silly it had been. I'd grown up in a comfortable home with not even a whiff of want, much less poverty. I'd approached life with the view of the pampered—expecting the right to a myriad of choices, never having had to suffer or do something I loathed in order to make a few dollars for my family. I realized how fortunate I'd been. Or unfortunate, perhaps, as I didn't appear to have as much figure-it-out spirit as my auntie Alice had. As much as I adored chicken rice, I'd never thought of trying to figure out how to make it. And there Auntie Alice was, curious about chicken rice, then questioning hawkers or professional cooks she met, trying to figure out on her own how to put the dish together.

The chicken, by this point, was almost done. Auntie Alice grabbed a chopstick and poked it through the bird at its thickest part. "If there's no blood, then the chicken is cooked," she said. With no blood in sight, she hoisted the chicken out of the pot and set it aside to cool, saving the water it had been boiled in. Heating a large wok over high heat with a little bit of cooking oil, she tossed in the snipped-up chicken skin that she'd saved and started frying it. "You must fry until it's crispy and all the oil has been extracted," she said, swirling the sizzling skin around the wok as it became smaller and smaller. Once the bits of skin had gotten about as small, brown, and crispy as they were likely to get, she gently removed them, replacing them with minced garlic, shallots, and ginger, frying the combination until its heady smell started hitting our nostrils. Next, in went the uncooked rice, which had been washed and drained, and six knots of pandan leaves from my mother's garden. Quickly, she fried up the mixture, trying her best to make sure that the rice grains were evenly coated, that the minced garlic, shallots, and ginger were getting distributed evenly. After just a minute or two, she moved the mixture to a rice cooker, added the cooking water from the chicken, and turned it on.

As the rice cooked, Auntie Alice set about chopping up the now cooled chicken and making the soup. There was still some water left over from boiling the chicken; into it, she tossed some *dong cai* (about one to two teaspoons, by my sense of *agak-agak*) and began bringing that to a boil. "You can put some little cubes of *tauhu* [tofu] in the soup if you want," she said, as she sliced up a few shiitake mushrooms to add flavor. Next, she heated a little bit of sesame oil in a wok, stir-fried some whole scallions in the oil until we could smell the scallions, then drizzled the oil over the cut-up chicken.

Soon enough, the rice cooker button popped and we were ready to eat. The chicken was delicious and tender, just as it should be. And the rice and soup, though not as flavorful as MSG-laden restaurant versions, were divine. As I nibbled on the rice, Auntie Alice asked why I wasn't eating much. "I need to lose weight!" I said, noting that I'd started to see an alarming rubbery tire around my waist as my year of cooking, bread baking, and eating progressed. "Aiyoh!" she exclaimed. "If you need to lose weight, that means people like us no need to eat already lah!"

With that, I began to really tuck in. Auntie Alice smiled as she watched me. "Cooking ah," she said. "If you do it with your whole heart, then it tastes good, you know. If you do it grudgingly, then better don't do it at all."

I thought back to the meals I'd made, the meals I hoped to make. Whenever I'd been rushed or busy or just plain stressed about putting dinner on the table, there hadn't been much enjoyment involved—making the meal was tiresome. If I tried to carefully yet quickly follow steps in a recipe, the food was often only okay, and the actual act of sitting down to eat always felt forced.

Auntie Alice was right. I had slowed my life down so I could try to watch, to listen, to learn. And slowly, I hoped, I was learning to cook with my heart.

CHAPTER FOURTEEN

There is a moment in the lives of eighteen-year-olds in Singapore when panic inevitably kicks in.

Singapore, a Commonwealth country, adopted the British school system decades ago, meaning that your entire academic career culminates in the taking of a single big exam at age eighteen. The A levels grade will determine which university you'll attend. Or if you'll be able to attend university at all.

Now, this may seem unfair to those used to the American school system, where cumulative grades and academic performance dictate your college prospects. But for someone who tends to perform best only when there's a fire ablaze under her butt, this Britty school system worked perfectly fine.

For my two years in junior college (the equivalent of eleventh and twelfth grades in American schooling), I threw myself into a host of activities—debate club, of which I was president, representing my school in national oratorical and elocution competitions; and student government, where I, a social butterfly at age seventeen, was fittingly drafted for the social events committee. Schoolwork was important, of course, and I did fine.

But it wasn't until a few months before the A level examinations that I really turned my focus to my studies.

Which is not to say that I turned my attention to *studying* per se.

Faced with this killer exam, almost everyone I knew was spending hours and hours "mugging," memorizing facts and essays that would answer the likely questions. This was particularly difficult for history, a subject in which we'd spent two years covering a wide range of topics—Singaporean, Mesopotamian, Thai, Japanese, Chinese history. Each year the exam entails writing long essays in response to five or six questions over the course of three hours. It was insanity to try to commit all of this information flawlessly to memory in order to answer just six questions—or so we thought. Kevin, my food-obsessed best friend, and I had a far better idea. Through a friend who'd recently done the A level history exam himself, we'd gotten our hands on a thick stack of papers on which thirty years of the exam questions, drafted each year in Cambridge, U.K., were printed. So we poured our energies into creating a giant chart on which we mapped out the questions asked since the early 1970s. Inevitably, a pattern emerged. It was like that exhilarating moment in *The Matrix* when all suddenly becomes clear. Instantly, we felt, we could see the exact sequence of questions that were asked every few years—and we could see what questions were likely to appear on our exam.

Oh, we had the best of intentions—initially. We'd mapped out thirty questions we should really focus on, and then a shorter list of fifteen, should we find ourselves with less time to study, and then an even shorter list of ten. And in case we found ourselves truly desperate and short on time, we'd made a list of six questions that we were almost certain would appear. Preparing only for those six questions would be foolish, we told ourselves. Yet weeks rolled by, and after cramming for our other exams, Kevin and I suddenly found ourselves at 2:00 A.M. the morning of our A level history exam, on the phone, hopped up on much too much Chinese tea, adrenaline and terror pumping through our veins, saying the words "Okay, I guess we have no choice. Which are the six questions again?"

The junior college cafeteria the morning of the exam was dark, lit only by the grayish glow of a few fluorescent lights. Huddled over the sea of lunch tables were our fellow classmates in powder blue Catholic school uniforms, all flipping through pages of notes with silent, frantic energy. "Oh my god, you guys are so dead!" Nette said as she surveyed our ashen looks, surmising that we'd stayed up all night and in the end done what we'd said we'd only turn to as a last resort: really focus on just six questions. Perhaps she was right. Our entire futures hung on a little chart that we had plotted out. What had we been thinking? Could this be the end of our academic careers? I steeled myself. We had believed in our chart. And our methodology had been thorough. Over and over, we had examined the pattern. There was a recurring sequence that simply could not be ignored. There was no way we could be wrong. Ignoring Nette, we flipped through our notes one last time before slowly trudging up the stairs to the examination room, a calm dread lacing every second. Finally, the moment came. I sat down at my square, gray desk and flipped over the exam to look at the questions. And immediately, I had to quell the urge to scream.

Our chart had worked—we had been right all along. Needless to say, we sailed through the exam. I scored an A. Kevin and I became heroes in our little circle. And this would be a tale of glorious triumph that we would share for years with anyone willing to listen.

It was this sometimes unorthodox approach to studying, to rigid Singapore life, that always made me feel slightly out of step at home, however. Particularly when it came to my father's somewhat by-the-book family.

Whereas I had busied myself thwarting the Singapore school system, my auntie Leng Eng was a bastion of success within it. Having started teaching in her late teens at Singapore Chinese Girls' School, Auntie Leng Eng worked her way up to vice principal, overseeing the entire primary school before retiring. She had terrified me when I was a child. Her generally stiff demeanor with just a whiff of sternness always made me feel that I was doing something wrong. Or that if I was merely *thinking* something wrong, she'd know right away. Now, when she invited me over for tea, I was a little apprehensive.

"So how are the cooking lessons going?" Auntie Leng Eng asked, once we'd settled into cushy chairs in her neat, high-ceilinged living room and the green tea had been poured.

"Good, very good! Auntie Khar Imm is a really wonderful teacher," I said. "I'm really learning a lot."

Auntie Leng Eng nodded with just the slightest smile. I felt heartened that she appeared to approve.

"When we were young," she began, "we used to dread the times when your ah-ma was going to make something, because it meant that we were going to be very busy. When she was making dumplings, we had to clean all the bamboo leaves. She would soak them in a big bucket, and I would sit there and have to wash leaf after leaf after leaf. Whenever she made anything, it would be by the hundreds, because she would be giving them to all the neighbors, the relatives, and all her friends. Later on, when the neighbors knew that she made such wonderful dumplings, they would place orders with her. If I'm not mistaken, she would make them by the thousands."

"Daddy never helped?" I asked, instantly drawing an incredulous look from Auntie Leng Eng.

"They were young," she said kindly. "Most of the time, I was doing the helping."

After a short silence, Auntie Leng Eng softly added, "She never thought of passing on recipes at that time. We were all young. We were all very young, still schooling. Later, when I started work, she realized that I was very busy, so she never actually told me, 'Oh, you better come and learn because I won't be around all the time.'"

The helping truly stopped when Auntie Leng Eng married, moved into her own home, and quickly had two young children to raise. "I just enjoyed the food," she said, smiling. "Every time she was done making she would ring me up and say, 'Oh, I've done this—you come and collect!' Then we all just enjoyed the eating."

I tried to imagine what it must have been like, growing up around all that cooking. I felt a fierce wistfulness that Auntie Leng Eng, who didn't cook at all herself, had never learned to cook from her own mother, whom I was admiring more and more as I spent more time learning her recipes. As I started to dwell on what a waste that had been, I realized I had been guilty of the reluctance to learn, too. I'd been in my Tanglin ah-ma's home many times as a child—and not once had I volunteered to help in the kitchen or expressed any desire to learn anything. Anne Tyler and Ernest Hemingway were far bigger heroes to me than my own grandmother at the time.

"Your ah-ma was very generous, you know," Auntie Leng Eng continued. "In the nineteen seventies, we had a neighbor who gave birth to a baby with, what's that condition where there's a lot of water in the brain? Hydrocephalus? His head was very big. The doctors predicted that he wouldn't live very long, and he had to undergo several operations. The mother already had a daughter, and she didn't want to look after him herself, so at that time the lady approached Ah-Ma to say, 'Can you look after my baby for me?' Ah-Ma was already looking after Uncle Ah Tuang, but she took this baby in also." Once the baby was in my grandmother's home, she kept him bundled up in a lengthy sarong fashioned into a mini-hammock and suspended from the ceiling by an elasticized length of rope in the middle of the living room. "Everybody was helping to rock him," Auntie Leng Eng said. "He became everybody's baby."

As Auntie Leng Eng spoke, she grew gentler, softer. I'd never spent much time chatting alone with her before—and now I realized that I should have, a long time ago. The vice principal demeanor was a veneer, one that quickly disappeared around those she loved. I just hadn't taken the time to be there for that.

"What was Ah-Ma's childhood like? Do you know?" I asked.

"Well, your ah-ma grew up in *bua gia hng*, which is 'crocodile area' in English," Auntie Leng Eng said. I'd heard snippets of this story before, but only that my Tanglin ah-ma had grown up on a farm in the northern part of Singapore, where many Teochews lived. "She was the youngest of three girls; there were six of them. Three girls and three boys. And she was the youngest of all of them. My grandmother had two husbands, I think. We were not too clear because we never asked about such things. But if I am not mistaken, the first husband passed away after she had two children, then she remarried, and when she remarried, she had another two boys and another two girls. Your ah-ma was the youngest."

When Auntie Leng Eng and her two brothers were in school, my Tanglin ah-ma began sending them away to this rural area during their long school holidays in June and December. "We were in primary school, and I remember they used to set up these *ge tai*, which were these traditional [Teochew] opera shows," she said, her eyes getting a little dreamy as she began to remember. "We were awed by all those figures in their bright costumes, and we were very taken with all the little stalls selling food around the stage. That was all just part of the fun."

My great-grandparents had stopped farming by that point. Roofs made with the broad, dried leaves of the tropical atap tree (a form of palm tree) were popular, and my rural family was earning its keep by sewing atap leaves together. "In the mornings, there was no show, so I also went to learn and help them sew," Auntie Leng Eng said. "They used these long rods to pick the atap leaves, folded them, and then stitched them together. It was very interesting. There was a group of ladies in the *kampong* [village] that did it. It was like a whole industry!"

Life in the *kampong* was different from life in downtown Singapore, where my far richer father's family lived. "All the buildings were very close to each other—you can peep into your neighbor's house!" Auntie Leng Eng noted. "Everybody was very friendly because you knew everybody in the area. We were like very, very special people because we were from the city."

As I tried to imagine my citified father and Auntie Leng Eng in this village setting, it occurred to me that I had no idea how my grandmother had left this existence. Though Singapore is a small country, it would have been highly unlikely that a farm girl could have crossed paths with a rich city boy, much less gotten married to him.

"They were match made," Auntie Leng Eng said. "In those days, your grandfather was supposed to be from a very wealthy family. My grandfather was in the rubber business, and he was the eldest in the family—he controlled the business with his brother and cousins. They had factories in Indonesia. Grandfather used to travel to Indonesia all the time. In those days everybody thought, *Oh, Grandfather was very rich, so it was a good match, you know*."

After Tanglin Ah-Ma married, however, the troubles began. Having married into a city family, my *kampong*-raised grandmother was scorned as a *sua deng*, or mountaintop person. "Country folk," Auntie Leng Eng explained. "She didn't have a very good time. Your grandpa's sister—she was quite domineering. And your ah-ma had a lot of hell from her. Your ah-ma had to submit to them and do everything in the house. But she was by nature a very forgiving person. She never bore any grudges, and she got along very well with everybody. She just kept quiet and did whatever she could."

With few resources, my Tanglin ah-ma turned to her cooking to win her new family over. "She had to cook for everybody in the family. So she improved her culinary skills all day," Auntie Leng Eng went on. "She used to grind rice with a millstone to make into flour, you know!"

The main person who adored my Tanglin ah-ma, and who thought her very good for his son, his family, was my great-grandfather, a man I'd heard only glowing reports of since I was a child.

"Yah," I said. "I've heard he was a great man."

Auntie Leng Eng paused, agreeing. But then she said, "he was an opium smoker—almost every day. I watched him. He would have friends who would come to the house. They would spread a mat on the floor, and they had these hard pillows shaped like a loaf of bread and they would be cooking the raw opium. Now, of course, I realize they were cooking opium, but as a young child I didn't know what they were doing. I was just attracted to the fragrance of the opium as they were cooking or puffing."

I was floored. The idea of my straitlaced Auntie Leng Eng as a child getting a contact high from opium fumes was mind-boggling. "There was one period when the government forbade people to smoke opium, but your grandfather was addicted. They then had to boil the raw opium in water in the middle of the night in the bathroom upstairs over a small charcoal stove. If you're awake, you can smell it lah. But they tried to hide the smell by hanging up *koo chye* [Chinese chives]. The smell of opium is almost similar to that."

I was still processing all this information about the model great-grandfather I'd thought I had. I'd been taught to be proud of him for decades. He'd left a tiny, impoverished village near Shantou as a young man, boarding a ship to Singapore in search of his fortune, and ended up building a very successful business, a trading company named Tan Yong Kee that thrived even during World War II. In all the family stories my father had told me—the legacy that he was passing on to me as his own firstborn—it was his father, my grandfather, who had been the shame of the family. My great-grandfather, the paragon. I could feel the cracks of my family racing open into a chasm.

"I was a courier for his opium, you know!" Auntie Leng Eng continued.

"What?" I said.

"Yah, I didn't realize it at the time," she said. "One evening I was asked to go in the car and the driver would bring me somewhere. They told me, 'Oh, you will collect a basket.' So I just dutifully went along and collected a basket. Later on, I realized I was carrying opium for them. My grandfather was arrested once, you know. He had to spend the night in prison for smoking opium. They came to the house to arrest him, and we were all so frightened. This was around the early nineteen fifties. In those days, to get arrested! We were just traumatized. After his arrest the smoking all stopped, but then he had opium deprivation and the illnesses started to come. I remember the day he passed away; it was pneumonia. It was a school day. I was in school, and when I returned home, he was lying on the tabletop in the house. Your uncle Soo Kiat was in primary school. He was so frightened he went to hide under the bed."

An addictive streak, it turned out, would run in the blood of the firstborns of my family. It was my grandfather's addictions that ended up breaking my Tanglin ah-ma's heart. This was a story I'd also heard in bits, told to me as a child by my father, still nursing his bitterness over his failed father. "Your Gong-Gong was a great gambler," Auntie Leng Eng said matter-of-factly. "Wine, women, and song—that's what he was all about."

My grandfather, she said, had a nickname, Ah Sia Kia, which means "rich man's son" or something like "spoiled child." "No sense of responsibility," she said. "My grandfather had a factory that produced some kind of resin. He got my father to work there, but of course, he was not interested in work. He was only interested in spending money. Your grandfather was a very intelligent person, very well educated in both English and Chinese. But he gambled away whatever he had." My father had told me this, remembering that, when he was a child, the family had almost been shipped back to China, so my grandfather could learn something about hardship and hard work. "This was just before 1949," Auntie Leng Eng recalled. "His father felt he wasn't doing anything good for his business, so he wanted to send him back to China and we all had to go back to China with him. I remember we were told to get all these warm flannel clothes."

Then, a stroke of luck: The Communists took over China and my great-grandfather changed his mind. My family remained in Singapore. Had this not happened, I most certainly would have been born in that tiny village in Shantou. I wondered how different my life would have been then. Would I have ended up in New York City? Would I have pursued writing? Would I have had any role in the world of fashion—other than perhaps working in one of the many garment factories that dot the cities of Southern China? It seemed unlikely. I thought back to all the times that I had criticized Chinese Communism in classroom debates or parties.

My family's troubles didn't stop with the thwarted move to China, however. When my great-grandfather died, a few years later, his much younger wife, whom everyone called Cantonese Ah-Ma because she was Cantonese, took over the household, banishing my grandparents and their three children to a single room on the second floor, forcing them to pay rent, and allowing them to use only that room for all cooking, eating, and sleeping. In this little room, my Tanglin ah-ma protected her family the only way she knew how—by taking in the neighbors' laundry for extra money and cooking simple meals. "She would make porridge with a little bit of salted egg and bean curd and some *chye poh* [pickled vegetables]," Auntie Leng Eng said.

What little money my grandmother earned, she was careful to hide from my grandfather, who would leave the house all day, return late at night, and try to pry any cash she might have from her fingers. "Just before every Chinese New Year, I remember, she would start saving up a little bit of money and send me to the pawnshop," Auntie Leng Eng said. "She would ask me to take out a few pieces of the jewelry that she'd pawned so she'd have a few things to wear at the holiday." It broke my heart to hear about my grandmother having had to pawn her precious items to put food on the table for her children, then scrimping and saving in order to borrow back a few pieces of jewelry to have some face at Chinese New Year. She lived in a big house along Emerald Hill, a lovely stretch of row houses in downtown Singapore, after all. As the wife of the firstborn son, she still had to have some pride.

"I used to have to do all this research for my father, you know," Auntie Leng Eng said. "He used to give me these note-books and have me record all the horse-racing statistics of each day. That was my job." It was becoming clear why Auntie Leng Eng pursued a life on the straight and narrow the very first chance she got.

"Did you have *any* fond memories of your childhood at all?" I found myself blurting out.

My auntie Leng Eng pulled out a photo album, pointing to a handful of black-and-white photos, square and small, with the ornately pinked white edges of 1950s photographs. In the pho-tos, my grandfather is in a park with his children—there's Aun-tie Leng Eng, dressed in her Sunday best. My father and Uncle Soo Kiat are small and yet unformed; both boys have pants so formal and high they seem to end just beneath their arms. It is a starched, dressed-up moment—one unlike the many fractured moments that bind their childhood together. And yet everyone is smiling. My auntie Leng Eng is beaming from ear to ear, my father has his "I'm smarter than all of you" smirk, my uncle Soo Kiat looks mischievous.

I felt relieved that at least there were, by some appearances, happy moments.

"There was this one time," Auntie Leng Eng says, "when

my father took us all to the amusement park. We were so excited, you know. It was a family excursion! But when we got to the park, he gave your ah-ma some money and said, Go take the children around the park and meet me back at this park bench at this time, and he went his own way. That evening, we went to the park bench, and we waited and waited and waited. He didn't show up. We were so scared, you know—it was so dark. We didn't know where he was, we didn't know what happened to him. And then finally, your ah-ma said to me, 'Go into that dance hall over there and ask your father to come out.' So I went inside, and he was dancing with this woman. I asked him to come out; I said we were waiting for him. He just said, 'Go, I'll meet you in a while.' So I went back out, and we waited and waited until it was very late. And then finally he came out and we went home together." I thought of my father as a young boy, his siblings with him, his mother, so virtuous and selfless, sitting in the dark on that park bench, waiting for my grandfather, Ah Sia Kia, not knowing when he might emerge from that dance hall. I suddenly understood why I had never seen a photo of myself with my grandfather, who had died the year after I was born. My father would spend decades loathing him. That night, perhaps, had been the beginning.

Auntie Leng Eng grew silent. Our tea had grown cold; twilight was setting in. We'd talked far more than we'd ever talked before. My mind was racing from all it had been absorbing all afternoon. My great-grandfather and my grandfather had both had addictive and selfish personalities. My father himself was prone to some of these tendencies. In fact, he and I, both firstborns, have always been alike in being drawn to risk, making sacrifices in order to live lives on the edge, whether by investing in the stock market or leaving loved ones to cross the world and seek success. As for gambling, I did tend to get weak-kneed around mah-jongg and blackjack tables. As a high schooler, I once arrived at a beach chalet my friends had rented for the week to find a mah-jongg table folded up in a room. We proceeded to play mah-jongg for three days straight, catching only a couple of hours of sleep here and there. By the third day, we were all so ill from staying up all night that we abandoned the chalet and went home. We had not seen the beach even once that whole time. What if this was intrinsically a destructive quality that would end up ruining me?

"It's getting late. I shouldn't bother you anymore," I said, starting to pick up our teacups to bring into the kitchen.

"No need, no need," Auntie Leng Eng said, gesturing for me to stop clearing up. "My maid will take care of it."

As I gathered my belongings, however, Auntie Leng Eng motioned for me to wait. Uncle Paul, her husband, disappeared for a moment, returning with a flat woven basket the size of a large bicycle wheel. "Your ah-ma when she died gave me the millstone that she used to grind rice into flour, but I didn't have room for it, so we gave it away," Auntie Leng Eng said, chagrined. "But this, I kept." Around this basket, my Tanglin ah-ma had gathered her children, and together, they had made *tangyuan*, the glutinous flour dumplings served in a lightly sweetened soup as a dessert or snack on special occasions. Because of its roundness, the dumpling is symbolic of unity of the family. And my grandmother used to have her children sit around the basket. Each would be assigned a section; each had to fill his or her section with the tiny white balls of dough. It was an activity even my father, the firstborn son, was roped in to do. Family is family, after all.

I lay my hand flat on the basket; it was cool to the touch. And I imagined my family. My auntie Leng Eng, my uncle Soo Kiat, and my father, whom I'd always believed had never cooked a moment in his life, gathered around the basket, carefully rolling little white balls, making unity dumplings, bound in a circle.

MY MOTHER'S SIDE OF THE FAMILY WAS GETTING EVER MORE enthusiastic about my quest.

"You *must*," I kept hearing over and over, "learn your ah-ma's *ngoh hiang*!"

As soon as any of my mother's relatives heard about my cooking lessons, anyone who'd ever sampled my maternal grandmother's cooking immediately ordered me to put *ngoh hiang* on the list. The dish, whose name is Hokkien for "five spices or fragrances," is a summer roll that's filled with a mélange of minced shrimp, mushrooms, pork, scallions, and crunchy water chestnuts, and flavored with salt, white pepper, and Chinese five-spice powder. The rolls can be steamed or deep fried—I don't think I need to say which version I prefer. Their origin is Hokkien, the dialect group of my mother's family, which originally came from Xiamen, a now cosmopolitan coastal city in southeastern China, and my maternal grandmother was well known for hers.

As soon as Auntie Alice could gather us together, she and I were back in my grandmother's kitchen with *ngoh hiang* ingredients at hand. I'd loved eating *ngoh hiang* as a child, but by the time I was a teenager, my grandmother had all but stopped cooking, preferring to leave it up to the maids to take care of things in the kitchen. In New York, I've ordered *ngoh hiang* whenever I've seen it on the menu at Simpson's restaurant, where he calls it Malaysian wedding rolls. But it had been more than two decades since I'd had homemade versions. My mouth began to water as I thought of the rolls, crunchy on the outside from a little deep frying of the bean-curd skin wrapper yet soft on the inside and bursting with the complex taste of five spice powder, a combination of star anise, cinnamon, ground fennel seeds, cloves, and pepper that's supposed to give you a flavor bomb of sweet, sour, bitter, and spicy all at once.

Once again, Auntie Alice had requested the presence of Erlinda, my mother's maid, as sous chef. Meekly, we sat by the kitchen counter as we watched my ah-ma direct her to *chop small small! Aiyoh, no! Smaller!* By now, Erlinda knew the drill and was patiently barreling along. The chopping was accomplished fairly quickly and painlessly. When the half cups of scallions and shrimp and two cups of water chestnuts had been minced, Erlinda turned to the half cup of dried Chinese mushrooms, which had been hydrated in water and then drained, chopping those up finely as well. Auntie Alice and I flitted about, gossiping about our relatives. "Has Alvin set a wedding date yet?" I asked. My cousin, her second son, had recently decided to marry the woman he'd been seeing in Dongguan, China. They'd been dating for years, and we'd all been hoping this would happen. "No, but I'm going up there to see them and her parents soon," she said with a hopeful wink.

Once everything was chopped up, the *ngoh hiang* making was a cinch. That morning my mother had gone to the tofu man in our neighborhood wet market—an open-air market where the freshest produce, fish, and meats are sold, an area that is hosed down so often that you can find yourself plodding through puddles as you shop—and purchased several large sheets of dried tofu skin. Under my ah-ma's watchful eye, we had carefully used scissors to cut these starchy sheets into six-by-six-inch squares and gently wrapped the stack of squares in a slightly damp towel to soften the sheets for easy folding. Taking out a large mixing bowl, we listened to Ah-Ma and mixed the minced pork, shrimp, scallions, water chestnuts, and mushrooms together, then added six teaspoons of corn flour and two teaspoons each of five-spice powder, white pepper, and salt.

The mixture looked good—it smelled great, too. Auntie Alice and I looked at each other, wondering how we would *agak-agak* this one to figure out whether it needed anything more. Ah-Ma pushed us aside to get at the bowl. I could practically see her thinking, *Novices!* Grabbing the mixing bowl, she pressed a finger to the meat and shrimp mixture, then stuck her finger into her mouth, tasting it. "Aiyoh, Mummy ah—cannot like that lah!" Auntie Alice cried out. "It's raw meat! You're not supposed to taste raw meat like that!" Ah-Ma just waved her away, instructing me to do the same. The way I saw it, I had a choice: Face *E. coli* or face my grandmother's wrath. The decision was pretty clear. Gingerly, I pressed my own finger to the meat, then licked it. I couldn't really taste anything. But I sure as hell wasn't going to tell my grandmother that and risk having to try again. "*Mmm,* it tastes good," I said, smiling way too broadly. Auntie Alice winced, then leaned over and whispered, "Well, you can always just wash your mouth out, in case there's bacteria."

Now that the mixture was perfect—going by Ah-Ma's *E. coli*–inducing test and my unsubtle fakery—we were ready to start wrapping. Ah-Ma took a slightly softened square, placed about five tablespoons of the meat-shrimp mixture on it, forming a five-inch log, carefully folded the delicate skin over the log, rolled it up, and sealed it. Because the skins were just slightly damp, the rolls sealed easily. Then she gestured for an oiled plate to be brought to her and set the roll on it, moving on to the next *ngoh hiang*. Auntie Alice and I joined in, rolling with such immediate ease that my ten-year-old cousin Matthew, who had set aside his homework and been watching us intently, asked, "Can I try one?" This was a little unconventional for a ten-year-old boy in Singapore—cooking barely interested ten-year-old girls—but he'd been watching the hive of activity, the barking, the chopping, the mixing, the rolling, all afternoon now. I could see why he might want in on the action. "Sure," we said, moving aside to make room for him at the counter. The boy, of course, turned out to be a *ngoh hiang* rolling whiz, applying the same focus and care to folding up these summery rolls that he did to creaming his younger brother at yo-yo stunts. "Look at Matthew," my beaming Auntie Alice said to Ah-Ma. "He's so clever!" I couldn't tell who looked prouder, Matthew, my grandmother, myself, Auntie Alice, or Matthew's mother, Auntie Donna. Somehow, this was a moment I'd not envisioned happening. I wondered if we might just have the beginnings of a little Jean-Georges on our hands.

With so many hands at the counter, in no time we had almost twenty rolls on various plates. "You can steam it or fry it," Ah-Ma said. "Or you can steam and then fry it." Since we weren't sure whether we would eat all of them that day, we decided to steam up the lot and fry those that we thought we might eat, preserving the rest for leftovers. We started a wok of water boiling, set a steamer rack on top, and quickly cooked the rolls for about ten minutes, setting about half of them aside while we deep-fried the rest. And my grandmother's *ngoh hiang* were as perfect as I'd remembered—lightly browned and crispy on the outside, with a tasty, crunchy filling on the inside. We sliced a few rolls into pieces and devoured them rapidly, saving a few for dinner.

By the time my kuku, whose home we were in, got back from work, we were almost ready to have dinner. All we were waiting for was the special treat he had ordered.

"You've never tried a Golden Pillow?" he asked incredulously.

I was flummoxed. Many thoughts ran through my head about what *exactly* a Golden Pillow might be—none of which I could share in front of Matthew or his seven-year-old brother, Zachary. I thought for a second. "Well," I finally said, "I guess I haven't!"

Soon enough, the Golden Pillow arrived—two, in fact. Each came in a box; Kuku carefully removed them one by one, placing each in a large bowl. I got my camera ready. The Golden Pillow turned out to be a bun about the size of a soccer ball. Using a pair of scissors, my uncle slowly snipped slits into the top of the bun. Steam instantly hissed out. Once the top of the bun had been cut open so that triangular slivers fanned out from the center like petals on a lotus flower, Kuku got to work on the star of the show—the bulging plastic bag of chicken curry that had been cooked within the bun as it baked. He snipped that open, and curry showered forth. "Eat it while it's hot," he said. We didn't need to be told twice. Grabbing bits of the bun and scooping curry onto our plates, we instantly dug in. The bun was sweet and just slightly spongy, the curry was flavorful and not too spicy.

"You should bring this to New York," Kuku said. "I think it would do well."

Surrounded as I was by my young cousins, my aunties, my kuku, and my grandmother, who loved me dearly, New York couldn't have felt farther away. And yet, there it loomed—the place that I now called home. The place I'd have to return to fairly soon.

Each time I went back to New York, however, I was returning with more and more of my true home. Bits of my family, dishes that I now knew how to make.

So, sure, the Golden Pillow could work in New York. But if not, I had a pretty mean *ngoh hiang* recipe.

A FEW DAYS LATER, ANOTHER "MUST" WAS FULFILLED.

I packed up a few *ngoh hiang* as a gift and met my uncle Ah Tuang, the man who had grown up with my father, regarding him as a brother. I'd not known much about Uncle Ah Tuang except that my Tanglin ah-ma had taken him in and raised him as her own. The family had been telling me, "You must go and see the Emerald Hill house," the town house in downtown

Singapore where my father, my grandfather, and my great-grandfather had lived. They'd been forced to give up the home decades ago when the owner sold it just as the area was being redeveloped into a trendy stretch of bars and restaurants. As astute as my great-grandfather had been in business, he had never had the foresight to buy any property, even this very home, which had been offered to him by the owner. It is a regret that my father and his siblings harbor to this day.

The spacious, two-story town house at 53 Emerald Hill Road was where my family's fortunes rose and fell. It was where my great-grandfather lived as he built his business, where his son would live as he squandered it. It was where my father lived as a young man, gathering up the courage to leave a comfortable teaching job to follow in the footsteps of his grandfather and strike out in the business world. It was where my parents first lived after they married; it likely was where I, my father's first-born, was conceived.

I don't remember much of this house, except that it had a large living room that opened onto a massive, open-air courtyard in the center. This was a handy form of ventilation for colonial-era row houses in Singapore. Uncle Ah Tuang parked as close to the house as he could get, growing increasingly excited as we got closer to the building. Tall, gleaming white, and pristine, the corner house was clearly well kept by a well-to-do family that seemed to have given it a recent paint job. "That window there—that was where the family lived when Cantonese Ah-Ma made everyone move upstairs!" Uncle Ah Tuang said, so excited to be back at the old homestead that he was jabbing at the air. "And here was where the drivers' sheds were," he noted, pointing to the side of the building as we walked around to the front. "Your great-grandfather used to have this big black car, and his driver slept and lived in this small shed on the side. There were several sheds there for drivers of other families. That's where my dad stayed."

Slowly, he explained that his father was a driver for a family in the neighborhood. He never married but wanted to have an heir—so late in life, when he heard of a woman in my Tanglin ah-ma's *kampong* who had gotten pregnant out of wedlock, he generously offered to adopt her child. That child was Uncle Ah Tuang. "My dad was very busy, so he couldn't really take care of me," Uncle Ah Tuang said. "So he asked your ah-ma to take care of me." Naturally, Uncle Ah Tuang became part of our family. In fact, in my grandfather's final years, he became the only person who would listen to his stories.

By the time Uncle Ah Tuang, who is more than twenty years younger than my father, joined the family, my grand-father's selfishness had run its course. He'd given up the gambling, the drinking, and the womanizing. Unfortunately, his family's patience with him had also run its course. "Nobody talked to him," Uncle Ah Tuang said quietly. "I was his only friend—me and this stray cat that he loved. Wah, he really loved that cat, man." Weakened by the vagaries of his youth, my gong-gong spent his waning days sitting on a chair in the living room, smoking cigarette after cigarette. "He had hemorrhoids, so he was only allowed to sit on this one chair," Uncle Ah Tuang said. "He would just sit there all day and talk to me because I was the only one who would listen."

This was the first I'd heard of this. I'd been told only the stories of a loathsome, selfish man with an addictive streak. The weakened, lonely shell he became had never been discussed. Before I could dwell on it for long, however, Uncle Ah Tuang had bounded away, eager to show me more of the neighborhood. "This was where we used to play in the alley," he said. "This was where the Pepper King lived. He was this really rich guy who owned a pepper empire. Or something."

"Uncle Ah Tuang ah," I began, suddenly thinking of a question I'd always wondered about, "my dad always says he and Uncle Soo Kiat were in a gang at Emerald Hill. Is that true?" His eyes widened, and a peal of boyish laughter immediately followed. "No lah, I don't think so," he finally said. "But they were young boys here long before I lived here—so I really don't know." (I made a mental note to ask my older family members when I saw them.)

"Did your dad ever tell you about the *meepok* man?" Uncle Ah Tuang asked. I shook my head. "It was the best *meepok*"—a tagliatelle-like noodle, tossed in a spicy sauce with fish balls, pork, and fish cakes—"in town, and the guy used to go through the neighborhood every day making this *tok-tok* sound. When you heard it, you'd have to run outside and order it. It was so good. I remember one time I was sick at home and your ah-ma bought some for me—*so* good." I'd had a large lunch that day but was feeling hungry all over again. I was starting to see where my obsession with food might have come from.

"You know there used to be a gambling den in the house, right?" Uncle Ah Tuang said at one point. "Your ah-ma used to have her friends over to play *see-sek*," the four-color card game.

"No!" I replied. My Tanglin ah-ma had been so scarred by

my grandfather's gambling, it floored me to think of her actually gambling herself, much less running any sort of pseudo-professional operation, even if it was to make a little money. So, both my grandmothers had gambling dens?

"Yah, and she used to make food for the gamblers—*pua kiao beng*," he said. Gambling rice? I was intrigued.

"What's in it?" I asked.

"It's basically rice that is easy to eat while you're gambling. You fry up cabbage, pork belly, mushrooms, and some other things; then you mix it all together with rice and cook it in a rice cooker," he said. "Very *shiok*," Uncle Ah Tuang added, using the Singapore slang word for "feels good." "You serve it in one bowl so gamblers can hold it in one hand and carry on gambling."

"Is it hard to make?"

"Very easy—even I can make!" he said. "Your auntie Khar Imm can also make. Ask her to teach you lor." *Pua kiao beng* was suddenly top on my list of dishes to learn.

As we rounded another corner, I finally asked the question I'd had on my mind. Uncle Ah Tuang had lived in my family home when my mother married into the Tans and moved in. I'd always wondered what happened between my mother and grandfather—had she really slapped him? Had that, perhaps, been the beginning of the end of my parents' marriage?

"Why did my parents move out of the house?" I asked. "Were they all really not getting along?" Uncle Ah Tuang, ever the peacemaker, ever the sprightly, jocular younger brother, paused for a moment. "Well . . . there was one really loud argument," he said. "But I didn't really hear what they were saying, and I didn't know what was going on.

"Anyway," he finally added. "It was so long ago."

And he was right—it was a long time ago. The events back then had already shaped us into the people we'd become. And it all had led somehow to this moment on a Saturday, me and my uncle Ah Tuang circling the old neighborhood with the tropical afternoon sun beating down mercilessly, thinking about the Pepper King and the old *meepok* man while mincing over the footsteps of ghosts.

Back at home, I was inspired to try to cook some of these recipes I'd been learning. My mother had bought a duck, and so I set about making soup. My Tanglin ah-ma's soup, by way of Auntie Khar Imm, that is. With my notebook by the stove, I slowly went through the steps—chopping up the salted cabbage, preparing the duck, tossing the ingredients in, and then leaving the concoction alone to "boil, boil, boil!"

Taking my first sips after the boiling was done, I thought, *Damn, this is not bad at all*. I packed the rest up in a thermos and dropped it off at Uncle Soo Kiat's office the next day. "For Auntie Khar Imm to try," I said. "See whether I pass or not."

The next day, the verdict came. "Not too bad," my cousin Jessie texted on behalf of her mum. "Just that not saltish."

Not quite the reaction I'd hoped for. But it didn't sound like a fail.

CHAPTER FIFTEEN

The first few times my family met Mike, they were perfectly polite.

Yes, he was a little older—our age difference spans fourteen years—and he was American, not some *guai* (Mandarin for "obedient") Singaporean boy that they'd always hoped I'd end up marrying. But he was half Asian—Korean, to be specific— and that, in the end, did count for something.

And so they were perfectly accepting as we fell in love, got engaged, and began planning a wedding . . . until one day my father happened to be in Honolulu for business and suggested meeting Mike's mother, who lives there. At the appointed cocktail hour, they met—my father and my future mother-in-law, Ai-Kyung Linster, a spunky, opinionated woman who unabashedly speaks her mind, often chasing a particularly feisty comment with "Korean women—we are all stubborn, you know!"

Though they were meeting for the first time without either of us there, drinks were going swimmingly. And then Mike's mother decided to test the few Chinese phrases she knew on my dad, who was suitably impressed.

"How do you know Mandarin?" he asked.

"I lived in Shanghai when I was a kid," she replied. "My grandfather was Chinese, you know."

This, suddenly, changed *everything*.

My dad immediately called my mother, barely able to contain himself. "Mike's *Chinese!*" he said. And as soon as my mother could get off the phone with my dad, she called me, bellowing into the phone, "*Why* didn't you tell us Mike's Chinese?"

"Um," I responded, "because he's only one-eighth Chinese? Why does that matter?"

But of course, to my parents, who had hoped for the tiniest thread of kinship with the person who was marrying their first-born, this mattered tremendously. And that was the moment Mike truly became a part of my family.

Mike's mother understood this perfectly as well. She had been thrilled from the moment we met, seeing as how I was Asian, not *haole,* as the Hawaiians call Caucasians. And her acceptance was instantaneous. As we sat in her Honolulu living room shortly after we had gotten engaged, one of her first questions wasn't about wedding planning or how work was going. Instead, she got right to the point: "When are you having a baby?" (I considered asking if it might be possible for her to let us get married first but thought better of it.)

It had been a few years since I'd seen her, Honolulu being something of a trek from New York City. So, leaving Singapore after about a month of cooking, I flew to Honolulu to meet Mike for a visit with his mother. Before I got there, he had told her about my cooking lessons in Singapore; by the time I landed, she was eager to corral me in her kitchen.

Although Ai-Kyung had emigrated to the United States from South Korea, just outside Seoul, she had spent several years in Shanghai as a girl when her parents worked for the Japanese Army's medical units there. As World War II ended, the family went back to Korea. There, years later, she met a handsome, tall Iowa engineer who was building power plants in the country. The relationship ended up not working out, but from that union, Mike was born and brought back to Iowa. Ai-Kyung stayed on in Korea, moving to Honolulu a decade later when she married another American.

Whenever we saw her in Honolulu, we were treated like royalty. After having spent so many years away from Mike—they reunited only when he was in his twenties—she treasured every minute with him, the son she had watched grow up only in pictures his father had taken care to send to her every year around his birthday. As a result, even though I'd been in Ai-Kyung's breezy apartment, which overlooks the famous Ala Moana shopping mall and the slender Ala Wai canal that outlines Waikiki, dozens of times before this trip, I'd always felt like a visitor in her home. Mike and I would perch on the best seats of the sofa—the ones with the fluffiest cushions, the best view of the television; Ai-Kyung simply wouldn't let us have any others. Never would she let me clear plates off the table, help in the kitchen, or clean a single dish. "Charlie will do it," she would say, waving to Mike's half brother, who lived with her, gesturing for him to take care of it later on. And always, the cooking would already be done by the time we got there—she rarely got to see us, after all. And she probably didn't think we wanted to waste any time watching her cook when there were picturesque beaches to be explored, tans to be worked on, sandy naps to be taken.

All this changed the moment she found out that I was learning to cook.

"Cheryl!" she cried when I walked in, grabbing me with her thin, strong hands, holding me to her in a firm, long hug. "You looking good! How are your parents?"

"They're good!"

"Your sister? Not married yet?"

"No, no. Still single."

There was a grimace. I could almost see her thinking, *Kids these days, I tell you.*

"Mike says you learning how to cook? I bought some stuff to teach you," she said, starting toward the kitchen. Clearly, I was to follow.

There was nothing bubbling on the stove this time, no smells of spicy Korean stews or Mike's favorite—steak—to signal that dinner was on the cusp of being served. Instead, carefully arranged on the counter were various ingredients: shredded chicken, garlic cloves, large, bunched-up sheets of dried, black-green seaweed.

"Seaweed soup," she said, holding up the crinkly sheets and waving them at me. "Korean recipe—good for women to clean the . . . *you know,*" she added, dropping her voice a few levels while pointing to her nether regions. "Good for making more milk after you have baby."

I could see where this was going.

Before I could protest, Ai-Kyung was off and running. "You take three pounds of chicken—whole chicken—then you boil it in a big pot of water," she said, holding up the bowl of chicken she'd prepped before we arrived. "Then you take the chicken out, drain the soup with a sieve, and you keep the water in the pot." The chicken, by this point, had been shredded coarsely. The seaweed had been soaked in cold water to just the right softness and then cut into small pieces. "Don't soak too long," Ai-Kyung cautioned. "Just twenty to thirty minutes. You want it a bit crunchy, not mushy." After soaking, "you massage the seaweed with your hand and rinse a couple times," she said. Then she tossed four cloves of bashed garlic into the pot of reserved broth, brought it to a boil, and turned down the heat to let it simmer, adding a scant teaspoon of Hawaiian sea salt and one to two tablespoons of soy sauce. "You put one in first," she said, pausing and raising her index finger to get my attention, "then you taste and see if you want more." After that, she let the broth simmer for thirty to forty minutes, added the shredded chicken, seaweed, and a dash of sesame oil, and suddenly we had a simple, clear soup that tasted clean and comforting at the same time.

"Good for ladies," Ai-Kyung said, as she watched me slurp up her soup, which was truly delicious. "After I gave birth to Mike, I had to take it every day. Make a *lotta* milk."

While the very well-intentioned milk-making soup was perfectly lovely, there were other Korean recipes I had my eye on. Whenever Mike craved Korean food, he wanted two things: *kalbi*, grilled beef short ribs, and *mandoo*, pork and cabbage dumplings. Specifically, he wanted *his mother's kalbi* and *mandoo*. The one time I'd tried to make *kalbi* at home in Brooklyn— with a recipe from the James Beard Award–winning Korean

American chef David Chang of Momofuku fame, no less—
Mike thought it was nice and all. But it just wasn't his mother's
kalbi.

Ai-Kyung, of course, was thrilled to hear this. "It's so easy!"
she said, laughing and turning away. I could tell she was touched
to hear that Mike missed her food.

Naturally, the next afternoon when we arrived, there was a
mound of beef short ribs on the counter. Working quickly once
again, Ai-Kyung started on the marinade, mixing half a cup
plus one tablespoon of sugar with one cup of water, three-
quarters of a cup of soy sauce, two tablespoons of sesame oil—
pausing for a moment to sniff at the bottle and say, "I hope this
is sesame oil!" before laughing and moving on—one tablespoon of minced garlic, and one teaspoon of coarse sea salt.
"Some people use mashed papaya or kiwi—makes it tender,"
she stopped to say. "But I don't like the papaya flavor. If you're
using papaya, though, mash it up before adding it in." Many
kalbi recipes call for apple juice as a tenderizing agent. Ai-
Kyung, however, had a secret alternative. "I like guava juice,"
she said, pouring half a cup into the marinade. Once she'd
mixed in three coarsely chopped scallion stalks—"Green parts,
too!"—and a one-inch piece of ginger, peeled and thinly sliced,
the marinade was ready to go. "Put it in the fridge for seven
hours or overnight," she said, squinting at the clock and realiz-
ing that this meant we wouldn't be able to eat until 10:00 P.M.
"Or at least three to four hours is fine."

Once that was done, she started on the *mandoo,* chopping
up two cups of cabbage, sprinkling sea salt on it, and letting it
sit for an hour or so. Then she mixed together minced chives,

green onions, minced pork, ground beef, sesame oil, soy sauce, salt, ground ginger, and a beaten egg. Ai-Kyung drained the cabbage, squeezing it dry with her hands, and added it to the mixture. Then, as Mike, Charlie, and Al, Ai-Kyung's husband, sat down to watch TV, she and I took the bowl of *mandoo* filling and sat on her veranda, which had a lovely fifteenth-floor view of Honolulu and the glimmer of sparkling blue just beyond the hotel skyline along Waikiki Beach.

Ai-Kyung took a round dumpling wrapper, showing me the package so I'd remember what kind to buy. *Mandoo* wrappers are typically a little thicker than Chinese dumpling wrappers, but Ai-Kyung prefers thinner skins on her *mandoo,* so she buys the Chinese versions. Holding a wrapper in her left hand, she dipped the tip of her right pinkie finger into a small bowl of water and ran it along the edge of the wrapper, wetting it. Then she scooped one tablespoon or so of filling into the center, folded the dumpling over, and sealed it with four tiny pleats. That was all it took. She placed the dumpling in a tray.

"I learned how to make these in Shanghai, you know," she said. "I was twelve or thirteen years old, and I saw my grandmother making them with the Chinese housemaid, so I sat down and learned. She used to make the skins herself. The centers should be thicker than the edges because when you fold it over you're going to have that heavy double layer on the edge if you have a very thick dough. We used to use a beer bottle to roll out the skins for making *mandoo.*" Because she learned to make *mandoo* in China, the versions Ai-Kyung makes are more Chinese than Korean. "I made it with tofu one time, Korean style," she said, wrinkling her nose. "I didn't like it."

Having learned how to fold dumplings from Auntie Khar Imm, I wasn't a complete dud at folding *mandoo*—which, I could tell from her slight smile, Ai-Kyung was pleased to note. With four hands and gradually growling stomachs, the filling disappeared quickly, and soon Ai-Kyung and I had more than a hundred *mandoo* carefully lined up in a series of tiny trays.

Ai-Kyung brought a pot of water with some salt to boil, tossed in a handful of *mandoo*, put the lid on, and brought the water to a boil again. When it was boiling, she added one cup of cold water, brought it back to a boil, and repeated. "When you've done it twice, the *mandoo* is ready," she said, mixing together soy sauce, apple cider vinegar, and black pepper for a dipping sauce while the *mandoo* was boiling. Removing the *kalbi* from the marinade, she sautéed it in a pan for three to four minutes per side and then set that on the dining table, too.

And suddenly, we were all eating—the very first home-cooked Korean meal that I'd actually helped to make. As his mother closely watched, Mike ate more than a dozen *mandoo* and half the plate of *kalbi*, all by himself. The next day, we were to return home, a fact that always saddened Ai-Kyung, I knew. But this visit, it had been different. We had made dinner together; together, we had fed her son, the man we both loved.

As we hugged our good-byes, I thanked Ai-Kyung for taking the time to teach me. "Oh, it's no big deal!" she said, wincing and pooh-poohing the thanks. But just as we were about to leave, she ran into the kitchen and emerged with a parting gift. It was a little plastic bag; in it was a bunch of dried Korean seaweed.

"So you know what it looks like," she said, winking, "how to find it in New York."

BACK IN NEW YORK, IT WAS NOVEMBER AND THE HOLIDAY season was getting under way.

Spending so much time in Singapore was beginning to take its toll on my social life in New York.

"Tan," Jesse, one of my dearest friends said, "we never see you anymore."

"Aiyah, you too busy for us now lah," Simpson complained. "Flying all over the world, too important lah."

Immediately, I set about trying to make things right. First things first. There was Thanksgiving, my favorite Western holiday. What's not to love about a festival that's all about getting together to eat? Having spent months in Asia, I wanted to include Asian elements in the menu—adding miso-rubbed turkey and persimmon-cranberry sauce to the lineup. In addition to cooking like a madwoman in the four days leading up to Thanksgiving, I flung myself into baking panettone bread to share with my friends.

This, however, turned out not to be the wisest of ideas.

This bread, it will drive you insane, make you tear your hair out. You may find yourself staring intently at an unrising bowl of taupe glop, thinking, *Just why, God, WHY?* I mean this for the folks out there attempting to bake it, that is. (If you're the sort who *buys* panettone in a store, then sure, go for it. I'm certain that's pretty harmless.)

I wasn't envisioning this at the time, of course—just the warm, glowing feeling I would get as I presented my friends with my festive, homemade holiday panettone. And so, with Ella Fitzgerald's "Christmas Song" burbling in my head, I merrily set about buying the ingredients—rye flour, pineapple juice, and bits of dried mangoes, cranberries, and pears. When I sat down to look at the recipe, I knew I was in trouble. This bread requires a starter that takes *five days* to make. And when that's done? The dough takes two more days.

A seven-day bread? But my holiday spirit was unflagging. And so, the baking began.

First, I started by making a seed culture—a mix of rye flour and pineapple juice, left to ferment and rise slowly at room temperature. Every day, I dutifully fed it a little by adding flour and pineapple juice or water and then just let it sit and watched it grow. This was happening so painfully slowly that I began to understand how it might feel to watch grass grow. Except that grass would be nowhere near as noxious. This recipe actually states at one point: "Do not be put off by the strong aroma of the dough." (Another favorite bit: "Try not to breathe as [the gas] escapes—the carbonic gas mixed with ethanol fumes will knock you across the room!")

After five days of this, however (with a very patient Mike politely ignoring the fumes and bowls of bizarre goo), the starter was ready to go. I mixed up a sponge using the starter, milk, and flour, and let that ferment overnight. Then I chopped up raisins, dried mango, papaya, cranberries, and pears; mixed those with orange and vanilla extracts and brandy; and let that sit out overnight. Now, traditional panettone calls for dried cherries, raisins, and apricots. Having never made panettone before, I, of course, decided to put my own tropical spin on it. What an unforgettable holiday gift that would be!

The next day everything got mixed together with more flour, sugar, yeast, and almonds, forming an incredibly liquid dough that just would not rise. After hours upon hours of staring at it and hoping for some action, I finally scooped some into muffin tins to make mini-panettoni and the rest into a large, round tin to make a cake-size version. Into the oven that went, and the moment it came out, I realized that my dreams of a lovely holiday gift to make up for ignoring—or igvoiding, as my sister might say—my friends were not to be.

How did it taste? Dry. Mealy. Sort of like "Big Waste of Time" encapsulated in a loaf.

I can think of a thousand things I probably did wrong. I should have used more flavorful fruits, such as dried cherries, instead of attempting my tropical take on panettone with mangoes and papayas. Perhaps my water was the wrong temperature. Maybe my apartment's aggressively tropical heating system ruined the dough. Whatever it was, I probably will never find out. (I'd decided then and there not to attempt panettone again.)

My friends politely nibbled at the bread when I set it out at Thanksgiving. (Perhaps their opinions had been slightly colored by the lengthy complaints and display of self-flogging I'd indulged in over the panettone the moment they sat down at the dinner table.)

Still, I felt like I wasn't connecting enough with my dear friends. The months I'd spent making Southeast Asian dishes meant it had been months since I'd cooked with Simpson, my

original teacher. I missed our time together in the kitchen—
even if it was just me watching his moves at the stove, picking
up tidbits.

A few weeks later, I was sipping a glass of sauvignon blanc
at Jesse's annual holiday party in Brooklyn, taking in the sight
of his bright Christmas tree with the stuffed panda perched at its
top and thinking about the time I'd spent away from my friends.
They respected my quest; they'd been nothing but supportive.
But they also missed me, and I missed them. I was reconnecting with my family, my friends in Singapore, but lives were
trundling along without me in New York. New girlfriends were
popping up, old jobs were being shed. Watching the party swirl
about me, I couldn't help but feel a disconnect.

Just then, my cell phone rang; it was Simpson. "I have two
pounds of foie gras in the car and some bread," he said. "Should
I bring it up?" The answer to a question like that, of course,
is *yes*, oh, yes.

Within minutes, Simpson was hauling up slabs of foie gras
and clearing a spot near Jesse's stove, inspecting his condiments
and pans before grabbing a skillet that he dèemed acceptable.
As I watched, Simpson drizzled a little olive oil on the pan and
swiftly sautéed the chunks of foie gras, turning them over and
over until they were suitably browned. Then he lay the foie gras
on a cutting board, slicing them into small strips, and placed
those onto little bits of crusty bread with a slight drizzling of
balsamic vinaigrette. A crowd started gathering. Jesse's spread
of cookies, pizza, cheese, and pulled-pork sliders had been delicious, to be sure. But here was a simple yet decadent dish that

had definitively taken his party up several notches, a snack that Simpson had just slapped together in minutes.

"This is amazing!" I said, scarfing down several foie gras toasts as I thought about just how much I'd missed Simpson's little treats, how much I'd missed watching him cook.

"Aiyah, it's nothing lah," he said. "So easy!"

Just days later, I would head back to Asia. And I realized how much I would miss him again.

"Soon," I promised, "I'll be done. Soon, we'll cook again."

CHAPTER SIXTEEN

The first sign that I might not fit in, I should have known, was the jellied sea worms.

We had just arrived in Xiamen to learn a bit more about ourselves and the part of China where our ancestors had lived. And after having traveled to this neon city in southeastern China filled with old Euro-Chinese hotels and sleazy expat bars in October 2008, my father, sister, Mike, and I felt somewhat invincible, ready to take on just about anything. We were in a restaurant that our host, a family friend who lived there, had proclaimed one of the best in the city. Xiamen was our oyster—or, as it turned out, our sea worm.

A waitress emerged with a plate, filled in the center with a pile of dark, chopped-up jelly, and plopped it onto the bright pink tablecloth, an ominous dark spot in a sea of Barbie effervescence. We looked at one another, not quite daring to ask. "They're sea worms—they live in the mud at the bottom of the ocean!" our host said cheerily, looking disappointed when we clearly did not recognize our cue to grab our chopsticks and dive in. "Come, come, you can*not* say you've been to Xiamen until you've eaten this dish." And so we did. Gingerly picking up a cube of jelly with chopsticks and trying not to think too hard about what I was about to put in my mouth, I closed my eyes and focused on the texture: slippery and slimy, yes. But it didn't taste like much more than a salty Jell-O, so it could've been worse. Except . . . Oh, wait. There was an odd rubbery bit—something like squid or octopus except that the fleshy substance produced an audible crunchy squish of a sound when you bit down and chewed. I smiled and politely crunch-squished for a few seconds before grabbing at a beer to wash it all down quickly. By the time we got back to the hotel, Daphne was covered in hives.

My maternal grandfather may have come from Xiamen decades ago, but it clearly wasn't home for us. Not anymore, anyway.

On this trip, the four of us had journeyed to southeastern China after years of talking about it. Flying in from New York, Hong Kong, and Beijing, we'd converged first in Shantou to find the village my great-grandfather had come from. The trip had been surreal—Shantou was an industrial city with a population of several million. The air was gritty. Cars and motorbikes paid little attention to stoplights and general cues to drive in the correct direction; we were horrified to learn that cars driving horizontally into busy traffic across a several-lane road were regular and accepted occurrences. The general lawlessness was disconcerting. And the Shantou portion of the trip had been capped with a harrowing, hours-long car ride to the tiny village we had been told was the right one, only to spend an hour in the dusty clan headquarters just off the village square, poring over its book of names without finding my great-grandfather's among them.

Flying out of Xiamen a few days later, I vowed to return. I promised to find my great-grandfather's village.

When I started cooking with them, Auntie Khar Imm and her sisters had offered some help, pointing me in the direction of the Tan clan association in Singapore that had organized my Tanglin ah-ma's funeral. "They'll know which is the right place," she had told me. And when I'd visited the association headquarters, barging into the tidy row house near Singapore's Chinatown that it occupied, ablaze with questions about my ancestral village, the gaggle of men playing mah-jongg and smoking cigarettes had looked bemused. "Women can join also," Michael, the president, noted in between puffs when he saw me looking around, wondering if I was actually allowed in the building. Even so, I thought it was a pretty clear signal.

Clan members would make their annual trip to the ancestral village in December 2009, Michael had noted. Would I like to come?

My father was slightly reluctant the second time. We'd been to the area, we'd tried to find the village. What could we gain from trying once more? In his early sixties, my father was slowly wrapping up his affairs at the moving company he now owned, preparing it for sale. Between entertaining potential buyers and going over the assets of the company, he was especially busy. Did we really need to be making this trip? "But, Daddo," I said. "We've been talking about going to Gong-Gong's village together since I was young! We have to do this."

With that, my father and I booked tickets and found ourselves hugging our hellos in the Shantou airport, nervous with anticipation. Michael had invited us to dinner with some villagers that first night, but my dad and I were too hungry to wait. The moment we checked into our hotel in the afternoon, we began craving *meepok*, the noodles tossed with bits of crunchy fried pork lard in a chili-soy–black vinegar sauce and topped with fish balls, fish cakes, and bits of minced or sliced pork, that Uncle Ah Tuang had mentioned. It's a simple dish made by the Teochews that we'd eat for breakfast in Singapore every day if we could. (More important, if our bodies could handle it.)

The noodles are not hard to find in Shantou, as you can imagine. Just half a block from our hotel, the Golden Gulf, we stumbled upon a promising display of fish balls in a refrigerated glass case on the sidewalk. When we peeked in the storefront, we spotted another promising sign: a massive banner that proclaimed its fish balls and noodles a "famous snack for long history in China." Now I'm not one for hyperbole, but I do admire chutzpah.

So Dad and I sat down for an afternoon snack, and the dishes began arriving. First, there was an assortment of fish balls that we'd picked out in the display case. They generally tasted the same—which was to say they were all good—mainly varying in degrees of springiness and density. (I preferred the lighter, springier ones.) We also had a few lovely fish "dumplings," in which the dumpling wrapper was made out of minced fish pounded with flour and then rolled flat. These were cut into squares, filled with scallions or minced pork, rolled up, and boiled—just delicious. Next up, we had regular dumplings filled with minced pork and chives and topped with a vinegar-pepper sauce that was slightly peanutty. And, of course, there was *meepok*.

Now, this version tasted very different from the *meepok* you'll find in Singapore. Instead of a salty, vinegary sauce, this was tossed in a peppery, peanut-based gravy that was similar to satay dipping sauces. Not that we were complaining—the noodles were tasty and very comforting. The perfect panacea for a rather long flight. As the eating wound down and we gauchely licked our spoons and chopsticks, I thought about the days ahead. We would travel to my ancestral village, take part in a ceremony commemorating the first Tans from centuries ago. We would meet our very distant cousins. We would be going home.

We paid our bill and wandered into the gray Shantou street. Outside, we flagged a cab. We were to meet Michael and the villagers in a restaurant near the village.

Our first meal with the villagers would be like all our other meals—filled with men. And me. We entered the private dining room of the restaurant to find ourselves penetrating a plume of cigarette smoke. Michael introduced us as fellow Tans—family—from Singapore and New York. I leapt into action, firmly shaking everyone's hand and telling them my name in Mandarin, Rulian. The village chief was there, a stout, comfortable-looking man who appeared to be in his sixties but had a full head of hair that looked dyed to unnatural blackness and the belly of someone who did not want for much. He gestured for us to take a seat at the dinner table. I headed straight for the chair in a corner at the farthest end, thinking nothing of it. The meal was a several-courser—fried tofu, fish, a heaping plate of noodles. We'd brought bottles of wine as a gift for the village head, so we shared several toasts. I was surprised they'd poured me a glass, too, and merrily drank along, clinking glasses with my new uncles.

They spoke Mandarin, yes, but were most comfortable with Teochew, a dialect I barely understood. By the end of dinner, however, I felt I was starting to get the hang of it. As we stood around outside the restaurant, the men embroiled in deep conversation, I nodded, listened, and smiled along.

"Do you know what they're saying?" my dad asked, looking amused.

"They're talking about the dinner tonight, right?"

"No lah! They're talking about what we're going to do tomorrow!"

I was suddenly glad I hadn't tried to say anything—not that I really would have known what to say in Teochew. (In fact, my Mandarin, which I rarely speak in New York or Singapore, wasn't functioning very well either. Shortly after, when I wanted to borrow a pen to write something down, it was fortunate that I thought to check with Dad about the wording. I had been about to ask the village chief if I could borrow his *bizi*, or "nose," instead of a *bi*.)

Just when I was starting to feel a little morose about the days ahead, however, one of the villagers asked, "Have you heard of this phrase, '*Teochew nang, paxi bo xiang gang*'?" Now, I'd heard one saying regarding *Teochew nang*, which means "Teochew people," and it was *Teochew nang, kacherng ang ang*. It's a popular saying in Singapore—a school yard taunt at times—that basically means "Teochew people have red backsides." I wondered if this saying was popular in China as well.

I wondered if I should ask. But I decided it might not be the best question on the very first night.

"No," I said instead. "What does it mean?"

"It basically means that Teochew people, you beat them until they're close to death but they'll still survive," he said. "We're strong."

I liked that—perhaps not as much as my red-behind saying, but I felt I was learning something about my people, about me.

In the car ride back to our hotel in Chaozhou, a picturesque historic city on the water, our driver said, "You see this car in the front? No license plate also can still drive." It was true; among the cars madly zigzagging across the intersection, this one had absolutely no identification. "Here," he said, proudly, "anything can happen. You want to do something, you can just do it."

I was beginning to like the sound of my people. It was starting to explain some things about my family and, perhaps, me. Shortly after, our driver slowed to a crawl. In the dusty blackness, I saw that a lorry had halted just before us. Not wanting to wait for the crowd to clear, the driver swung his steering wheel and darted around the lorry. As we slowly passed, we saw a flash of bright red and understood what had happened. The lorry had struck a girl in a red parka. Two young men had run onto the road—one grabbed her hands, one, her feet. Together, they were hoisting the wide-eyed, terrified girl like a limp doll as they hurried back to the side of the road. Our car barely missed hitting them.

Before we had gone to China, we had been warned about the "gifts" we'd likely have to give. Both my grandmothers had made pilgrimages to their ancestral villages before, and both had come back with little more than the clothes on their backs; once a reasonably well-off overseas Chinese person goes back to visit less well-off relatives, the pressure to shower them with money and gifts like refrigerators and microwave ovens is intense. So my father and I were prepared when Michael took us aside and said, "You should give something—nothing big, just a token." We should give a small cash donation to the village chief, he said—"the amount, up to you"—as well as a few cartons of cigarettes. And he knew just the place to buy them—the little tea and cigarette store the village chief owned.

My father and I looked at each other; we had expected this. And a small donation and a few cartons of cigarettes seemed appropriate.

The next morning, the chief's son came to the hotel to give us a ride into the village. On the way there, Michael filled us in on our people. "Sanitary ware is the big business here," he said, pointing to giant billboards that advertised bathtubs and toilet bowls.

"Our people are famous for making toilet bowls?" I whispered to my dad. "Eew."

He stared straight ahead, trying not to laugh. "Well, it's a good business, you know," he whispered back. "Everybody has to shit."

It was hard to ignore the poverty that was all around us, however. Streets were in dismal condition, filled with potholes, and all along these streets were buildings that had been half constructed and then abandoned. Toilet bowls didn't seem to be creating a real business boom for our people.

After about forty minutes of lurching through traffic, just

after we passed a gaggle of women squatting in a canal by the side of the large main road, ankle deep in water as they scrubbed away at clothing, we pulled up to a familiar tiny road, a narrow sliver that would wend its way to the heart of my ancestral village. My dad and I looked at each other—we had been here before. This was the exact same village we'd come to the year before. We had been right all along!

This time, however, we had an English-speaking guide whom the villagers had found to help us. "My name is Fiona," this young woman said tentatively. "Hello, I am Rulian," I volunteered. "I can speak Mandarin." She looked a little relieved.

The next day the village would hold its annual celebration to honor its ancestors—the reason Michael and other clan members from Singapore were in town. As the chief and the elders got down to the business of planning the festivities, Fiona, my dad, and I set about exploring the town.

"Do you know much Teochew?" Fiona asked. I confessed that I didn't.

"Well," she added, "the Teochew that's spoken in your village is known as a particular kind of Teochew. It's very soft and tender. People say it's like listening to lovers' whispers."

I thought back to the Teochew I'd grown up learning. I knew how to wish my parents happy new year, and I knew how to swear. Neither of these sounded remotely like lovers' whispers to me. I decided I would try to speak as little Teochew as possible while I was there.

Lovers' whispers or not, the village scene was heartbreaking. Dirt and trash cluttered the streets. Too-skinny chickens scratched and pecked at invisible bits of food in thick layers of dirt and mud. Several generations of families crammed into one or two tiny rooms, with the women holding tubs and squatting over drains to wash vegetables or fish for dinner. Within minutes, we found the village market; the vegetable aunties lay wan produce on plastic sheets on the dirt, sitting on stools and propping their bare feet up right next to their greens. Butchers and fishmongers set out their meats on wooden tables; flies descended on everything. The local candy merchant had a prominent display of "Kemt" and "Marlbovo" brand cigarette-shaped sticks of chewing gum.

Soon enough, it was time for lunch. Back into the village chief's car we got. I found myself suddenly resentful of his relative wealth. (And girth.) And our meal turned out to be another several-courser featuring pricey soups, fish, and seafood in a private room on the outskirts of town. We piled into a restaurant's private room, exhausted after a long morning walking around the dusty village. The village head gestured to us to seat ourselves. I started toward a chair in a corner, a seat I usually prefer, when my father pulled me aside.

"You know," he whispered, "in China, the most senior person at the meal sits facing the door."

Now, in all the meals we'd had thus far in China—two of which the village head himself had attended—that prime seat had been the one I'd taken. In fact, it was the one I had been making a beeline for before my father saved me.

Shamed, I vowed instantly to be more sensitive, more subservient, as an obedient Chinese daughter should be—for the remainder of the trip, anyway.

When a platter of salmon sashimi hit the table, I was a little surprised. We were, after all, in a restaurant that served traditional Teochew food.

I picked up my chopsticks, snagged a slice, dipped it in soy sauce, and lifted it to my mouth. That's when I noticed everyone around me averting their eyes as they picked up pieces of salmon; piled on slivers of fresh garlic, ginger, and chili; and carefully dunked the mounds into a bowl of soybean dip.

I was beginning to feel that I wasn't quite fitting in. Earlier that day, in fact, Michael had taken me aside. "Today ah," he said, "you must call everyone Ah-Chek or Lau-Chek, okay?"

Uncle and senior uncle, of course. I was chagrined that I'd forgotten such basic niceties. It turned out I also needed to tame the outgoing journalist in me, fade into the background a little, and let my father be the first to shake everyone's hand.

Also at lunch that day, a bottle of whiskey was opened and shared. Even Fiona and I were offered small amounts. There was much laughter, storytelling, and many, many toasts.

I thought things were going well. I raised my glass several times, merrily clinking it with my ah-cheks and lau-cheks. Once again, however, my father whispered to me. "When you toast someone older than you, your glass needs to be lower than his as a sign of respect." Of course, in the many toasts I'd shared, this had not been the case.

I dejectedly began to wonder what they must think of this unruly, Americanized female. I also questioned whether I had any real connection with this place that had been my ancestors' home.

Just then, however, the conversation steered toward Barack Obama. As the chatter took a slightly negative turn, someone stopped, gesturing toward me and shushing the others because they might be offending the New York girl.

Immediately, however, one of the ah-cheks piped up. "I know she's American, but she still has black hair!" he said in Teochew. "She is still Chinese."

JUST HOW CHINESE I WAS WOULD BE CHALLENGED THE next day.

The village was a hive of activity the moment we arrived, once again in the chief's plush car. The clan association's great hall had been dressed up for the ceremony for our ancestors. Two massive lambs had been slaughtered, skinned, and were splayed on high benches near a massive altar bearing tablets noting our ancestors' names. On top of each lamb was a large, skinned pig, splayed as if caught in a bizarre sex act. Flies were all around. I started to feel ill.

We were a curiosity, hailing from faraway Singapore—but I was the far bigger curiosity for many of the villagers. I was a woman, yet I was being shown some modicum of the respect that my father and other men were. I had traveled from afar, after all. And, while they weren't exactly sure what I did, they knew I did something professional in glitzy New York. I shrugged off the questioning looks and decided just to act as if I belonged.

Michael took my father aside for a short conversation and my dad returned looking grim. "The donation now is a 'suggested amount' of at least 1,000 yuan," he said. The figure was about 150 U.S. dollars—certainly far more than any amount that we would have considered a mere "token." "What should we do?" I asked, feeling terrible, as this whole trip had been my idea. "No choice," my father said, shrugging. "We just have to pay." This "family" that we were seeking out and reconnecting with suddenly seemed like a bad idea to have in our lives.

Just then, however, the festivities started up.

Villagers packed into the great hall, women largely in the back or standing by the side, reserving the front rows for the men. The elders took turns kneeling on the ground, reading words off large sheets of thin pink paper. "They're calling to our ancestors, asking them to join us," my dad whispered. Just then, we both noticed a tall, skinny man at the center of the activity. Wearing a long brown robe, he looked like he was in his seventies or eighties, and he was dutifully obeying as the master of ceremonies called out various instructions, prompting him to get up, kneel, and make shows of respect on our behalf to our ancestors, who were, presumably, now present.

When this man turned around to face the audience, my father's eyes grew massive. "He looks exactly like my father!" he whispered. "Quick! Take a picture!" The man became our new obsession. I sprang into action, snapping as many pictures as I could of him. I'd seen some pictures of Gong-Gong, and I could tell that my father was right. This man was a dead ringer for my grandfather. "Maybe my grandfather had another son in China before he left?" my father wondered. I pondered the possibility; it wasn't inconceivable.

As we watched the ceremony unfold, with me understanding very little of it, my father grew very quiet. And when it ended, we wandered the halls of the association, looking for my faux grandfather. Finally, we found him in a back room, sitting down to eat with a large group of men. Gingerly, my father approached him, introducing himself. *"Wa see Tan Soo Liap—Singapore lai eh,"* he said, gesturing to ask whether we could have a picture taken with him. The man raised his eyebrows, looking puzzled as he touched his hand to his chest, the universal signal for "A picture with me?" My father scooted behind him before he had a chance to change his mind as I whipped out my camera. "Smile!" I said in Mandarin. And the man did—displaying a broad cavity containing only two teeth. I was shocked. My doppelgänger grandfather was different, after all. My actual grandfather had had access to great dental care in Singapore and had a handsome smile throughout his life. I was beginning to see the life he—and possibly I—would have led had my great-grandfather never left.

While the village elders had planned an elaborate lunch of lamb, lobster noodles, and pricey fish maw, my father had other ideas. He'd struck up a conversation with a young woman holding a toddler while waiting outside for the ceremonies to start. The woman and her family were regular villagers who couldn't afford to be part of the feast that was under way. Instead, her family was going to make *char kway teow,* a stir-fried flat noodle that I'd grown up eating in Singapore. Would we like to join?

My father and I followed this woman, wending down narrow lanes, dusty and quiet. Her name was Tan Neo Soon—we all had the same last name in this village, it turned out—and she was just twenty-two. With bright eyes and an impish smile, Neo Soon looked far younger than her age. She appeared to belong more in a mall on a Saturday, trying on lipstick with her high school girlfriends. Instead, she was here in a small Chinese village, balancing a three-year-old son on her hip and nipping away to a nearby room that was her makeshift work studio whenever she could. There, she unpacked large boxes of plastic and glass parts, assembling coffee presses by hand to be sold in larger cities nearby.

When we got to her home, my father and I suddenly felt like giants. Neo Soon, her husband, her sister, her parents, and her grandmother all lived in a row house so tiny even Hobbits would not have found it a luxury. Their living room, I realized, felt slightly bigger than my closet of a kitchen in Brooklyn, which I often complained about. Their "kitchen" was in an open-air back alley, next to a well from which all their water came. Neo Soon's son sat on the stone paving of this alley, playing with a utensil, while his father started on lunch. "He's the one who cooks," Neo Soon said sheepishly. "He learned from his mother." Neo Soon and her husband, Cai Chu Ju, had met while working in a stainless steel factory years ago, and when they'd gotten married, they'd made the unconventional move of having her husband—who was from another village, as indicated by the fact that his last name was Cai and not Tan—move in with her family instead of the other way around. This was simply a practical matter; her family had more space. I looked around at the miniature living room and the alleyway kitchen and wondered what "less space" looked like.

Working quickly, Chu Ju chopped a whole cabbage into slender, long slivers, heated up a little cooking oil in a wok, and stir-fried those slivers. After they'd gotten a little soft, he added a bag of cooked noodles and stirred it all together before adding soy sauce, a smidge of monosodium glutamate, and a few shakes of a chocolate brown powder I'd never seen in any of my aunties' kitchens. "What's that?" I asked, pen poised, notebook in hand. *"Sha cha fen,"* Chu Ju replied, showing me the packet. I continued to be perplexed—*sha* is the word for "sand." I had no idea what *cha* was, and *fen* is powder. When my father saw me panicking, he swooped in to help, taking off his glasses so he could squint at the ingredients, listed in Chinese characters. "Well, I think it's five-spice powder mixed with onion powder, garlic powder, ground peanuts, and a few other things," he finally said. It also turned out to be the main flavoring agent for the noodles, which were done in a matter of seconds. Once the ingredients had been adequately heated through and stirred, lunch was ready.

Their tiny dining table was only large enough for three people to comfortably sit down to eat—and Neo Soon insisted I sit the moment the noodles were set out, practically shoving me onto the seat when I began to politely resist. With her grandmother, sister, and husband watching carefully, I took a small bite of the noodles. It wasn't the most flavorful dish I'd had. I imagined trying it back in my New York kitchen jazzed up with shrimp or slivers of pork belly perhaps. And maybe a few dashes of oyster or chili sauce. In Neo Soon's home, however, I realized they had to make do without these accoutrements. This was all they had—and it wasn't much. *"Hen hao chi ah!"* I said to Chu Ju, praising his food. Then I wiped my mouth and said I wasn't very hungry after all, gesturing to Neo Soon's grandmother to please sit down and eat. The platter of noodles wasn't huge, after all—and there were many mouths to feed that day.

Standing out on the road, my father reflected. "My grandfather's wish was to come back to the village and die here," he finally said. "I told my grandfather I had come back for him."

I nodded, silently. All these years later, we had fulfilled his wish.

Surveying motorbikes and cars racing by in terrifying zig-zags, my dad suddenly smiled. "Imagine if I got knocked down and died here," he said. "I'd also be fulfilling my grandfather's wish."

"Choi!" I said, suggesting that it was time that we go back into the great hall for the annual picture-taking session.

In the Singapore clan association building, and throughout the village's meeting rooms, I had seen these pictures. In them, rows of stern-looking men in stiff suits are seated on benches, staring straight at the camera, largely unsmiling. When the camera was whipped out, I was unsure whether I should join them—even though I desperately wanted to. My dad moved aside, making room for me. "Of course you should be here," he said.

Michael and the elders looked at me with disapproval. I knew I really shouldn't have been in that picture. But I was my father's firstborn, after all. I had my great-grandfather's blood. Ignoring the stares, I stood unflinching as the camera flashes went off.

I HAD ASKED MANY QUESTIONS DURING MY TIME IN THE village. Why do overseas Chinese call Shantou or mainland China *dengsua*, which means "long mountain," for example. "Perhaps because as their boats sailed away from Shantou, they'd look back at the long mountain range in the mist and wonder how long it would be before they saw it again," someone had volunteered. (It was also likely that it referred to Chinese people, called Deng Nang in Teochew, and the mountain range from which they came.) Where did the Teochews in our village come from? "A family of seven brothers who emigrated from Fujian Province centuries ago and formed seven small villages—ours was one of them," the village chief had said.

Before we left, however, I had one final question. I hadn't been sure whether I would ask it. But it was one of the few Teochew phrases I had heard while growing up. I had to know if it was something that was commonplace here or just something said in Singapore.

"Lau chek ah," I said to the village chief as we made our good-byes. He already looked a little miffed by my refusal to pry myself from his all-male photo session, so I figured I had little to lose.

"We have a funny Teochew saying in Singapore," I began. "It's *Teochew nang kacherng ang ang.* Do you say that here also?"

His face instantly puffed up. "I've never heard of that before!" he sputtered out.

"Oh, okay, thank you," I said, gathering my things and getting ready to scurry out. "For everything."

The trip back to *dengsua* had been as eye-opening as I'd hoped. My first instinct had been right; we may have come from there, but there certainly wasn't a place for us in that village anymore. Definitely not for me. My great-grandfather had given us, given me, a tremendous gift when he left almost a century ago to find a better life in Singapore. As our car sped away, I looked out at the long mountain range in the blackening sky and said a silent thank-you to the great-grandfather I'd never before known.

CHAPTER SEVENTEEN

My love for all things Italian had been etched on my heart decades ago.

Granted, the seeds had been planted by the smoldering Roberto Baggio and formidable Walter Zenga of the 1990 Italian World Cup squad. But the love affair continued through little discoveries: a hearty bowl of cioppino, filled with fish and delicately balancing briny sea flavors with sweet, sweet tomatoes; an effervescent Bellini, sipped at Harry's Bar in Venice after a long twilight stroll along the city's picturesque canals.

It was through baking bread, however, that this affection truly deepened. Through the Bread Baker's Apprentice challenge, I was introduced to *casatiello*—a light, spongy loaf that came studded with dry-cured salami cubes and heavenly pockets of melted provolone; and pane *siciliano*—hearty, pecan-hued, crunchy breads in the striking shape of giant *S*'s. The week I met *panmarino*, I knew this was it—the bread I had been looking for. This garlicky bread made with mashed potatoes and fresh rosemary was intoxicating from the moment the dough hit the oven and its scent began invading the crevices of my apartment. By the time I slipped the first sliver into my mouth, I knew I had found it. This was the one I was bringing home.

I had tried to explain my bread-baking quest to my aunties and mother—making homemade loaves was something I'd never considered within the realm of my abilities. Bread was something you bought at a store—an item so basic that it didn't warrant the (sometimes) days of effort that went into each loaf. This was certainly something my mother believed, too, even though she was a great lover of bread—buns filled with red-bean paste or airy clumps of sweet pork "floss" (dried pork that's somewhat akin to beef jerky), or topped with shredded cheese and baked to crispy perfection, had been staples in my Singapore home since I was a child. And while I had always favored heaping plates of salty noodles for breakfast, my mother liked nothing more than to begin her days with a cup of Nescafé coffee and a slice of toast with a hefty layer of salted butter scraped on and a generous Chinese soup spoon of sugar sprinkled on top. "Bread? Might as well just buy, right? So *leceh*," she would say, using the Malay word for *troublesome*, when I told her of the wheat breads and braided loaves I was attempting.

From the time that I pulled my very first bagels out of the oven, however, I'd realized that there was true magic in the smell and taste of freshly baked bread, still hot from the oven. And I had hoped to be able to share that revelation with my skeptical family. After a steak and potato dinner left me with a mound of leftover mashed potatoes, I decided to pull out Peter Reinhart's recipe for *panmarino*. The bread is incredibly easy to make—on the first day, you make a *biga*, mixing flour, yeast, and water, and let it sit. On the second, you cut that *biga* into pieces, let it rest and rise, then mix it together with more flour, salt, black pepper, chopped fresh rosemary, roasted garlic, mashed potatoes, olive oil, and water; then you knead it, form it into two round boules, and let it rest some more to rise. And then into the oven it goes. It was so easy that I started to wonder whether it would be any good. The combination of the sweet, softened garlic with sharp bits of rosemary and the slightly salty, potatoey bread was just perfect, however. You could set this bread out with cheese and ham for a pre-dinner snack but, really, it's more than flavorful enough to stand on its own.

Shortly after making—and rapidly devouring—my first *panmarino*, I began whipping together more mashed potatoes for several more loaves. And, shortly after that, I found myself wedging myself into a seat on a plane headed for Singapore, carefully tucking away a large tote bag stuffed with bread and absolutely reeking of garlic. I was a true hit on that plane with my fellow passengers, I'm sure.

From her first bite, I could see that my mother understood. She'd carefully toasted a small sliver and buttered it slightly. Her eyes grew large as she thoughtfully chewed for a moment. "How did you make this?" she asked, listening quietly as I quickly walked through the steps I had taken. "Wah, so clever ah," she added, before leaping up to quickly bundle up the rest of the loaf. "Daffy and your daddy must try this," she said. "Better keep it for them." She proceeded to guard over her loaf with great ferocity, instructing Erlinda not to serve it to anyone. Only my mother was allowed to slice it up and parcel it out in tiny, buttered slices—it was that precious.

I thought back to the days I had spent sweating at the

counter in my Brooklyn kitchen, kneading pillowy mounds until my arms and fingers hurt—or desperately trying to hang on to my jumpy KitchenAid mixer and prevent it from jitterbugging off the counter as it strenuously mixed massive gobs of dough. I thought of the failures I'd encountered, the whole days it had taken to get the smell of smoke out of my living room—and the fact that I'd kept at it even though the quest had seemed, at times, plain silly. Watching my mother and her prized *panmarino*, I knew it all had been worth it.

ONE DAY, MY MOTHER SAID THE WORDS I NEVER THOUGHT I'd hear. "I think you should meet your father's new wife."

It had been a few weeks since I last saw my father, when we had traveled to Shantou together. With the holidays approaching, however, Ketty and my father had some errands to run in Singapore and were due for a short visit—a trip that pained my mother, I knew, from the way she never spoke of it. "Well, I'm not sure that I want to," I said. But someday soon, I knew, this woman who had entered our lives would be in charge of my father's life, should his health weaken. "You don't want to regret not having a relationship with her if she's suddenly the one who decides who gets to see him if he gets really sick," Mike had suggested. "I'm just saying . . ."

I wasn't sure what to do—so I consulted with Willin.

"You know," he said as we sipped glasses of sauvignon blanc while sitting in rattan lounge chairs at his hilltop bar, Wild Oats, before his dinner shift one night, "I have this friend whose elderly uncle married this very young Chinese woman less than half his age. The uncle was the eldest son, so he was in charge of the family assets—everything was in his name—and they had this big house in China that belonged to the family. After he married this woman, he went to China to see the house with his new wife. And then, mysteriously, he fell down the stairs and died!" he added, dramatically using his fingers to punch quote marks in the air as he said the words *fell down*. "And then the new wife inherited the house and now the rest of the family doesn't have access to it anymore!" he finished, practically shrieking.

"*Maybe*," he said firmly, quietly, "you should meet your father's new wife. Just so you know what she's like."

That settled it. I immediately called Le Bistrot du Somme-lier, a little French place I thought my pâté-loving father would like, and made a dinner reservation.

The night of our dinner, Mike and I squirmed in our seats, waiting for my father and his wife. Mike leaned over and stroked my back—my uncharacteristic silence was telling of the anxiety coursing through me. I texted Willin, telling him that Mike and I were bundles of nerves, wondering what on earth we would have to say to Ketty. "I'm not involving myself in this—I don't want to get tied to this in any way. I'm on your mum's side!" he immediately texted back. And then, right after, his final bit of advice, reminding me of his friend's sad tale: "Quick, push *her* down the stairs before it's too late."

We ordered wine and then decided not to drink it, feeling it would be disrespectful if half the bottle disappeared before our elders showed up. And soon enough, my father appeared, spritely and beaming as he effervescently pumped Mike's hand and hugged me before stepping aside to introduce his wife.

With her long black hair and smooth alabaster skin, this woman with the slender, girlish figure looked younger than I was. She spoke little English, I had been told, so I introduced myself as Rulian. There was little more to say. As we looked through the menu, my father spoke at breakneck speed, filling us in on her likes (shopping; The Gap; simple, healthy foods like fish and rice) and dislikes (anything ostentatious; rich, Western food like pâté, which she worried would shorten my father's life). I suddenly recalled that I had known that about Ketty; I wondered if that had subconsciously been a factor in my choice of restaurant.

"But you like pâté!" I said.

"I know," my dad said, "but I can't eat too much of it."

We decided to get some for the table anyway, since it was a specialty of the restaurant. I was feeling better about this dinner. The man sitting across from us at the dinner table was still ordering like the father I knew, at least.

With my Mandarin being so-so at best, I was unable to say anything much deeper to Ketty than, "What did you buy today?" ("Just a few T-shirts.") and "What do you like about Singapore?" ("It's very clean."). And since Mike understood no Mandarin, the conversation largely took place in English, as my father enthusiastically filled us in on their life together in China, pausing every few sentences to translate what he said in Mandarin to Ketty. As dinner whizzed along, I realized it wasn't going terribly, after all. My father was happier than I'd seen him in a while; Ketty, who was carefully watching his pâté and wine intake with a whiff of thinly disguised disapproval, didn't seem like the shoving-down-the-staircase sort. Mike looked over and gently squeezed my hand.

As Mike signed the bill, my father leaned back, smiling as he sipped the last of his wine. "You know, Cheryl," he said, "you're actually supposed to call Ketty *houma*." The Mandarin word for second mother. My mouth actually fell open in surprise. Ketty looked around the table nervously, then giggled and said, "*Buyong ah!*" I instantly agreed. There was no need for this. We had taken a step that night—but for the moment, it was just that, a step.

Outside on the street, as Mike and I watched my father and his bride wend their way in the darkness toward their nearby hotel, I noticed they were strolling hand in hand. "Your father was so happy," Mike said. "You did a good thing tonight."

I suppose it was just as well that I hadn't listened to Willin.

A few days later, I made my way to Auntie Khar Imm's house for my final cooking lesson. With Christmas and then Chinese New Year approaching—and with the recent arrival of her second grandchild, a sister for Giselle—my aunt's workload had increased. There was more cleaning, more babysitting. The cooking lessons, sadly, had to come to an end.

The dish for the finale was an obvious one: *pua kiao beng*, my Tanglin Ah-Ma's gambling rice. Or, as Auntie Khar Imm called it, "*Landuo fan lah!*" Lazy rice did seem like an appropriate name for it, given that it was designed for easy eating so that gamblers didn't have to get up from their tables midgame in order to fill their stomachs.

As always, Auntie Khar Imm had prepped the ingredients before I got there. The dried mushrooms had been soaked in water for four hours until they were soft enough for easy dicing. The pork belly had been cubed, the shallots had been minced, the cabbage had been shredded and was soaking in a basin of water next to her sink. "The prawns," Auntie Khar Imm said, holding up a handful of dried shrimp. "You soak them a little in water until they're soft." I watched as she washed the rice she intended to use, rinsing it out a few times until the water she was swirling it in didn't grow cloudy anymore. Placing that rice in a rice cooker, she pointed out that she was pouring enough water into the cooker so that the water level was three-quarters of an inch above the top of the rice.

Then the frying began. She began to pour cooking oil into the wok before pausing to reach into a cupboard to pull out a measuring cup. I was surprised—I had thought I was supposed to *agak-agak*. "*Ni xihuan* measure mah!" she said, smiling. Yes, she was right—I did like measuring. I felt a pang as I realized that this would be our final cooking lesson.

After pouring a half cup of oil into the wok and heating that up, she mixed in the shallots, frying them until they turned brown—this took about ten minutes by my estimation—and then removing them and setting them aside on a plate. Then she fried the mushrooms in the same oil, removing them and setting them aside after five minutes. Next, she added the pork belly cubes to the mixture, frying that together until the meat browned. Then she added the dried shrimp, shallots, and mushrooms back into the wok, mixing it all together and taking out a measuring spoon to scoop a half tablespoon of salt into the wok, and an eighth of a teaspoon of monosodium glutamate. After

===

mixing that all up, she added the cabbage and stirred it all together for a minute. Turning off the heat, she carefully dished the mixture into the rice cooker, making sure to stir the entire mixture together before pressing the "cook" button.

As we waited for the rice to cook, we sat around the dining table, sipping from mugs of warm water.

"I met my father's wife, you know," I said, watching as her eyes widened and her hand flew up to cover her mouth.

"Wah, really?" she said, thinking about what I'd said for a moment. "So what did you think?"

"She's not bad," I said. "My Mandarin is not very good, so I didn't have much to say."

Auntie Khar Imm took another sip of water, thinking again. "I met her also," she finally said. "I thought she was very pretty. Beautiful skin; nice girl. Just like you. Just like your mother."

Her words weighed on me as we packed up the rice and I prepared to leave. She was right—Ketty was a nice girl. She would never be my *houma*, my second mother. But perhaps it was time to start seeing her as family.

SINGAPORE MAY BE A COUNTRY FILLED WITH A DIVERSITY of religions—Taoism, Hinduism, Islam, Buddhism. However, when it comes to Christmas, everyone, regardless of race or religion, jumps right in and celebrates.

Orchard Road, the main shopping street in Singapore's downtown area, is strung up with Christmas lights from beginning to end. An endless stream of cars and pedestrians clogs the street during the entire month of December as Singaporeans turn out to madly shop and check out the massive—and usually gaudy—holiday decorations that malls put up, each shopping center hoping to outdo the rest in the annual contest for the best-decorated mall.

Amid this festive hive of activity, my family was going through a little meltdown. Except for a handful of Christmases when either I or my father hadn't been able to get enough time off at work to fly to Singapore or New York for the holidays, my family had always spent Christmas together. This year, however, Daddo had decided to stay in Beijing with Ketty, a decision we had all thought we were fine with—until Christmas morning, when we woke up to unwrap a mountain of gifts. Faced with a pile of crumpled wrapping paper, we did the annual photo shoot where each person piled on all the gifts they'd gotten that day—artfully perching them on the body, on the head, on the arms—and had a picture taken to document that year's bounty. Giggling over our pictures, we realized there were none of my father that year. Under the tree, his presents remained wrapped.

Over the phone, my father told us he missed us. And knowing that it was hard to say good-bye and hang up, he said to me, "Remember when I brought you to college for the first time? Remember what I said?" Of course I remembered—it was a phrase that had come to mind the many times a day that I thought of my parents, my sister, my friends in Singapore so far away, with sharp stabs of longing.

"I'm as far as the telephone," he had said. "Whenever you miss me, just look at the telephone. I'm always there."

To quell the tears, we set about preparing our Christmas Day lunch. For years, Auntie Jane, my mother's younger sister, had been in charge of Christmas. At her trendy apartment near Orchard Road, we would gather, filling our plates with turkey, glazed ham, noodles, and her famous potato gratin. After she retired and moved to New Zealand, however, the Christmas dinners my mother's family used to have had become a some-time occurrence. This year, Daph and I had decided to take over, inviting Auntie Alice, Ah-Ma, our cousin Benny, his wife, and their daughter, Bernice, over for lunch.

Like Auntie Jane, we took the easy route for the basics: the ham, gravy, stuffing, and log cake had been ordered from the Tanglin Club, the British social club to which my parents belonged. And Auntie Alice had offered to make Auntie Jane's potato gratin for old times' sake—this invention involved cubed potatoes tossed with diced onions and button mushrooms that were topped with bits of pork and chicken sausage and then drizzled with decorative squirts of mayonnaise before going into the oven.

Around plastic garden tables on my mother's sunny front porch, we perched on stools, filling our plates over and over. Sure, Auntie Jane wasn't there. Neither was my father. Or my kuku and his family, who had decamped to Denver to visit family.

But there were enough of us. And the stories flew out fast and furious.

"I still remember when you were living in Taiwan," Auntie Alice said. "You were just a baby—one or two years old. We went to visit your parents and we were all in a restaurant and you asked your parents for something and they said no. You just threw yourself on the floor, just screaming and crying. You wouldn't get up, you know! I thought, 'This Tiger baby ah!'"

"Yah lah, this one, always so stubborn," my mother said, as the laughter around the table subsided.

I noted to Auntie Alice that her new daughter-in-law might be having a baby soon. "Another Tiger in the family!" I said. She instantly stopped laughing, looking a little horrified.

"Aiyoh," she quietly said, shaking her head, "our family has been mostly filled with such peaceful animals so far."

As the afternoon waned, we packed up the leftovers and said our good-byes. Ah-Ma hugged me and clung to my hand, pulling me toward her as she stroked it firmly. I braced myself for the conversation I had been expecting to have.

"You should find a boyfriend," she said in Mandarin, looking intently at me. "You're not getting any younger."

"Hah?" I said, unsure of what she meant. Hadn't she meant to say "baby"?

"You need a boyfriend," she said again.

I wasn't sure what to say.

"Aiyoh," Auntie Alice said. "I think she thinks you're Daffy."

And she was right—even after Daffy and I told her who we were, she did not believe us, squinting at both of us carefully, repeatedly pointing at me and saying, "This one is the second one, right?"

After a few minutes of this, the laughter turned into an uncomfortable silence. My grandmother was not just forgetting old recipes—she was, perhaps, starting to forget who we were. As we stood in the driveway waving our good-byes, I hugged her once again, grateful that I had come home.

CHAPTER EIGHTEEN

With Chinese New Year approaching, my year of cooking was rapidly coming to an end.

As I entered my auntie Khar Imm's family's kitchen once again, I could feel it. The wheel had come full circle. A year ago, I had entered this kitchen fearful and uncertain, with little sense of my family and whether I still fit in it. Now, just a year later, I knew the pineapple tart–making drill the moment I stepped into the room. No one had to explain anything to me. I simply jumped in wherever I could, rolling out dough, filling holes in the cookies, rolling out balls of pineapple jam, and hoisting trays of pineapple tarts over to Auntie Khar Imm, who once again was manning the stove.

Still, of course, there were new things to be learned.

"Lu-Lien ah," Auntie Khar Imm called to me when I arrived. "Try this," she said, pushing a jar of deep-fried green and beige strips in my face. I took one and chewed on it. It was crispy, salty, delicious. It would have been fantastic with beer or a cold soda. "Mmm, what is it?" I asked. It turned out it was sheets of seaweed attached with a mix of flour and water to summer roll skins, cut into bite-size strips, and deep-fried. My aunties had sampled them somewhere and decided to experiment with making them at home as a Chinese New Year snack this year.

And instead of pig's trotter stew as a lunch snack, my aunties were sweating over a different set of ingredients on the stove this time, methodically deep-frying *ikan bilis* (anchovies) in hot oil and setting that out on the dining table with a platter of fried eggs, a large bowl of chili, and coconut rice. *"Nasi lemak,"* Jessie explained. I was surprised. This dish of rice and fried anchovies that I sometimes trekked to a hawker center to buy for breakfast was Malay—not a recipe that would have been passed down from my grandmother. "Wah, so good ah! Know how to make *nasi lemak* all!" I said.

"Aiyah, just try lor—see how it tastes," Jessie said. A few seconds later, after Jessie tasted the rice, she bundled it all up and put it back in the rice cooker, adding more coconut milk. "Not enough," she said. "Must cook longer." I realized I was witnessing the process of *agak-agak* at its best.

As involved as I was in the Chinese New Year tart-making process, I was most nervous about the dinner I had been planning for the third day of the new year. "What are you going to cook?" Auntie Khar Imm had asked. "Well, some of this and some of that," I'd said, as mysteriously as I could. "You'll just have to come and eat!"

I'd been planning this meal for months—a dinner for my father's side of the family in my parents' home. I knew how much my aunties had put into teaching me to cook over the past year. I wanted to thank them properly. I also wanted to bring them all together.

While I was planning to make a medley of "greatest hits" from both sides of my family, I wanted to surprise my aunties with a few additions that they hadn't taught me. As a child, I'd grown up having *bak kut teh*, a peppery pork rib soup, as an occasional Sunday treat. "This is Teochew, you know," was a refrain I'd always hear just before my father slurped up his soup. In the past year, I had asked all my relatives if they knew how to make this soup my father so loved. None of them did. This was when Uncle Willin came to the rescue. "Hmm," he said a few days before Chinese New Year began. "I've made it in my restaurant. I don't know how 'traditional' it is, but I like it." Although we had eaten our way through much of Singapore, I hadn't cooked with Willin in all my months there. With my year of cooking coming to a close, I begged him to teach me.

"Aiyoh, I'm not even Teochew, and this is a Teochew dish! You should learn from a real Teochew!" he protested.

"Aiyah, can lah. You're a chef!" I said. "I want to learn something from you!" And that settled it.

On a clear, hot day, just after his lunch shift, I met Willin in a swanky Cold Storage supermarket on downtown Orchard Road to pick up pork ribs, garlic, peppercorns, and a bag to hold the peppercorns in the pot of soup. I wondered what my Tanglin ah-ma would have thought of us buying these ingredients at this gleaming, pristine store, where prices were surely far higher than in the wet markets where most Singaporeans bought their meat and produce. A short drive later, we were at the stove in the kitchen of Relish, one of Willin's restaurants. He didn't have much time, so we worked quickly. Bringing a large pot of water to boil on his industrial stove was a cinch.

Then he quickly blanched the ribs under hot water before tossing them into the pot along with the little bag of peppercorns and a whole head of garlic. Then we let the soup boil for forty-five minutes, until the broth turned pale brown.

As Willin worked, he told me how he had come upon the recipe. "Just from tasting and thinking and experimenting in the kitchen," he said. "It's very easy." And it was true—the soup was simple yet delicious.

"I'm going to make this for my family," I said, after having several large sips.

"*Don't!*" he said. "I'm not Teochew! Your family is going to hate me for trying to teach you something Teochew if they don't like it!"

I thought about my auntie Leng Eng, my uncle Soo Kiat, the formidable Auntie Khar Imm trying Willin's *bak kut teh* and thought perhaps he had a point. To be safe, I decided to try it out on my mother's Hockchew family and see how it went.

The plan was to make the traditional reunion dinner—which gathers the family together on the eve of Chinese New Year—for my mother's family, then cap the New Year festivities with a dinner for my father's relatives on the third day of the year. I began several days before the meal, making a giant shopping list for my mother and starting with the *otak*. With my notebook in hand, I went through Auntie Khar Imm's steps, blending together the lemongrass, the shallots, and the chilies to create the sauce mix, adding in the chopped-up mackerel I now was unafraid to touch. On the list were braised duck, gambling rice, my grandmother's *ngoh hiang*, my auntie Khar Imm's salted vegetable and duck soup, and my mother-in-law's *mandoo*.

For the first meal, I thought I had everything under control. The *ngoh hiang* looked lovely; the braised duck was just the right color. The *otak,* though a little spicy, was a beautiful shade of orange and tasted just like versions you'd buy in a store. I was proud of how well everything was going—until I hit Willin's *bak kut teh.*

When we were in Willin's kitchen, I had watched him pour salt by the tablespoon into his own broth, dutifully writing down "about two tablespoons of salt" in my notebook. In my own home, however, as the dinner hour approached, I began to get more panicked, especially when my mother started bounding in every ten minutes or so, asking, "How's everything going?" As the minutes ticked by, the soup wasn't taking on enough flavor, I thought. I didn't have extra ribs or extra peppercorns. So instead, I grabbed my mother's box of salt and shook it like a madwoman into the broth, tasting as I went along.

When my ah-ma and my kuku and his family arrived, we were ready. Before dinner began, there was the traditional "*lo hei,*" in which the family gathers in a circle around a large platter of raw fish salad, each person holding a pair of chopsticks in hand, picking up bits of the salad and tossing it high up in the air. The salad, called *yu sheng,* is made up of ingredients that have lucky-sounding names or symbolic meanings—the word for fish, for example, sounds like abundance or prosperity; sesame seeds indicate a year of flourishing business. Kuku had ordered our *yu sheng* from the Four Seasons Hotel—not being traditionalists, we had always gathered to toss the salad without knowing what we were doing exactly, besides tossing the ingredients as high as we could to ensure that our abundance, flourishing business, and good health would reach soaring pinnacles in the coming year.

This year, however, Daphne had printed out instructions off the Internet, guiding us along as each dish was added. As the slivers of salmon sashimi went onto the platter, she announced *"Nian nian you yu!"* prompting us to follow along in chanting the Mandarin words implying "This year, you'll have abundance." As chopped peanuts were scattered about the platter, she called out *"Jin yin man wu,"* wishing all of us precious gold and eternal youth in abundance. After julienned daikon, carrots, oil, pomelo, and several other ingredients were added, the plum sauce went in. Most of us knew what accompanied this. *"Tian tian mi mi!"* we called out, wishing a sweet year ahead to everyone at the table. With loud cries, we dug our chopsticks in, tossing bits of fish and vegetables as high as we could into the air, hoping fervently for a good year ahead. Once the reunion dinner dishes started coming out, my family ate ravenously, pausing to marvel that I'd actually made these dishes.

"Wah, quite good ah!" Auntie Donna said, smiling. I was starting to feel good about everything—until they dipped into the soup. All around the table, eyes were squinting. If they hadn't been so intent on not hurting my feelings, I'm sure they would have spit out the soup. It was far, far too salty. Daphne helpfully tried to move my grandmother's bowl of soup away from her so she wouldn't sample it. But it was too late. *"Jin giam ah!"* she shouted, wincing and sticking out her tongue as she frantically looked around for some water to wash away the intense taste of salt.

I decided to take it off the menu for my father's family dinner.

(I also decided not to tell Willin, chirpily texting him "Dinner went great! Thanks for the BKT recipe!" the moment it ended.)

Before the big dinner for my father's family, however, there was one more family event: the traditional lunch on the second day of the new year at my auntie Khar Imm's home. I was growing increasingly stressed over how my dinner would fare, my father's family being rather fussy about food in general, not to mention the food that I was trying to make using my sainted grandmother's recipes. Sitting at Auntie Khar Imm's dining table, I started to feel a gnawing pain in my abdomen. She had made Teochew braised duck, together with lovely chocolate brown eggs and tofu steeped in the salty gravy—it was perfectly done and amazing over rice. We could not stop eating it.

Surveying the lunch table, my dad made a pronouncement. "Tomorrow, you all better eat before you come. Stop at McDonald's or something," he said. "Your dinner is not going to be as good as this, for sure!"

I felt my face start to redden, but he was right. How could I possibly outdo the teacher? Perhaps this had been madness all along. Amid the laughter, Auntie Khar Imm leapt to my defense. "Aiyah, don't listen to your daddy!" she said, smiling. "I'm sure it'll be very tasty!"

The next morning Willin texted me. "How are you doing? Everything OK?"

The outpouring of my insecurity began. How would I ever compare? My aunties were phenomenal cooks. My grandmother had been a goddess in the kitchen. Why did I think I could do this?

"That's the thing about being measured" against others, he immediately replied. "Since everyone knows they are great cooks, you have nothing to lose if you don't cook as well. Everyone knows you don't cook like that daily unlike them but if you do, everyone will be amazed. Either way, you win, so no sweat!"

Willin's words would ring through my head for the rest of the day, as I chopped, steamed, stirred, and boiled. I was so frazzled that at one point I peeked out to the dining room and noticed that not only was my sister sitting at the table wrapping *mandoo* but my father and Mike had joined in the process as well. I had never seen my father cook in my life. Just as I started to tear up, my dad showed me one of his dumplings; it was a *mandoo* wrapper filled with spicy orange *otah* filling instead of pork and cabbage. "I'm calling it *jiao-tah*," he said, referring to the Mandarin word for dumplings—*jiaozi*—and combining that with *otah*. "I think it's going to be a hit!"

As the afternoon raced by, I felt like I had everything under control. Then, at 5:00 P.M., with guests arriving just two hours later, I suddenly noticed that my massive pot of salted vegetable and duck soup wasn't boiling. This would be because I had completely forgotten to start the process—the duck wasn't even in the pot. The salted plum and tamarind leaves were still on the counter. I could not believe it. This was a process that should take at least two hours, more if you wanted your soup to be flavorful. I started to feel shooting pains in my head. I couldn't believe I had screwed up one of the compulsories. Ignoring my second braised duck, I turned my attention to the soup. How could I get it to be more flavorful in this shorter period of boiling? In a panic, I tossed in extra chunks of smashed ginger, extra tamarind leaves, an extra sour plum. It would just have to do. By the time this was done, I checked back in on my duck to find that its skin had burned through and was firmly stuck to the wok. This was turning out to be nothing short of a disaster.

Right about then, I noticed the piles of softened clear vermicelli and sliced cabbage, carrots, bean curd, and shiitake mushrooms that I had scattered about the kitchen counter in little bowls. The *chap chye*! Just a few weeks earlier, I had begged my Auntie Alice for some time in her busy schedule before she flew to Dongguan to spend Chinese New Year with her second son. I'd wanted to learn to make my mother's family's *chap chye*, a dish of mixed vegetables and tofu with clear noodles that's eaten for luck during the New Year festivities, but my mother, crazed with school homework, had been too busy to teach me. The dish is easy enough to make—the prep is what takes the most time. But with my soup catastrophe, a slightly burned duck, and the trauma of hard-boiled eggs that weren't peeling right since I hadn't boiled them long enough, I was in no frame of mind to set all that aside and whip together *chap chye*. I considered skipping it altogether—we did have an awful lot of food on the table. What was one dish less?

"*Chap chye* must eat one!" my mother clucked. She was right—it was a good luck dish. In fact, during Chinese New Year, my mother often adds *fu chook*, a black fungus that looks exactly like clumps of human hair, to her *chap chye* for added luck. (The name of the fungus sounds like the Chinese word for prosperity.)

Even so, I simply could not muster the energy to pull together a dish of *chap chye*. Standing in the kitchen, I began to

understand how it must feel to be on the precipice of a meltdown. My head was pounding. A film of sweat coated my entire
body. My T-shirt had glued itself to my skin. My hair was a
tangled mess bundled up into a raggedy ponytail. From the way
my mum was looking at me, I could tell I had a manic look in
my eyes. "Go up and change," she said, waving me out of the
kitchen. So I took a break, putting on a cheery pink floral Tracy
Reese blouse and a comfortable black skirt. I washed my face,
combed my hair, and spritzed on a few pumps of Paris by Yves
Saint Laurent, the perfume I've worn for years to job interviews
and major meetings—situations in which I aim to walk in feeling as if I own the world. With a dash of lip gloss, I was looking
halfway normal, so back down to the kitchen I went.

My mother was at the stove this time, whizzing about
quickly and surely, grabbing bits of cabbage, carrots, and vermicelli, and flinging them into the wok with the confidence of
Rachael Ray. Despite her many protestations over not really
knowing how to cook, of course, she did all along. And it was
lovely to watch. I was stunned—and very grateful. With her
stepping in, the *chap chye* would be made, after all. She even
tossed in bits of the good luck fungus, which I've loathed and
avoided for years but certainly didn't mind in the least this
Chinese New Year.

Biting my lip and feeling completely terrified, I began
setting dishes out on the table. There were my two braised
ducks—one looking okay, the other looking charred and a little
too caramelized. The gravy for the duck was peppered with
tofu and chunks of mushy yellow bits from several disintegrated
hard-boiled eggs. I'd not boiled them long enough, making

them impossible to peel cleanly. My grandmother's chicken curry had turned out to be a bit of a disaster. I had used canned coconut milk instead of fresh to save the step of squeezing the milk out in cheesecloth. This meant that the much more concentrated canned milk made the gravy incredibly thick; instead of it being like a thick soup, it was a little like ectoplasm. And the salted vegetable and duck soup—I had no idea how it tasted. I was just hoping for the best.

I did, however, stand by my *otah*, my *mandoo*, my gambling rice, and the pork adobo, a dish that I love to make in my Brooklyn home, which I'd added to the mix.

The moment my family arrived, I hid in the kitchen, peeking out periodically.

First Uncle Soo Kiat circled the dining table, then Uncle Ah Tuang, who enthusiastically pointed at the salted vegetable and duck soup, saying, "Good, good—you made this. This one is a *must*." Auntie Khar Imm's eyes widened when she saw the spread. "Ma ah, these are all your dishes!" my cousin Jessie exclaimed.

Among all the guests, however, there was a face I wasn't familiar with. It was a woman my family called *Niajeh*, a cousin of my Tanglin ah-ma's who had grown up with her and cooked with her. The moment I saw her, I grew even more terrified. Niajeh was a legendary cook, and she had known my grandmother. How could I possibly measure up?

Willin's words, however, piped through my mind. There was nothing more I could do. The dishes had been made. I went out to watch everyone eat.

"This one, only okay," Uncle Soo Kiat said, pointing at the gambling rice. "But this one," he added, gesturing to the *otah*, "very good!" I started to feel relieved. I was so afraid that I could barely eat, but as I sat at the long table in my family's garden, watching my aunties and uncles—even Niajeh—wolfing down my *otah*, my duck, going back for seconds, I started to feel like perhaps I hadn't screwed up. More important, I realized that the point hadn't truly ever been the food.

There was my family, several branches that had been fractured over time, rarely spending time with one another, sitting around a dinner table, everyone thoughtfully chewing and picking apart each dish. I watched as my father held court, my sister flitted about, seeing if anyone needed refills of wine or water, and Mike could not stop eating. Even my mother, who had been adamant about not seeing my father's family ever again in the wake of the divorce, was smiling.

I realized that I was glad—no, I was thankful that I had come home.

As the meal wound down, Uncle Soo Kiat started telling me about Niajeh and her amazing *mee siam*, the Malay noodle dish that's spicy and sour all at once. "It's the Indian kind of *mee siam*," he said. "You really cannot find it anywhere else now."

"I'd love to learn," I said.

"Well, she lives in Australia. Maybe you should go there next!"

I wasn't sure what the future held, if a *mee siam* adventure in Australia was in the cards. All I knew was that, for one night, we were there, together, eating a meal culled from the women who had made me—my mother-in-law, my auntie Alice, my auntie Khar Imm, my mother, my ah-ma, my Tanglin ah-ma.

As my aunties left that night, I gave them long hugs good-bye.

And when Niajeh asked for Tupperware to bring leftovers home, I almost teared up once again.

"When will you come back?" my aunties asked.

I said I wasn't sure.

"Thank you," I finally told Auntie Khar Imm. "Thank you for everything."

"No need lah," she said. "You passed already."

EPILOGUE

I was leaving Singapore with a heavy heart this time. I wasn't sure when I'd be back. But at the same time I knew I'd learned so much that I'd be carrying bits of my family back with me to Brooklyn. And this included bird's nest soup, something that I'd never thought I'd be eager to learn.

For decades, this clear, sweet soup with floating bits of gelatinous "bird's nest," which look alarmingly like clumps of cloudy phlegm, had been the bane of my days in Singapore. Bird's nest is not cheap—the Chinese fervently believe in the healing properties of the soup, which is eaten hot or cold, usually as a dessert. My mother always says it's what keeps skin looking youthful, and it restores the body's energy. As a result, I usually see a bowl of it on my bedroom table the very morning after I arrive from the long journey between New York and Singapore. (For a while, during my teenage years, my mother took to believing that the body best absorbed the bird's nest if you drank the soup while half asleep; she took to rousing Daphne and me at ungodly hours of the early morning and attempting to shove spoonfuls of it into our mouths even before we had time to fully open our eyes.)

Beautiful skin and great health, however, is still never enough to get me to finish the bowls of it she makes without complaining bitterly. The idea of eating what essentially is birds' saliva is simply not worth the Shangri-la youthfulness it supposedly offers.

As my year at home drew to a close, however, I realized that my time ahead in New York was devoid of bird's nest soup. The euphoria I thought I'd feel wasn't there. Instead, there was a pang. "Mommo ah," I said one afternoon. "Can you teach me how to make birds' nest?" If she had been sitting on a chair, I'm certain my mother would have fallen off it. "You sure?" she asked. "Yeah," I said. "I should learn."

The process of making bird's nest soup was simple—you need, in essence, just four main ingredients: water, bird's nest, rock sugar, and pandan leaves. My mother adds a little ginseng to hers for added health benefits, but it's really not necessary. "You soak the bird's nest in cool water for half an hour to one hour," she said, speaking slowly so I could write everything down. "Until the hairs all come out—once they're loosened then you take tweezers and you pluck all the hairs out." This seemed like a very essential step—I suddenly thought of all the mornings when I had wailed and complained whenever she'd tried to foist this soup on me. I now realized how difficult it had been. I remember watching her bent over a bowl, squinting hard into a semi-clear glob for long stretches, tweezers in hand, meticulously pulling out hair after hair. My mother always was driven in this task; she would only pause now and then to quickly rub her tired eyes. I had always chosen to ignore this whenever I saw it—if I didn't think about her painstakingly preparing the bird's nest, I wouldn't have to think about eating it in my very near future.

"After all the hairs have been plucked out, you drain it and 'wash it clean,'" she said. "Then you put the bird's nest, three to five pieces of pandan leaf, and eight or nine small pieces of ginseng into a pot and put enough water to cover it—just boil over a small fire for half an hour. Toward the end, add rock sugar to taste."

"How much sugar should I add?" I asked, before I could stop myself.

"Aiyoh, you don't ask me how much lah—very difficult to tell you one!" she said. "Just until you think it's sweet enough lah."

It seemed simple enough, once the hair part had been dealt with, that is. "Oh, when you make it ah, make at least five pieces," my mother said, noting how the nests were generally sold in bits that were about three inches long and about two inches wide. "You make just one or two—it's just wasting time to make. Make more."

My mother looked at me keenly, seeming to wonder whether I would actually bother to do all this back in Brooklyn. "It will cool you down, help you *bu shenti*—strengthen your body," she said. "Mummy always sees you running around, so busy. You'd better take care of your health, okay? Listen to Mummy."

I promised that I would try.

"Cheryl ah," Auntie Alice said in a phone call the day before I left. "So how did your dinner go?"

"Good, good," I said, telling her about the text that I'd gotten from my cousin Jessie the next day: "Thanks Cheryl for your dinner. the food was great. . . . especially the braised duck . . . my mum said yrs is so much better than hers. . . . You Won her heee . . . heee . . . real good. . . ."

"Wow!" Auntie Alice said. "Not bad ah! Clever already ah!"

I started to say "No lah, no lah" before she cut me off.

"You know, there's this Chinese saying: *Jingde liao chu fang ye jingdeliao dating,*" she said. "It means you are skilled enough to be in the kitchen but also skilled enough to be in the great hall."

"What does that mean?"

"It means you can do both—you're a superwoman!" she said, laughing. "You have really grown up, Cheryl."

Recipes

TANGLIN AH-MA'S PINEAPPLE TARTS

Makes about 100 tarts

Quantities aren't exact. My aunts don't use a recipe, and they laughed at me the first ten times I asked them for this one. The initial set of instructions they gave me for pineapple jam was "Aiyah, you just juice the pineapple, add sugar, and then boil, boil, boil!"

For the jam

4 pineapples
2 to 3 pandan leaves* knotted
   together
1 long cinnamon stick, broken in two
At least 2 ½ cups sugar,
   depending on desired sweetness

*Leaves from the pandan tree, also called screw pine, can be found frozen in some Asian grocery stores.

Peel the pineapples, dig out the eyes, and chop the fruit into chunks. Run the chunks through a juicer. Place the pulp in a wok or pot with a large surface area and heat it on the stove.

Add the juice until the mixture has the consistency of porridge or grits; add the knotted pandan leaves and cinnamon stick. Bring the mixture to a boil and keep it there for 3 hours, stirring often. Halfway through, taste the jam, and add sugar by the ½ cup until the jam is as sweet as you desire. (Note: The amount of sugar needed will vary greatly depending on how ripe the pineapples are.)

The jam is done when the pineapple mixture has changed from bright yellow to brownish ocher and most of the liquid has evaporated, leaving a dense but moist jam.

For the pastry

3 sticks plus 2 ½ tablespoons butter at room temperature
About 4 ¾ cups flour
4 egg yolks, plus 1 yolk for brushing onto pastry

Preheat the oven to 350 degrees.

With a mixer on low speed, combine the butter, flour, and egg yolks, mixing for 3 to 5 minutes.

Place the dough in a cookie press fitted with a disk featuring a circle of diamonds. Press the cookies out onto greased baking sheets. Form small balls of dough and press each one into the hollow of a cookie, forming the base of the tart.

Beat the remaining egg yolk with ½ teaspoon of water. Brush the rim of each tart generously with this mixture. Take a scant teaspoon of jam (more or less, as desired) and form a ball, then press it into the hollow of each tart. Pat the sides of the jam to create a small dome.

Bake for 15 to 20 minutes at 350 degrees, until golden brown. Remove the cookies from the baking sheets and cool on a rack.

AH-MA'S *KAYA*

Yield: About 4 cups

10 eggs
½ to 1 cup sugar, depending on how sweet you like it
Milk from shredded pulp of 1 coconut
    (squeeze milk out in 2 batches)
3 pandan leaves, tied in knots

Crack the eggs in a bowl; whisk them together. Add ½ to 1 cup of sugar and coconut milk and mix it up well. Transfer mixture to a glass bowl, add knotted pandan leaves, then perch that bowl atop a steaming rack in a wok.

Steam the mixture for 45 to 60 minutes, untouched (if using Ah-Ma's method), until the desired consistency is reached. If you are using the method E-Ma and I experimented with, stir occasionally.

When you remove the *kaya* from the steamer, stir it, let it cool, and spread it over toasted bread. The consistency should be smooth and creamy.

TANGLIN AH-MA'S *BAK-ZHANG*

Yield: About 40

2 pounds glutinous rice

1 pound pork belly

2 pounds pork leg

2 pounds shallots, peeled

¾ to 1 cup vegetable or corn oil

10 cloves garlic, peeled and minced

4 ounces dried Chinese mushrooms, soaked in water for 2 hours, drained, and cut into ¼-inch cubes

1 tablespoon salt (or more, to taste)

4 tablespoons sugar

1 tablespoon white pepper

2½ tablespoons ground coriander

2 to 3 tablespoons dark soy sauce

80 to 90 bamboo leaves and string

10 pandan leaves

Wash the rice and soak it in a tub of water for at least 5 hours.

Bring a pot of water to boil, place the pork belly and pork leg in the water, and cover. Cook it until it's 50 to 75 percent done. (Poke a chopstick in. If it goes through easily, the meat is ready. You want it to be solid enough to be easy to cube.) Then chop the pork into ¼-inch cubes.

Place the shallots in a food processor to chop them, not too fine. Heat about ¼ cup of oil in a wok. When the oil is hot, add the garlic and fry until it's slightly brown. Remove the garlic, then add the shallots to the same oil and fry until soft. Add more oil (½ cup perhaps), and fry some more to mix. Remove the shallots. Then add the mushrooms to the same oil and fry for about 10 minutes or until the mushrooms are soft and the water they release has evaporated. Add the pork and fry it all up together. Add 1 tablespoon of salt, fry it a little, then add the garlic and shallots. Add the sugar, white pepper, and coriander, and fry it all together for about 20 minutes, then taste. If you'd like any more of any of the spices, add them now. Finally, add the dark soy sauce and fry until everything is well mixed. Remove from the wok and set aside. Let the filling cool for a few hours or overnight.

Soak the bamboo leaves in water to soften them.

Drain the rice and set it aside.

Take 2 bamboo leaves and fold them in the center so you form a triangular hollow, with the ends of the leaves pointing upward. Place in the hollow 1 or 2 tablespoons of rice (or more if you'd like), then 3 or more heaping tablespoons of meat mixture (or more, if you'd like), and top it with 2 or 3 tablespoons of rice, until the hollow is filled. Then fold over the leaves to cover the top of the hollow, twist them to seal, and tie the *bak-zhang* with string.

When all the *bak-zhang* have been wrapped, heat a large pot of water with the knotted pandan leaves. When the water is boiling, place the *bak-zhang* in the pot and boil them for 90 minutes.

Bak-zhang can be kept in the refrigerator for a week or the freezer for up to 2 months. Serve with chili sauce on the side.

SIMPSON'S *POPIAH*

Makes 4 rolls

3 tablespoons canola oil

12 peeled, deveined shrimps

1 tablespoon sesame oil

3 tablespoons minced shallots

1 tablespoon minced garlic

1 pound julienned jicama

2 tablespoons preserved
soybean paste

1 tablespoon oyster sauce

1 teaspoon sugar

1 ½ cups water

Salt and pepper

4 (8-inch-by-8 inch) *popiah*
(spring roll) wrappers

4 lettuce leaves

4 ounces julienned
five-spiced tofu

2 tablespoons minced
scallions

For sauce

1 tablespoon Sriracha chili sauce

1 tablespoon preserved soybean sauce

In a pan, heat 1 tablespoon of canola oil over medium heat, add the shrimp, and sauté until they are cooked through. Remove the shrimp from the pan and set aside.

Add the remaining canola oil and the sesame oil, heat over medium heat, add the shallots, and cook until soft but not brown. Add the garlic and continue cooking for another 30 seconds; stir constantly to prevent the mixture from browning. Add the ji-cama, 1 tablespoon of soybean paste, oyster sauce, and sugar, and toss evenly. Add the water, turn the heat to low, and let the mixture cook for 15 minutes or until the jicama is soft. Season with salt and pepper. Strain the mixture, set the solids aside to cool, and reserve the "juice."

Lay a sheet of *popiah* skin on a clean surface; put a piece of let-tuce on top; place the cooled shrimp, jicama, tofu, and scallions in the middle; and gently fold the extra skin over to form a roll. Continue making the rolls.

Add Sriracha sauce and the remaining soybean sauce to the juice.

Slice up rolls into ¾-inch-thick slices; serve with dipping sauce on the side.

AUNTIE KHAR IMM'S SALTED VEGETABLE AND DUCK SOUP

Yield: 6 to 8 Chinese soup bowls of soup

¼ head salted mustard greens
½ duck, cut into large pieces
2 sour plums
1 (2-inch-long) piece of ginger, peeled
2 tamarind leaves
2 tomatoes

Cut the mustard greens into large chunks and soak for 30 to 60 minutes. Snip off as much of the duck skin as you can (the more skin you leave on, the oilier the soup will be). Heat a pot of water. When it's boiling, blanche the duck in it for a few seconds.

Put 2 to 3 inches of water in a large pot. Bring the water to a boil and then add the duck, sour plums, ginger, and tamarind leaves and bring it to a boil. Simmer for 45 minutes. Add the mustard greens, then simmer for 40 minutes. Add more sour plums and tamarind leaves to taste. Add the tomatoes and boil for about 10 minutes longer. Serve with rice.

AUNTIE ALICE'S
TEOCHEW BRAISED DUCK

1 whole duck

2 level Chinese soup spoons (each is about 1 ½ to 2 tablespoons) five-spice powder

2 level Chinese soup spoons salt

2 level Chinese soup spoons sugar

10 to 15 thick slices of peeled galangal (ginger can be used as a substitute)

15 cloves of garlic, peeled and lightly bashed

1 Chinese rice bowl (slightly over 1 cup) dark soy sauce* (add more if you like the taste)

*Note: Dark soy sauce can be purchased in many Chinatowns in U.S. cities.

Trim the duck, cutting off its head, behind, and feet if you're not planning on eating the feet. Wash it thoroughly inside and out.

Mix together the five-spice powder and the salt and rub it all over the outside and inside of the duck. Let the duck marinate for at least 2 hours in the refrigerator.

Heat a large wok over low heat and add the sugar, stirring until it melts. Add the galangal and garlic, frying the mixture until it is brown. Add the dark soy sauce.

Lightly rinse the marinated duck—this will make the end product less salty. Slide the duck into the wok, then coat the top of the duck with the sauce and turn it over. Add enough water so that the liquid comes halfway up the sides of the duck. Bring the mixture to a boil and cover.

Uncover and turn over the duck every 15 minutes. After 50 to 60 minutes, see if you can poke a chopstick through the fleshiest part of the duck. If the chopstick goes through fairly easily, the duck is ready. If not, cover and continue boiling until the chopstick pokes through easily.

Once it's ready, turn off the heat and let the duck sit, covered, for 10 minutes. Then slice it up and serve it with rice, with the sauce on the side.

AUNTIE KHAR MOI'S
PANDAN-SKIN MOONCAKES

Makes 60 small mooncakes

For the filling

3-pound bag of lotus-seed paste
Melon seeds
Salted egg yolks

For the skin

8 ½ ounces all-purpose flour that has been steamed for 10 minutes, then dried

6 ounces Prima Flour Top Flour (a super-fine flour; cake flour can be substituted)

3 ½ ounces mochi flour

7 ounces confectioners' sugar

4 ounces shortening

14 ounces pandan water

A few drops of green food coloring

To make the filling, mix the lotus-seed paste with the melon seeds for crunch. Then form into little balls, a little less than 1 ounce each. Hollow out each ball and fill it with about a quarter of a yolk. Then roll it back up.

Measure out 60 (approximately 1 ounce) balls of the lotus-seed paste filling and set aside. Using a stand mixer, mix together the three kinds of flour and confectioners' sugar. Then add the shortening and gradually mix in the pandan water. Mix until the dough is stiff but also soft. Add a few drops of green food coloring and mix well.

Divide the dough into 60 balls weighing 9 ounces each. Roll each ball into a flat circle, place a ball of lotus-seed paste in the center, turn it over, stretch out the skin, and seal so the paste is entirely covered.

Place the ball sealed side up in a mooncake mold and use your palm to smooth it out. Tap the mold on the counter to loosen and remove the mooncake.

Mooncakes should be stored in the refrigerator. If you're planning on eating them after 1 week, store them in the freezer.

MY MUM'S GREEN BEAN SOUP

Yield: 8 to 9 cups of soup

7 to 8 cups water
3 pandan leaves, knotted loosely
1 cup dried green beans (also known as mung beans)
1 to 1 ½ cups peeled and cubed sweet potato
2 tablespoons pearl sago (add more if you like sago)
3 tablespoons sugar (add much more if you like it sweet;
   my mother doesn't make hers very sweet)

Add the water and pandan leaves to a pot and bring to a boil over medium heat. Rinse the beans, add them to the pot, and boil for 25 to 30 minutes, adding the sweet potato halfway through.

Then add the sago and sugar, and boil for 10 more minutes. The soup is done when the beans have split and the sweet potato has softened.

Serve hot or chilled.

TANGLIN AH-MA'S *OTAK*

Makes about 80

2 to 3 thick stalks lemongrass

2 pounds shallots

2 ounces blue ginger or
galangal

2 ounces yellow ginger or
turmeric

2 tablespoons toasted,
crumbled belacan

2 ounces candlenuts
(macadamia nuts can be
substituted)

3 ½ ounces dried chilies,
boiled in hot water for
15 minutes to soften

12 chili padi, also known as
bird's-eye chilies (add more
if you want it to be spicier)

¾ tablespoon plus
¾ teaspoon salt

1 ¼ cups vegetable or canola
oil

Fresh banana leaves,* cut
into 8-inch-by-5-inch
rectangles

2 pounds mackerel

3 ½ cups coconut milk

8 eggs, beaten

1 ½ tablespoons sugar

2 tablespoons ground
coriander

2 tablespoons tapioca
flour

¼ teaspoon monosodium
glutamate

*Note: If you can't find fresh banana leaves, you can scoop the fish
paste into a bowl and steam it.

Thinly slice the lemongrass, shallots, blue ginger or galangal, and yellow ginger or turmeric, and blend them together in a food processor with the crumbled belacan, candlenuts, and a little water. Remove the paste, transfer it to a large wok, and fry over medium heat.

Blend together the softened dried chilies and chili padi in the food processor with about ¼ cup of water. Add the chili mixture to the paste in the wok. Add ¾ tablespoon of salt.

Keep frying the paste. After 30 minutes, start gradually adding about 1 ¼ cups of oil to the mixture while frying. You want the mixture to get really dry. The best way to tell whether there's still water in the paste is to add oil by the ¼ cup and then inspect to see if white wispy strands appear. If you see the wisps, there's still water in the mixture.

After about 90 minutes, the paste should be dry enough. Remove it from the wok and let it cool overnight.

The next day, fill a large wok with water and bring it to a boil. Soak the banana leaf rectangles in batches in the water for 1 or 2 minutes to soften the leaves. You want them to be pliant enough to be folded with ease.

Cut the fish into smaller-than-bite-size pieces. In a large mixing bowl, whisk together 4 to 5 cups of the chili paste (add more if you like it spicy), the coconut milk, eggs, sugar, coriander, tapioca flour, monosodium glutamate, and ¾ teaspoon of salt. Add the fish to the bowl and mix well.

Take a banana leaf, position it on your hand so its veins are vertical, then scoop 2 to 3 tablespoons of the fish mixture onto the leaf so it forms a slender vertical strip along the middle. Make sure the paste does not reach the ends of the leaf; you don't want it to spill out.

Fold over the left side and then the right side of the leaf so you have a long, slender *otah* that's about 1 ½ inches wide. Secure the top and bottom with sharp toothpicks. Repeat with the rest of the mixture.

Steam the *otah* for 10 minutes and serve them with rice or bread.

AI-KYUNG LINSTER'S *MANDOO*

Makes 100

Dumplings

2 cups shredded cabbage
2 cups minced chives
1 cup chopped green onions
1 pound minced pork
1 pound ground beef
2 tablespoons sesame oil
1 tablespoon soy sauce

½ teaspoon salt
¼ teaspoon ground ginger
1 large egg, beaten
Mandoo, gyoza, or round
　　Chinese dumpling
　　wrappers

Dipping sauce

1 cup soy sauce
½ cup apple cider vinegar
Black pepper, to taste

Lightly salt the cabbage and set it aside.

Mix the other filling ingredients in a large bowl.

Wring out the cabbage until it is very dry and add it to the mixture.

Take a *mandoo* wrapper and lay it flat on your palm. Dip a finger into a bowl of room-temperature water and lightly coat the edge of the wrapper with water. Scoop a scant 1 tablespoon or so of the filling into the center of the wrapper. Fold the wrapper in half, lightly press the edges together to seal, and then fold 4 small vertical pleats into the edge so the *mandoo* will seal tightly.

Add a bit of salt to half a pot of water and boil. Add the *mandoo*, in batches of 12 for a regular-size soup pot, then cover the pot and bring the water to a boil again.

Add 1 cup of cold water, cover the pot, and bring it to a boil a third time. Do the same one final time. Remove the *mandoo*.

To make the dipping sauce: Mix a 2-to-1 ratio of soy sauce to apple cider vinegar. Add freshly ground black pepper to taste.

ACKNOWLEDGMENTS

Thanks, first and foremost, must go to my two grandmothers: Tanglin Ah-Ma, who fed me well and whose pineapple tarts inspired this journey into my aunties' kitchens; and Ah-Ma, who loves all her "smelly puppy" grandchildren with such tender ferocity.

The journey would never have been possible without my parents and sister. Thanks to my father, Tan Soo Liap, for never letting me beat him at Scrabble; my mother, Cynthia Wong, for teaching me to read; and Daphne, for being my partner in crime, confidante, and just about the best sister anyone could have. I miss you dearly every day.

Special thanks to two women who opened their hearts and kitchens to me: Auntie Alice and Auntie Khar Imm, I remain in awe. I am also grateful to Auntie Leng Eng, Uncle Ah Tuang, Uncle Soo Kiat, Ai-Kyung Linster, Auntie Donna, Auntie Hon Tim, Auntie Khar Moi, Ng Geak Tieng, Jessie, Kuku, Matthew, Zachary, Uncle Paul, Auntie Sophia, Valerie, and Auntie Jane. And Erlinda, our trusty sous chef.

To Simpson Wong and Willin Low, two amazing chefs and truly great friends.

To Jeanette Lai, Kevin Cheng, and Regina Jaslow, who have loved me, saved me, and cheered me on for more than twenty years now. I would be a mess without you.

And my dear New York friends for their patience and support during my year of traveling and writing—and, basically, ignoring them: Brian Fidelman, Jesse Pesta, Robert Sabat, Robert Christie, Henry Wu. Greg Morago, I adore you. In Washington, D.C., thanks to Laura Sullivan, Kris Antonelli, Rachelle Pestikas, and Laura Smitherman—I love you all.

I would not be where I am today without the mentorship and teachings of my journalism editors. I've had the good fortune of working with a few of the great newspaper editors of my time, and I consider myself lucky to also call them my friends: John Carroll and Paul Steiger. Thanks, too, to my *dalaoban* Marcus Brauchli, whose work and career have been an inspiration. As well as editors Bill Marimow, Tony Barbieri, Diane Fancher, Michael Gray, Edward Felsenthal, Elizabeth Seay, and Felix Soh. Last but not least, to an editor whom I love dearly and who shaped me greatly: the incredible and incredibly sweet Mary Corey.

At Medill, thanks to John Kupetz, Roger Boye, Pamela Cytrynbaum, and the late Dick Schwarzlose.

I have so much gratitude for the Asian American Journalists Association, whose members have offered me support and love for more than a decade. I can't list everyone but special thanks to Jeannie Park, Albert Kim, Abe Kwok, Ed Lin, David Ng,

Victor Panichkul, Charles Price, Mei-Ling Hopgood, Sachin Shenolikar, David Oyama, Charles Christopher Chiang, Randy Hagihara, Joe Grimm, Donna Kato, Jessie Mangaliman, Sharon Chan, Craig Gima, and Keith Kamisugi, who was so very helpful with the launch of www.cheryllulientan.com.

I can't offer enough thanks to my family at Yaddo, the artists' colony, where I completed this book. Elaina Richardson, Candace Wait, Mike Hazard, Jim Ryall, Cathy Clarke, and the rest of the Yaddo staff provided the serenity and nourishment that made writing a breeze. And I owe gratitude, of course, to my Yaddo mates, who gave me a bubble of encouragement and invaluable advice during a few very crucial weeks. Your art inspired me; your faith nudged me toward the finish line: John "Nonny" Searles, Nicholas Boggs, Gordon Dahlquist, Lucy Puls, Peter Mountford, Zachary Keeting, Noa Charuvi, Gretchen Somerfeld, Thomas Cummins, Darren Floyd, Silvia Pareschi, Jonathon Keats, Andrew Solomon, Rebecca Pappas, Steve Giovinco, Rachel Cantor, Emily Mast, and Cleopatra Mathis. And special thanks to Robinson McClellan for the gift of PIG.

Thanks to the thoughtful Daphne, Leonard Lee, Jeremy Tan, Ryan Page, and Doris Truong for sending generous care packages to help with the writing. And a big thank you to Ng Aik Wye, the Singapore Tourism Board, KF Seetoh, Aisah Omar, and Auntie Jianab for all their assistance.

Major thanks to Hyperion and the people there who have been a true joy to work with: Barbara Jones, Allison McGeehon, Claire McKean, and my editors Sarah Landis and Leslie Wells.

My deepest thanks and love go to my indefatigable agent Jin Auh and the Wylie Agency. Thank you for loving this book from the very beginning.

And, of course, Mike. Sweetie, I hope I thank you enough every day.